THE WRITER LAID BARE:

MASTERING EMOTIONAL HONESTY IN A WRITER'S ART, CRAFT AND LIFE

LEE KOFMAN

First published in 2022 by Ventura Press
PO Box 780, Edgecliff NSW 2027 AUSTRALIA
www.venturapress.com.au

All rights reserved. No part of this book may be reproduced or transmitted in any form or by any means, electronic or mechanical, including photocopying, recording or by any other information storage or retrieval system, without prior permission in writing from the publisher.

Copyright © Lee Kofman 2022

A catalogue record for this book is available from the National Library of Australia

The Writer Laid Bare
ISBN 9781920727550

Cover design by Alissa Dinallo
Typesetting by Midland Typesetters
Printed and bound in Australia by Griffin Press

The paper in this book is FSC® certified.
FSC® promotes environmentally responsible, socially beneficial and economically viable management of the world's forests.

Lee Kofman's *The Writer Laid Bare* is an inspiring exploration of the joyful – and painful – art of writing.
Christian White
Author of *The Nowhere Child* and *The Wife and the Widow*

The Writer Laid Bare is the creative friend that every writer needs. The writing process is demystified with insight and self-awareness, its difficulties and joys delineated, its braided paths outlined with grace and open-hearted generosity. It is an elegant book to read, practical, inspiring and encouraging all at once. For readers, it is a book to enjoy for its revelations of the writing life, for writers it is a book to keep on your desk as you write and to pick up and read whenever you stop writing. I will be recommending *The Writer Laid Bare* to all my writing students.
Patti Miller
Author of *Writing Your Life and The Memoir Book*

The Writer Laid Bare is a rich and delicious distillation of Lee Kofman's experience, wisdom and reading. Part writing memoir and part writing manual, this beautiful hybrid is simultaneously accessible and erudite, and Kofman's voice is refreshing in its honesty and vulnerability. I know it is a book I will be thrusting into the hands of other writers, as well as a book I will keep returning to – not just for the perfectly curated advice from some of the world's best writers but for Lee's personal writing journey and her reassurance that in our pursuit of emotionally honest writing, we are not alone.
Melanie Cheng
Author of *Room for a Stranger* and *Australia Day*

The Writer Laid Bare takes us on an intimate journey into the magical, and often challenging, terrain an author inhabits. Kofman courageously shares with the reader her own probing writerly journey of self-discovery.
Leah Kaminsky
Author of *The Waiting Room* and *The Hollow Bones*

ALSO BY LEE KOFMAN

Split: True stories of leaving, loss and new beginnings
Imperfect
Rebellious Daughters: True stories from Australia's finest female writers
(co-edited with Maria Katsonis)
The Dangerous Bride
I'll Love Christina (in Hebrew)
Single Woman, 32 (in Hebrew)
Scars (in Hebrew)

photo by Tizia May

Dr Lee Kofman is a Russian-born, Israeli-Australian writer, editor, writing teacher and mentor based in Melbourne. She holds a PhD in social sciences and MA in creative writing. Lee is the author of three fiction books and two memoirs, including *Imperfect* (Affirm Press, 2019), which was shortlisted for Nib Literary Award, and *The Dangerous Bride* (Melbourne University Press, 2014), co-editor of *Rebellious Daughters* (Ventura Press, 2016) and editor of *Split* (Ventura Press, 2019), which was longlisted for ABIA Awards – anthologies of memoir by prominent Australian authors. Her short works have been widely published in Australia, US, UK, Scotland, Israel and Canada; her blog was a finalist for Best Australian Blogs 2014.

FOR PETER BISHOP WHO TAUGHT ME
HOW TO TALK ABOUT WRITING
AND FOR LUCA EFRON, MY DARLING BOY

‘The writer has to be like a firefighter, whose job, while everyone else is fleeing the flames, is to run straight into them.’

– Jonathan Franzen

CONTENTS

PROLOGUE: INTO THE FLAMES

Every now and then I get a particularly cheerful student in my writing class. While everyone else bemoans the 'ginormous', as my children are fond of saying, effort that writing requires, this student will sit back, smiling mysteriously, or perhaps incredulously. At some point, they will raise their hand to tell us, not so much smugly as rather innocently, that writing is a sheer joy for them. That whenever they sit at a computer or open a notebook (or, nowadays, a voice recorder) the words just pour out of them, as if of their own accord . . . This is the one student, however, I am sorry to report, who is usually made of the least writerly material, as my once-jealous class inevitably discovers when they begin sharing their works.

Writing is *meant* to be difficult. Many writers, I am sure, would nod vigorously at Thomas Mann's famous suggestion that writers are those for whom writing is more difficult than for other people. Writers understand the weight of words and this understanding weighs on us. We know that each minute choice we make matters, that to express something truthfully and vividly is a feat. We know that writing that emerges with the greatest ease, is often clichéd, unattuned to nuance. As Philip Roth said, when you're writing 'you're looking . . . for what's going to resist you. You're looking for trouble.'

It is no wonder then, that for many of us, writing is foremost an act of self-doubt, a breeding ground for self-loathing, a boot camp. That's why writers are more likely to be nervous wrecks than wise philosophers calmly observing reality (as I assumed during my teenage years). On the other hand, our neuroses tend to be of the perfectionist kind; as such, they make our work better. Or as the bestselling American novelist James M. Cain puts it, if a writer doesn't lay awake at night worrying about their work, 'the reader isn't going to, either'.

There are difficulties and there are *difficulties*, however. The most painful as well as dangerous to our art, I believe, are the difficulties associated with emotional honesty – the times when we lose touch with our viscera, with how we perceive ourselves and the outer world; or when we are reluctant to share what we find there. I am speaking from experience. There was a time, just after I turned thirty, when I grew so despondent about my writing that I made up a word to describe what was wrong with it: *nonesty*. To say that my works were 'dishonest' didn't feel right, because they didn't contain outright lies. But they emanated a subtler stink, one more difficult to get rid of. I sinned more by omission than commission. There wasn't *enough* honesty in my prose.

What I mean is that I airbrushed whatever I wrote, fiction or creative nonfiction. I smoothed the edges of even mildly controversial topics. And I skimmed only the surface of my characters' minds: *Does she love him or not? He is a loner because he had a difficult childhood.* I failed to explore the ambivalences and gradations inherent in romantic love (she may love him a little and need him a lot) or that a solitary nature is likely to be formed by a mix of factors (is he also an introvert with a rich inner world?). I wasn't sufficiently in touch with the complexity of human thoughts and emotions. Or, as the editor of my then-latest book put it in an email: 'You've taken your readers on a fascinating tour through the main streets of your novel but foregone visiting the hidden alleys.'

Some of my nonesty was habitual, an extension of my personality. In real life, too, I often try to tidy up the mess of the human condition. Just recently, when a mother at my children's school asked where my accent was from, I automatically said 'Israel' instead of explaining that it's a mixed Russian-Israeli accent. (I was born in Russia and moved to Israel as a teenager.) Still, as a young writer I had times when I was more vigilant about my 'nonest' tendencies and had more courage too. A book of short stories I'd written before that novel was uncomfortable and probing; it examined the poor choices otherwise decent people make – to plagiarise another's work, betray a friend, commit violence. I wrote those stories because I was possessed by them and wanted to exorcise them from my system. I didn't really believe anyone would publish them, so it was easier to write as Jonathan Franzen thinks writers should: 'like a firefighter, whose job, while everyone else is fleeing the flames, is to run straight into them.' But at thirty, more published and more self-conscious, I was no firefighter. Assuming this time that what I wrote was likely to be read, I felt more exposed and frightened to say things that are not usually said in polite society.

On top of that, at the time I was a recent arrival in Australia and in the process of changing countries and languages I had lost touch with my gut. Being self-aware is always hard work, or at least it is for me; however, I struggled even more during those years when I had just begun writing in English. In a language not yet embedded in me viscerally I found it harder to unpick my feelings and experiences into their molecular components. And if I wasn't sensitive to my own complexities, how could I have the insight to describe those of others, be they real or fictional? How could I reflect meaningfully on others' anxieties – their idiosyncrasies, biases, conflicting desires – if I couldn't properly analyse my own?

Creative writers of any genre are at their best when they continuously study themselves and their perceptions of the world, when they cultivate what I think of as hyper-self-awareness as well as hyper-courage in order to describe their findings truthfully. But during my 'nonesty period', I was nowhere near ready to do anything of the kind. I craved publication and recognition as an author in Australia so much that I worked to please more than to say something authentic. (Funnily enough, this was actually antithetical to my dream of recognition, as it is the writing that endangers us that has the best chance of moving readers.)

My lack of deep reflection extended into the writing process itself. I sort of 'forgot' that difficulties in writing are a natural part of creating; every challenge appeared to me as a catastrophe, yet more proof that I had no more books left in me. I wasn't connected to my shifting needs – the conditions I needed to work at my best in my new country in my new language. I wasn't even clear on whether what I was trying to write was what I really wanted to write or thought I *ought* to.

At least I was aware of my creative failures. I wrote in my diary:

> Nonesty is when your typing fingers are not in sync with your memory, or your heart. Nonesty is when you describe what you are *supposed* to feel. It is when you are so focused on finishing a work that you don't ask yourself questions, because they are a waste of time.

I went on struggling like this for four years. Or rather, this was more than a struggle: it was a crisis. Another diary entry from that time: 'Nonesty makes me feel alienated from myself, both as a writer and a human. It makes me feel as if I am homeless.'

That crisis, which I now understand to be a full-blown writer's block, began dissipating only when I finally admitted to myself what I wanted, yet feared, to write about – my experiences of non-monogamy. And even when I began writing a memoir about that, it took me a while to learn to approach my subject with honesty and nuance.

By the time I finished that book, *The Dangerous Bride* (it took five years), I came to appreciate the critical importance of self-awareness, deep reflection and moral courage for writers – three concepts I now fit under the umbrella term of emotional honesty. So, when my publisher, Jane Curry, suggested I write a book about writing, I immediately knew through which lens I wanted to examine this artform. I wanted to write the kind of a book I once needed myself, as I strongly suspect timely advice would have spared me years of wallowing in despair. If only someone back then pointed out that my difficulties weren't a sign that I couldn't write; that struggling with authenticity, candour and self-understanding is something writers must do, often throughout their entire lives. Not all of us naturally know how, or dare, to write like firefighters.

Truisms come to us easier than an unmediated view of reality. It may feel true, and safe, to write that children are 'innocent', for example. No risk here of attracting outraged comments on Goodreads or Twitter. But anyone who cares to observe a kindergarten playground with eyes and ears wide open soon discovers that while some children are innocent others are far from it. Those *others* can confront us with a darkness we don't wish to see. And even with the so-called innocent children – is there innocence to every aspect of their existence? Then, what *is* innocence anyway? And is it always a virtue?

These are the kind of difficult questions that writers committed to an emotionally honest practice face. We don't have to answer them with absolute authority, perhaps nobody can, but we must at least ask them. And in the process, we'd do well to acknowledge that none of us comes to our observations from a neutral place. We bring to the kindergarten playground, and to our writing desk, a lifetime of baggage along with various other limitations. Some of these limitations are external (the Twitter-fear) while others are intrinsic to who we are, like my tendency to simplify complex phenomena. In this book I explore these various barriers to what I see as the writer's chief job – to go wild and rid our writing of conventions, including ideological ones, that prevent us from exposing the demons and angels inside us.

No doubt such writing is taxing intellectually and emotionally – something our blissfully ignorant student, whose words pour and pour out, would eventually learn. This book explores how to push through the various creative and emotional obstacles towards vivid, clearly articulated and authentic storytelling, and how to discover the optimal writing conditions you need to remain motivated and work well. It is my belief that from the moment we conceive a piece of work to when we farewell it, finished, into the outside world, the principles of emotional honesty can help us do our artistic best as well as reduce some of the stresses inherent in the process of creation.

Perhaps these principles can even apply to better a writer's private life. The obvious, and under-discussed, fact is that writers have obligations other than writing. We write around and despite our families, peers, friends and lovers. We write between money-paying jobs and unwashed dishes, thirsty house plants and tantrum-throwing children. And . . . surprise, surprise – sometimes we don't write. Even writers can get tired or, God forbid, depleted, just as mere mortals do. Sometimes all a writer wants is to watch *The Bachelor* or light up a joint. This, too, is a part of a writer's story and we need to be honest about that.

I explore the various pathways to an emotionally honest writing practice through the experiences of writers I have known and studied, through what I've observed as an editor as well as a teacher of writing, and through my own trials and numerous errors – especially the ones I committed while working on *The Dangerous Bride*, the hardest work I've ever written.

Finally, this book is meant to be an enquiry into the mystery of writing, not its ultimate solution. Creativity has many faces, varying from writer to writer. That's why I suggest you treat *The Writer Laid Bare* as a hardware store that has a range of tools for you to choose from in order to build, or expand, your own singular writer's toolkit. Firefighting is not for the fainthearted, so you'll need all the ladders, hoses and torches you can get.

PART ONE:

HONESTY IN (THE WRITER'S) MIND

'I certainly don't. I get a fine, warm feeling when I'm doing well, but that pleasure is pretty much negated by the pain of getting started each day. Let's face it, writing is hell.'

– William Styron, when asked if he enjoys writing.

Once upon a time I killed a novel. It was a sexy, slinky, burning tale. In my mind, that is. It was a love story between a troubled man and a woman who was placed at his mercy by unfortunate circumstances. In theory. In reality, I was so afraid to fail that I overstuffed the novel with secondary characters, sub-plots and themes until I had no energy left for my protagonists. On the page they turned up pale and gaunt, one-dimensional. Nothing happened to them, as I was preoccupied with 'realising the themes' and wrangling the stories of minor characters. That was, when I was writing.

Most of the time I spent not writing but researching and subsequently felt that to justify all the hard work, I ought to put everything I'd learned into the book. That task, too, proved to be so weighty that when I wasn't researching, I was *planning* the book, to cope with the overload. The problem was, writing pre-planned chapters is as tedious for me as doing my tax return. As if all this wasn't lethal enough, I also discussed my novel with anyone who cared to listen, and with every conversation, that mysterious magic I'd initially felt about the story leaked away until I forgot why I wanted to write it in the first place.

All that happened long ago, during the 'nonesty time', when I was out of touch with how my writing process works. More recently, that novel has resurfaced in my mind while I've been writing other books. I've taken a great deal of notes for it and wrote a new synopsis, altering the plot significantly and culling the secondary characters. The names of protagonists are now different, and so is the man's ethnicity. And yet. The novel's weather is the same – the claustrophobia of that relationship, the self-destruction, the erotic doom . . . I often visualise my works as if they are paintings, and the novel's palette is still the same too – the silver and khaki of Australian bush with occasional splashes of crimson.

Whenever I'm thinking about having another proper go at writing this story, I enter the mood of my protagonists: I feel claustrophobic (and a little erotically doomed). I am haunted by the possibility of failure, just as I was years ago. Yet this time I hope to approach the story with greater self-awareness, notice sooner when anxiety is leading me astray and if the book still doesn't work, to realise this early on and put the novel to (a final) rest.

This first part of the book is concerned with mastering just this facet of emotional honesty – awareness of the patterns and challenges of the writing process. Sometimes such awareness can be depressing, like in this (not atypical) account by Albert Camus:

> It takes years to find your real voice, your tone and the truth in your heart. People believe that this is given at the beginning, and a writer's work is to translate this given. Not at all! The writer's work consists of writing with as much effort as possible, and at the end of this labour it sometimes happens that he finds what he sought for so long inside himself. Creation is not a joy in the vulgar sense of the term. It is a servitude, a terrible volunteer slavery – and the joy much resembles that of great visionaries: it has an odor of melancholy.

That from a winner of the Noble Prize in Literature!

Melancholic odour notwithstanding, Camus never stopped writing. The most successful writers harbor the least illusions about the writing process. However grudging, their awareness that creation is never far away from failure, that shaping their innermost dreaming into compelling stories requires not only a talent but also enormous tenacity and patience, surely helps them persevere. Such awareness normalises creative difficulties. Where I viewed my novel's problems as insurmountable and so killed a story that wanted to live, wiser writers conceptualise writing as an ongoing process of problem-solving (for example, you can ditch your secondary characters . . .), approaching it as they would any other challenging yet possible task.

The difficulties inherent in the creative process – fear, fatigue, lack of motivation or discipline and so on – are mostly commonplace, but how we solve them varies among writers. Extensive planning proved to be dangerous for me, but the American writer Louise DeSalvo describes in *The Art of Slow Writing* how she cannot get enough of planning. She has a notebook to record ideas, a journal where she regularly reflects on her writing progress, a daily work planner and a schedule of long-term goals. The more you talk to writers, the more gradations of planning you find. (Although I've never come across anyone with more elaborate and time-consuming rituals than DeSalvo's.) The same can be said about any other aspect of creation. Yet there are so many myths about how writing *should* be done that it can be difficult to identify our own pathway. This is, however, what a writer needs to do and the earlier the better.

Knowing where you belong on the planning scale, or how to recognise your writing subject, or even what beverages (herbal tea? cognac?) are most effective to woo your muses, can make the entire difference between completing a work and giving up. In the following chapters we'll examine these and other aspects of the writing process. We will do this not in order to control it, but to submit to it – to learn to fit into the natural contours of our creative skin rather than stretch or shrink it. To use another metaphor, emotional honesty for a writer, in the sense of self-awareness, is like a miner's lift – it eases and speeds our descent into the mind's murky underground where creative impulses dwell.

WHERE WRITING SPRINGS FROM

In 1930, at the age of thirty-six, the poet Vladimir Mayakovsky shot himself. (Not an unusual occurrence among Russian poets . . .) His now-famous suicide note reads, 'Mother, sisters, friends . . . forgive me. This is not the way (I do not recommend it to others), but there is no other way out for me.'

And this is often how I feel about writing. I do not recommend it to others, because of how difficult it is. (Not to mention, occasionally fatal!) Sometimes I wish I could be a chef instead. Cooking gives me reliable pleasure and, despite the universal reputation of grumpy chefs, I think this would have been a happier life (for starters, I've never heard of 'chef's block'). But there is no other way out for me. No matter that my study is often my torture chamber. No matter that sometimes my laptop screen turns into a mirror to my troubled soul and says to me, 'Who is the most talented of them all? Definitely not you.'

So why do I write?

This question becomes particularly urgent whenever my work gets rejected or I receive yet another meagre royalties update, or become paralysed by fear at the idea of starting a new work, or my pile of research notes reaches the height of Mount Everest – in an inverse ratio to completed manuscript pages. And most recently, in the face of the biblical flavour of current times, punctuated by bushfires, floods and a pandemic, when it has become even easier to lose faith in what I do and it seems chefs are far more essential to our survival than writers. When it feels frivolous to be a writer, as my writer-friends and I have been saying to each other. Now more than ever I must dig deeper to get to the heart of the 'why', so as not to let go of what tears me apart but at the same time reliably keeps me intact.

Writing – my double-faced Janus. My curse and my blessing. It cures me of boredom but also robs me of inner peace. There is always something inside me brewing, some idea or work-in-progress that occupies large swathes of my brain during my waking hours and sometimes invades my dreams in a way that's equally exciting and troubling. Perhaps, being a writer is like falling in love, and falling, never hitting the ground. Is this a sustainable way to live?

It's not just me. Most writers, it seems, are nowhere near as fortunate as Stephen King, who not only gains riches through his words, but also writes with consistent joy, the bastard. (In his memoir *On Writing* he says that it is *not writing* that feels like work for him!) King is one of those lucky escapists who are so immersed in their storytelling that they have little space left for anxiety to kick in. But for many of us writing is inseparable from the drama of self-doubt. And yet, in some aspects, our lot might be better than that of others (that lack of boredom, for example). To relish and believe in our vocation we need to be aware of our blessings so easily obscured by the daily grind of writing. So, why do we write? Let's unpack some common reasons and see where you belong.

*

One popular proposition is that the writing drive originates in our wounds, especially those incurred in childhood. Freud championed this view in his famous essay 'Creative Writers and Daydreaming'. There he argued that writers are essentially driven by the desire to alter an unsatisfactory or unpleasant reality, usually rooted in their unfulfilled childhood wishes, which they satisfy explicitly or in metaphorical disguise in their creative works. If we look at the biographies and memoirs of successful authors, unhappy childhoods are indeed abundant and loom large in these writers' oeuvres. The Israeli writer Amos Oz, for example, who as a child lost his mother to suicide. In his memoir, *A Tale of Love and Darkness*, Oz writes that the one impulse that underpins his otherwise diverse works is, 'the desire to grant a second chance to something which could never have had one'. In a way, his oeuvre is a sublimation of his impossible wish for his mother to live on, to live a happier life.

My own childhood, spent in the shadows of communist dictatorship and lengthy hospitalisations, is yet another illustration of Freud's suggestion. But there were also other, less unfortunate, conditions that spurred my writing. I was born in a place where books were a natural habitat of the mind, in the absence of other entertainment and on account of their state-driven affordability. In the Soviet Union, even truck drivers were fond of referencing Tolstoy. (In fact, I preferred their references to those of my teachers, who often divorced the texts from irony, stripped them down to bare Tolstovskian moralism.)

The Soviet Union not only popularised books (albeit, selectively – Tolstoy and Australia's own communist Katharine Susannah Prichard were in; George Orwell and Solzhenitsyn were banned), it also bred graphomania – an obsessive need to write. Much of the available literature was state-sponsored propaganda and those books resembled each other, making it seem as if writing was easy. Many citizens tried. Artless poetry in particular was a national disease. So, when the writing affliction hit me first at the age of three, no one was surprised. Or concerned. I recited my poem in front of Siberian village babushkas: 'The blue bird flies up to the sky/The blue bird flies high.' The audience was impressed.

In addition, our home was bookish even by Soviet standards. It was crammed with various collected works – Chekhov, Conan Doyle, Hugo . . . As I was often bedbound on account of serious childhood illnesses, and surrounded by family members who read voraciously, I learned to read by the age of four and first tackled *War and Peace* at eight. (I skipped through the war, though, concentrating on the romance.) From its dawn, my existence was so enmeshed with words on the page that it felt only natural to insert my own words into the conversations with my well-thumbed friends that lived on our bookshelves.

But I also *needed* to write. I needed to escape the physical pain and loneliness of my sickbed and my early realisation of my mortality, as well as the tedium of Soviet life. In my early years, reading and writing afforded me an alternative space in which, as per Freud, to fulfil my wishes – for a freer, brighter life.

To this day, at difficult times writing is my city of refuge. So when my newsfeed tells me that the worldwide death toll of COVID-19 has just bypassed three million, and businesses are collapsing everywhere, and I once again question the point of being a writer, I can also tell myself that now writing becomes more essential than ever. It may feel as if the world doesn't need my words, but *I* do. Yet I also need to write in happier times. Why?

*

Not a few literati have explored their reasons for being possessed by writing. One seminal essay on this, titled 'Why I Write', comes from Orwell – that writer the Soviet authorities didn't approve of. Despite the title, Orwell's ambition was greater than self-understanding. He wanted to compose a definitive list of reasons. He offers four, arguing that these 'exist in different degrees in every writer, and in any one writer the proportions will vary from time to time, according to the atmosphere in which he is living'. Here is my summary of these reasons:

> 1. Sheer egoism. Desire to seem clever, to be talked about, to be remembered after death.
> 2. Aesthetic enthusiasm. Perception of beauty in the external world, or in words and their right arrangement.
> 3. Historical impulse. Desire to see things as they are, to find out true facts and store them up for the use of posterity.
> 4. Political purpose. Using the word 'political' in the widest possible sense. Desire to push the world in a certain direction.

The first of these reasons isn't something writers like to own, yet it is a powerful, and indeed common, motivator. When Gertrude Stein was asked why she wrote, she candidly replied, 'For praise'. For Federico García Lorca it was to be loved. 'Being an egomaniac and a narcissist, I had to make my inner world public,' John Banville announced publicly. And the Norwegian writer Karl Ove Knausgaard wrote: 'I'd always carried that inside me, the desire to be someone.'

I am no different. Writing first became bound with vanity for me around the age of twelve when the Soviet authorities, exasperated by the shenanigans of my dissident parents, finally allowed us to leave the country. As I began adjusting to life in Israel and to adolescence, my reasons for writing changed. I had an embarrassing accent and scars from my operations; I was a freak, I decided. It was then that writing became a primary means of forging a more attractive self. When my journalism and short fiction began appearing in a popular youth magazine, writing elevated me from Freak to Journalist, and later, when my books were published, to Author. This impulse to be recognised through writing is still there. I love *being* a writer with all this entails, often enjoying the egotistical things writers do, like giving interviews and lectures or participating in festivals.

All of Orwell's other points ring true for me too. The beauty of language is intrinsic to my sense of wellbeing – the making love to words when I write and the shaping of sentences out of their flesh. I claim the historical impulse too, particularly given that I come from two countries whose histories are often misunderstood in the wider world and sometimes deliberately skewed. I even sometimes want to push the world in some direction, one that doesn't fit with the mores of our times, although I am also wary of this impulse, as I'll discuss in later chapters.

But, Orwell, there are more sources from which writing springs.

*

The American writer Anna Quindlen thinks that writing is a writer's 'way of becoming something else, something more, something greater'. Quindlen is not referring to the vanity impulse but to that old-fashioned word I am fond of – wisdom. The kind of wisdom some of us can access only through writing.

Quindlen's proposition resonates. I also write because my verbal communication often fails me, in all three languages I speak. My speaking-self lacks nuance, it betrays me. My tongue is too quick and susceptible to generalisations. I blurt stupid things, or things that show me as someone I don't think I am. But once I start pinpointing my words onto the page, I consider my options more carefully before choosing a position. Writing slows my mind down. It helps me figure out what I really think, to calibrate my moral compass. I take more care to express my realisations; I pay attention to subtlety and qualification. Outside those years of writer's block, I am also more honest when I write, wear fewer masks, try less to please. I am bolder on the page, quirkier and funnier than in real life. My better self, I believe, resides in my works.

Some scientists think creative writing can also promote the wisdom of *self*-understanding. According to this research, the most significant psychological benefits occur not during the initial outpouring, but when we revise and, in the process, gain some distance from the sensitive material. Studies show the reflective writing phase helps reduce pathological cognitive patterns, such as dichotomised thinking, instead encouraging a new, more dynamic understanding of our experiences.

Potentially, these benefits are available to writers of fiction as much as to writers of creative nonfiction. 'All art is a kind of confession,' James Baldwin famously suggested, meaning that any literary work is rooted in our (external and/or internal) lives. Thinking along these lines, Jonathan Franzen argues in his essay 'On Autobiographical Fiction' that 'Kafka's work, which grows out of the nighttime dreamworld in Kafka's brain, is *more* autobiographical than any realistic retelling of his daytime experiences at the office or with his family . . . could have been.' I don't know if Kafka's work helped him deal with his personal demons, but I do know that crafting the chaos of my internal and external life into coherent sentences and storylines gives me some sense of control. I've also noticed that when something, for reasons I don't understand, moves me so that I have to turn it into art, I grasp the reasons for my obsession once I revise the writing, cutting out excessive emotions and clichés, reaching for more precise language to describe the experience. So, I suspect that although I've never earned much money through my writing, I must have saved quite a bit of what would otherwise have been spent on therapy.

But there is a price to pay when you write to understand. Too much understanding can be perilous to the writing drive. Every time I gain self-knowledge, I also lose some of the inspirational fuel. For instance, having written my previously inexplicable obsession with Anais Nin into a book, I am no longer seized by an exquisite, aching longing when I revisit Nin's diaries. There is a satisfaction in solving such puzzles, but I've never liked being overly known, not even to myself. If all my mysteries were solved and converted into psychological platitudes (yes, Nin represents the bohemian, creative life I longed for as a repressed adolescent), why would I keep writing?

*

Even this web of reasons I've tried to untangle doesn't fully explain why I write. To be more definitive, I must evoke my teen years, when things were less muddled, when I simply revered writers. I believed they had the gift of clairvoyance, knew things about this world non-writers didn't. I thought they wrote to decipher the secrets of the universe, to find life's meaning. I was definitely looking for meaning in my adolescent notebooks decorated with drawings of beauties, always beauties, and sometimes roses. There I wrote bad fiction and even worse poetry, and copied quotes that inspired me.

> I don't believe in God, it's an infirmity, but not to believe in God is a belief.
>
> – Marguerite Duras

I believed in literature. I wrote a note to myself: become a writer or disappear into a black hole.

Even though I've since lost some of my loftier convictions, deep down I am still a believer. I cannot speak of my need to write without reaching into the spiritual realm that Orwell, the self-declared atheist that he was, omitted from his list (perhaps despite himself, considering that on his deathbed he requested to be buried in a churchyard). Some others, though, have spoken about this dimension of writing. Karl Ove Knausgaard is one.

In his masterpiece, *The End*, Knausgaard suggests there is a certain psychological void in today's secularised society: 'When we closed the door on religion, we closed the door on something inside ourselves as well. Not only did the holy vanish from our lives, all the powerful emotions associated with it vanished too.' His argument resonates. It seems to me that many of us, non-believers, long for the experience of the sublime once found in prayers or so-called moments of enlightenment. It's just that today we reach for it through such substitutes as extreme sports, sex, political devotions or body modifications. Or artistic pursuits.

My most powerful reason for writing is just that: I write to experience the holy and also, not unlike those practising organised religion, to have a scaffold to build my life around. My writing, after all, is the only consistent thread that runs through my patch-worked life of multiple languages, countries, lovers, degrees and occupations. It stitches my disparate parts together, giving me some sort of coherence. And, like faith, it infuses my days with a pleasurable purpose. A tram ride is an opportunity to collect dialogue snippets, and to take notes about bodies and their language; a taxi ride is an occasion for in-depth character study. The pleasure I take in watching films is amplified as I absorb lessons about plot development. Then, as paradoxical as this may sound coming from a writer often crippled by fear and doubt, I find writing uncommonly grounding. The self-sufficient solitude, and the temporary quietening and focusing of the mind that writing, like prayer, affords are all precious to me.

Once, when I briefly considered stopping writing (what inadequate words to describe the turmoil of trying to give up a lifelong obsession!), a recurring dream began haunting me. It replayed an event from my childhood when I was dismissed from a school play as retribution for my parents' dissident activities. I had a small role and had attended only a few rehearsals, but I was already addicted to the rustle of my crinoline dress, the sound of my feet on the stage and the elevated viewpoint being there afforded. I never completely got over that dismissal from the only school play I was ever invited to do. I took that dream, which recreated that excitement and the subsequent devastation of my expulsion, to be a vivid reminder that I am unable to live without the drama of writing, particularly those occasional writing highs when I transcend the world and my busy mind. As much as writing causes me pain, nothing matches those rare hours, when the words flow smoothly and it is all pure, mindless sex, with blood flushing my face, my head buzzing, legs trembling, as I soar towards the sublime . . .

I suppose not-writing for me is even less sustainable than the tough slog that writing is. I hang onto this hard-won understanding that I am not that different from Scheherazade; that I, too, tell stories for my life. And perhaps next month everything will turn brighter. Perhaps the world and I will regain some equilibrium. Even then, it is better to hold onto the list of whys as a sort of insurance policy – for whatever blue days are to come.

FINDING YOUR SUBJECT

In the autumn of 2006, I was doing my first writing residency in a yellow house in the Blue Mountains called Varuna, which once belonged to the novelist Eleanor Dark. Every night we, the fortunate guests, feasted on the Varuna cook's curries and other culinary wonders. Every night my housemates – a poet who wrote villanelles, a novelist who was also a yogi and a terrifyingly prolific New Zealander who whipped up plays, poetry and fiction – discussed their daily writing progress. Every night I sat mostly silent. After dinner I lay on the monastically narrow bed in the former maid's room I was staying in, reading and crying myself to sleep.

While everyone else moved ahead, I was going nowhere. My book had no clear direction, even though I'd been writing it for two years. When I'd dragged my suitcase up Varuna's steep pathway, I was eager to set my fingers in typing motion, greedy for all the hours stretching before me, hopeful that a fortnight away from my busy life would help me to finally capture that elusive work. But it rained heavily when I arrived and, at first, I blamed my failings on the gloom of the weather. Later, when the sky cleared, I blamed the wealth of Varuna's library for overwhelming me. What was the point of writing anything new? I fought that thought by perusing books by Gail Jones, Sasha Soldatow and Brian Castro, hoping to spark my fire with their bewitching prose, but nothing helped. Good writing became a mystery I was unable to solve.

Towards the end of my stay, I gave up writing altogether. I took long walks in the mountains. I bought a halter dress with blue flowers. I called my husband many times a day and sat in my garden studio, looking at yellow roses and cockatoos luxuriating in the comfort of well-established trees. I, too, had comfort: generous windows, a large desk, a sofa to daydream on. I sat in that studio that was every writer's fantasy, feeling even more miserable than I did at night. My only happy day was when the New Zealander, satisfied with her output, took me along for a trek to the Three Sisters. The air was moist and warm, the foliage laden thick with silvery spiderwebs, and neither of us mentioned writing for the entire trip. Soon after, I returned to Melbourne, feeling my life was devoid of meaning. I did have a good dress though.

*

To explain my failure to write in the magic of Varuna, I have to tell you about a period that preceded that stay – my early years in Australia when I didn't know what to write about. The life baggage I'd arrived with seemed too foreign, even compared to that of other migrants; Russians, Israelis and especially Russian-Israelis like me are as rare as unicorns in Australia. I worried nobody would care for my stories if I wrote about what I knew. At the same time, I didn't feel 'qualified' to write about my new country.

Soon, however, I noticed that the locals I met seemed fascinated by my childhood spent in Odessa's dissident circles under the watchful eye of the KGB. It seemed like *this* was a kosher subject for a book – something that local readers would be interested in. All the signs were there to the extent that I was awarded a major literary grant and, later, that residency at Varuna to support the writing of my 'Russian memoir'.

I had other reasons for writing that book. The story of Soviet Jewish dissidents, which once made headlines in the West, had been largely forgotten. As per Orwell's writerly motivations, I wanted to rescue it from oblivion. I also wanted to pay tribute to the courage of my parents. I was clearly *meant* to write that book. So, I worked and worked on it. For writing it always felt like work, never pleasure, and my prose reflected that unfortunate state. Still, it took me several years to let go of it. Even after coming back from Varuna, when it became crystal-clear I wasn't passionate about the work, I persevered for some time – out of duty, 'just to finish' it, and because I didn't know what else to write. Or rather, because deep down I did know and was afraid of the subject.

*

Emotionally honest writing practice begins with the choice of themes. Or as V. S. Naipaul put it: 'Half a writer's work . . . is the discovery of his subject.' Before finding his, he grew so insecure in his writing ability that he would write with a pencil – a more tentative instrument.

There is plenty of advice out there for writers to help with such discoveries, like John Marsden's *Everything I Know About Writing* book, which includes 'the great feature: 600 extraordinary topics, guaranteed to have you or your students writing'.

> Topic 368: Describe a time when an animal you've known has shown courage, loyalty, affection . . .

I hold the ubiquity of such advice responsible for many mediocre books being written, and sometimes published. Fortunately, or unfortunately, I don't believe anybody can direct us to our subjects. Premade topics don't make delicious stories. Isaac Bashevis Singer talks along these lines: 'every writer must write . . . the things he is pondering about, brooding over. This is in part what gives writer his charm. And it makes him genuine. It's only the amateur who will take hold of any topic.' Elena Ferrante describes in *Frantumaglia* how she chooses her subjects in this spirit: 'The question in every story is the same: is this the right story to seize what lies silent in my depths, that living thing which, if captured, spreads through all the pages and gives them life?'

Writers cannot rely on another's advice, but they can hone and sharpen their intuition. During the years that followed my first sojourn in Varuna, I gathered some sharpening tools, or tenets, that help me to discover my themes.

*

My first tenet is **write about what is urgent**. Good literature, I believe, arises out of a pressing need to express something. Isn't creative writing all about being possessed, seized, obsessed? The legacy of a few holy fools? It's like sexual desire: you cannot sensibly choose what to be attracted to. Urgent subjects reside in our blood and marrow – whether we write about ourselves or not, they are bound to who we are, to our personal history, our passions or concerns. I cannot picture a serious artist working on a matter they are merely curious about; they must be driven to explore.

Memoirists write directly about what matters to them, whereas fiction writers might sublimate their obsessions. The American writer Kate Christensen describes in her memoir, *Blue Plate Special*, how she wrote her wounds into her novel *In the Drink*: 'My narrator, Claudia . . . was a helpful, comforting embodiment and extension of my own troubles; I made her problems much worse than my own, and so I was able to subsume my fears, channel them into my work.'

The channeling doesn't even have to be that direct for the novelists to bring what matters to them into their work. Jonathan Franzen, who rarely fictionalises events from his life, nevertheless views his fiction as 'extremely autobiographical, and . . . I consider it my job as a writer to make it ever more so. My conception of a novel is that it ought to be a personal struggle, a direct and total engagement with the author's story of his or her own life.'

Few people have a large number of fierce preoccupations of the kind that are fit to power a story. However, following what is urgent shouldn't limit the number of works an author can produce. As Bashevis Singer tells us, 'a writer can describe countless variations' on a topic they are passionate about. As if speaking to that, Graham Greene writes in his memoir, *Ways of Escape*, that all his novels are variations on 'the high romantic tale, capturing us in our youth with hopes that prove illusions, to which we return again in age in order to escape the sad reality'. Most of Chekhov's stories and plays can be summarised along the lines of 'it's a story about bored, unfulfilled, defeated people'. Yet I can never get enough of Chekhov, which I find encouraging as I, too, am drawn to writing about the same themes time and again – the dark side of eros, Russia's pull, the female body. I used to worry about repeating myself. Now I nurse my obsessions. I trust that if they return it is because I haven't exhausted my investigation of them yet.

Even when a writer knows what is urgent, what they brood over and grapple with, they don't always have the courage to follow their subject if it causes them discomfort, which such subjects often do. Equally common is the anxiety that the topic that quickens our heartbeat isn't of interest to others nor 'worthy' of literature. Amos Oz in his younger years, for instance, was ashamed of his desire to write about ordinary lives in provincial places. And sometimes it is difficult to resist fashions or vanity or the want to please; to ignore such questions as: What subject shows me as the most moral, and generally superior, person? What is easiest to write? What sells?

However, as difficult as it can be to pursue what's urgent, it is also foolish not to. Paradoxically, books devised with an audience in mind are unlikely to appeal. Writing that lacks authorial desire is usually dishonest and flat. Conversely, books conceived out of some innate need are more likely to crackle with electricity and be urgent for readers too, even if their subject matter is supposedly pedestrian. As the renowned American literary critic James Wood puts it, 'the vitality of literary character has less to do with dramatic action, novelistic coherence, and even plain plausibility – let alone likeability – than with a larger philosophical or metaphysical sense, our awareness that a character's actions are deeply *important*, that something profound is at stake.' Important to whom? Whose stakes are these? Foremostly, the author's. And if the author cares deeply about their subject, chances are high that readers will care too. (Read Oz's early fiction about ordinary lives and you'll see.) Even more or less formulaic bestsellers are likely to originate from an internal drive. The mega-selling Stephen King and Patricia Highsmith, for instance, describe in their respective books *On Writing* and *Plotting and Writing Suspense Fiction* how they write foremost for *themselves*.

*

I am done with lukewarm, pragmatic relationships to my works. I won't commit to a subject unless I am haunted by it. Except that sometimes nothing haunts me. Nevertheless, I can be burdened with a generalised urgency to write with no outlet to release the pressure. In that case, I have my second tenet: **just wait**. I'm thinking here again about Highsmith, who argued, with her characteristic aplomb, that our innate subjects 'cannot be sought after or strained for; they appear'.

Waiting for such 'appearances' is a common operational

procedure as Robert Dessaix's survey of notable Australian authors demonstrates. Dessaix writes that the only shared denominator in his respondents' creative processes was that 'everyone . . . had a sense . . . of going to the sacred glen and waiting to be approached.'

The idea that waiting is useful for cajoling our muses goes against the advice of many writing manuals and teachers uncomfortable with creative pauses, urging us to just write – something, anything. For some writers forced writing may work, but I believe cultivating patience is better. Trust me, the muses will appear, often when you least expect them to.

Stories abound about these appearances when, say, an overheard sentence or a film scene sparks an idea for a work. For instance, here is how Helen Garner's true crime book, *Joe Cinque's Consolation*, was conceived: a journalist told her about a murder of a young man by his girlfriend and Garner felt immediate affinity to the case. Only later, already working on the book, did she understand why that case came to haunt her. It hit close to home. At the time, she was grieving her divorce and wondering what *she* was capable of, what possibly terrible things.

Anecdotes such as Garner's are usually told as if they are lucky accidents. But are they? She had good reasons, Garner writes in *Joe Cinque's Consolation*, not to pick that story; it echoed the themes of another book for which she had been viciously attacked by certain feminist ideologues. Yet Garner followed the haunting, at her peril, just like Hamlin's children followed the piper. To me, rather than a fortuitous accident, this story is a testimony to emotional honesty in action – Garner's trust in her instinct.

Not all writers possess a natural ability to recognise those initial stirrings for what they are. Salman Rushdie, for example, describes in his memoir, *Joseph Anton*, how he spent thirteen years searching for his subject, the migrant's wandering identity. His might be an extreme case, but still – I suspect for every 'appearance' there are many more untold stories of unknowingly missed opportunities. That's why, when I wait for my subject, I try to be actively attentive, to notice how urgency manifests in me.

Sometimes it arrives as a spatial image. A landscape forms in my mind, and I want to experience it and its mood. That was how that murdered novel I'd mentioned revived. One day an image of dense bush with sky-scraping trees appeared in my mind, with my protagonist there, looking up into the foliage, feeling some comfort at being hidden away from the big bad world but also melancholy, for her refuge was fragile, tense, temporary. I wanted to go there, to smell the moss and eucalyptuses, to peer at the greenery alongside my character. But many other things can move writers to signal the arrival of the subject. An impressionistic painting, a dream, a tune or sentence that suddenly forms in our head. Let's trust these stirrings, those moments of mystery. Let's interrogate them. What might be drawing you to them? Are they pregnant with your tale?

*

Anyone's patience can run out sometimes. If (or when) this happens, you might like to stoke your attentiveness by trying my third tenet: **write what you need to understand.** Like most of my writing tools, I acquired this one the hardest way: through trial and error. It took me a while to see that my Russian memoir didn't work partly because I was writing it in order to 'educate' – about life in the Soviet Union, Russian Jews, the struggles of dissidents . . . A noble agenda perhaps, but an agenda nevertheless. Where is the urgency in *that*? I mean the visceral urgency. This, I now think, doesn't reside in the answers we already have when we begin writing, but in the questions we must resolve – foremost for our own sake. Or as Robert Frost famously said, 'No surprise for the writer, no surprise for the reader.'

This isn't to say that writers can't feel urgency about social issues. I am, for instance, urgently concerned about climate change. I have strong opinions and, who knows, may write a newspaper article about the dangers of mining. But to attempt a literary work warning against mining? At best, it would read like the Soviet state-sponsored literature. No good artwork I know of waves an accusatory finger or 'teaches'. Readers might gain knowledge on various subjects, but this would come as a side benefit to being involved in the narrative, not a primary aim.

And does this mean I should never write about climate change? Of course not. The question is not whether writers can write about issues that concern them but from what angle to approach these. Creative writers are not polemicists. They don't air their opinions or 'share lessons they've learned', as the cliché goes, but explore the dimensions of the issues which they are conflicted about, the facets they still need to understand. The Guyanese-British writer Fred D'Aguiar, for example, is concerned with race relations and his verse novel, *Bloodlines*, he says, originated in the following question: 'Can love emerge in the middle of despotism? In particular, during US plantations mid-nineteenth century slavery. I wondered if love could happen between a black woman and her white male captor.'

Similarly, if I were to write about an issue I care about – be it Soviet Jews or climate change – my starting point would be to consider, as Socrates would have it, what I don't know but must find out about these topics, and I would treat this material as the pathway into a new work. Considering the enormous scale of the environmental disaster we are facing, can individual actions count? And even more urgently – how should *I* act in the face of this crisis? I wish I could answer these questions. But I cannot. This is where my conflict, and perhaps my subject, lies. And the mining? I suspect if I ever wrote about environment, my views on mining would get some acknowledgement as an aside to the main subject – the quest to understand how to live in the twenty-first century.

*

My last tenet is **write what makes you blush**. Karl Ove Knausgaard speaks along these lines in his interview for *The Paris Review*:

> Concealing what is shameful to you will never lead to anything of value. This is something I discovered when I was writing my first novel, when the parts that I was ashamed like a dog to have written were the same parts that my editor always pointed out, saying, This, this is really good! In a way, it was my shame-o-meter, the belief that the feeling of shame or guilt signified relevance.

Art, unfortunately for writers, often emerges from the caves of shame. It is there that we find what constitutes the themes of great literature – internal conflicts, so-called immoral desires, childhood wounds. Such material contains the kind of human experiences we don't normally discuss in polite society but are intrinsic to our species. This is what good books give us: a conversation about what it *really* means to be human, with all the inherent darkness and confusion.

Knausgaard's shame-o-meter can help us find our subject: we can consider what we don't want the world to know about us, or to discover we are capable of imagining for our characters, and then write against our better judgement. Usually, such subjects are also the ones urgently pressing from within to be let out to the light, understood better and perhaps even resolved. A word of caution, however. Shame is not the same as trauma. Trying to make literature out of our wounds while they are still bleeding, when the pain is acute, can be psychologically damaging. Besides, to make an artwork requires a certain distance, an ability to approach our topic without great heat – something hard to do when the feelings are still raw.

On the other hand, to write shame-inducing stuff isn't as hard as choosing a less painful subject, because the latter wouldn't lead us anywhere artistic. That's why I eventually dropped that Russian memoir and began writing about the non-monogamous relationships of my past, tales that were seething in me.

I didn't want to tell the world about my bedroom life. More so, I worried that writing this story would be social suicide; even in these permissive times non-monogamy was still a taboo. Many of my normally open-minded friends raised their eyebrows when I told them what I was doing. One, usually a hyper-liberal woman, wondered: 'Who's got time for such things?' She said, when couples she knew had spare time, they engaged in environmental activism. Was she implying that non-monogamists were all climate change deniers? This response was perhaps extreme, but the consensus seemed to be that my topic wasn't worthy. At best it was light, perhaps even comical, and frivolous. I should have been writing about child abuse, historical accounts of convicts, the diminishing polar bear populations . . .

Still, I kept writing my unworthy story and nobody died apart from my writer's block (although it was a slow death). There were other factors that helped to annihilate it and I'll discuss them later, but these wouldn't have been effective if I hadn't had the right subject to begin with. So now I share Franzen's conviction that 'literature cannot be a mere performance . . . unless the writer is personally at risk . . . unless the writer set himself or herself a personal problem not easily solved; unless the finished book represents the surmounting of some great resistance it's not worth reading.' I also think that the best writing is an expedition into the unknown, the urgent and the uncomfortable. No writing manual with 1001 writing topics can guide us to where we need to go, as bravely as we can, deep into the wilderness of our battered heart.

INTO THE WILDERNESS

We've all heard this old, old story: 'In the beginning God created the heavens and the earth. Now the earth was formless and empty, darkness was over the surface of the deep, and the Spirit of God was hovering over the waters.' A writer can relate. The uncertain time when we first approach our subject, the formlessness. The emptiness. The darkness. I wonder what God was feeling when she began writing our tale. Was she, too, paralysed by all the possibilities? And by all that was still untold?

Every time I start a new work I suffer anxiety, but the beginning of *The Dangerous Bride* was particularly agonising because of how prolonged it was. Two years into my memoir, I still had no shape for it, and I felt overwhelmed by all the thinking and research I'd already done, not to mention the shame I felt about my subject matter. I decided to take a break to reconsider whether I could actually do this book and reread what I had: a 25,000-word jumble of ideas, snippets of scenes, character sketches, quotes from my research and reflective passages. This is how my typical page looked:

I turned to him and even through the haze of phosphoric darkness I could see in his face the ancient ruins of our marriage.

Artistic imagination occasionally breaks away from tragic clichés in favour of a more complex exploration of non-monogamy.

During his visit to Perth in 1922, DH Lawrence was overtaken by an uncanny terror in the face of what he called 'the spirit' of this 'raw loose' place.

The softly spoken English of the mystery writer I met was remarkably clear of slang and brimmed with words like whippersnapper. He seemed to belong to another era, that of genuine gentlemen. In short, he seemed like a man who could do no harm to a lady.

Much of the content was transcribed from my notebooks, scraps of paper and café napkins stained with the green of avocados and brown of god-knows-what, because in those years my writing was akin to a commitment-phobic lover. It rarely arrived when we had a date at my desk. The best sentences came when I wasn't chasing them, of their own accord, during my lunch breaks at work, or in the gym, or just before I fell asleep. Wherever it would be, I immediately scribbled them down, because the lover was so fickle I never knew if he would come again.

Notetaking has always been my natural way of entering a new work. It helps me to exorcise the terrors of the blank page and to absorb my subject. Having said this, often I begin a work even before I've put a single word down, first brooding over it for some days or weeks. The brooding sets my subconscious in motion to work on the budding project. At the same time, I might also stimulate my conscious appetite by doing some preliminary research. The writing of this very chapter, for instance, began with my re-reading of Joan Didion's famous essay on keeping notebooks.

Some time into the brooding and the researching, ideas and random sentences begin forming in my head. Nowadays my fickle lover is more reliable, but I am still fearful to lose these thoughts, so I always keep a notebook in my handbag and another by my bed as well as pens and paper in my car and in the kitchen. At some point, I gather my various jottings in one file along with research quotes and even copied paragraphs from my previous works if they fit the subject, because plagiarising my own writing can be my crutch to get past my fear of beginnings, even if most of the reappropriated material gets discarded in later drafts. These muddled files are the seeds from which the seedlings of my first drafts grow.

My intuitive, chaotic way of easing myself into a work is common among writers. Helen Garner, for example, describes the initial sketches of her remarkably concise novel *The Children's Bach* as 'HOPELESS MESS' (the capitals are Garner's). It's just that this phase rarely takes as long as two years. No wonder I lost hope with *The Dangerous Bride*. However, taking a break from it, then reading what I had in one sitting, gave me new perspective.

I discovered my file wasn't as formless as I assumed. It contained a rough sketch of several early chapters, plus fragments that would belong later in the story. There were also ideas and themes there to be threaded throughout the book, such as my religious upbringing and its impact on my love life. Then, some of the prose snippets felt so urgent and conveyed so precisely my experience that I turned them into engines to drive the writing of longer passages. Take this sentence: *The girl was a willowy, pretty redhead with serpentine lips; her plastic uniform was dangerously short.* I believe this imagery captures the heady cocktail of Eros, theatricality and risk that non-monogamy was for me. The sentence propelled me into writing the story of my first visit to a fetish club, where I met and kissed that girl, and it became the first chapter of my memoir.

*

Once I resumed writing my memoir, I could see that it wasn't just my anxiety that had long prevented me from finding some, even tentative, form. The story I wanted to tell was complicated emotionally and factually, involving multiple characters and several storylines. For these reasons, my work needed to go wild for a long time before I could work out how to tame it.

See, when we write well, even if we have a plan, many of our words surprise us as they rise from our guts, smeared with blood and undigested risotto, slapping themselves wetly onto our pages, naming things we don't want to be associated with. *These* words are our best material. There is even some neuroscientific evidence of this, that creative activity in its initial stages is an intuitive process. It has little to do with the analytical part of the brain. The brain at the time shows far less inhibition than usual. Instead of following the well-worn pathways, it exhibits a heightened activity of alpha waves, which are responsible for making new connections. Interestingly, the visual artist Max Ernst described his creative process, in similar if unscientific terms, as 'the chance meeting of two remote realities on a plane unsuitable to them.' To enable such chance meetings, the cognitive scientist Guy Claxton advises (in *The Wayward Mind*) during early creative phases 'to encourage a state of mind which is not the "winner takes all" mode of focused, purposeful attention, but one that delays foreclosure, and permits wider exploration of a priori less likely – e.g. less stereotyped or conventional – associations.'

My way of encouraging this state of mind, when the oddest and most interesting ideas, sentences and metaphors emerge, is note-taking. Note-taking is a less committal form of writing, so naturally my language is more dishevelled, and my mind is more open to weird ideas and unexpected narrative directions. I've also noticed that if I take notes on the same topic or scene between long intervals (because I've forgotten I've already considered the same thing), the ideas and even prose scraps I come up with are often almost identical. This affirms my belief that notetaking is a more thoughtful, and reliable, process than it seems. That it is a pretty accurate transcription of what's inside us.

Those two years of furious scribbling, when my thoughts weren't yet straightjacketed by a certain vision or structure, helped me to make the book more complex, and crazier, than it would have otherwise been. And, my fretting notwithstanding, I also enjoyed working like this, because my intuition kept dropping enticing mysteries into my lap for me to solve. For instance, one day I absent-mindedly copied the following quote by the Russian poet Osip Mandelstam into my file: 'The spiritual disposition of a poet inclines to catastrophe'. Why did I feel this belonged? My book wasn't about doomed poets. Or was it? As I soon found out, Russian poets of the early twentieth century, Mandelstam included, were no strangers to non-monogamous love. Then, my own spiritual disposition, as well as that of some other characters in my book, surely inclined us to . . . well, various (love related) catastrophes.

*

Some writers are natural planners or at least work in ways more orderly than mine. They might have some design, an outline, or even without a plan they might still write chapter-by-chapter or scene-by-scene while unsure yet how the scenes fit together. However they do it, gifted writers let wilderness enter their work one way or another before ordering it into its final shape. They might take notes *alongside* their more methodical writing, or daydream or meditate before their writing sessions. Or they might peruse images that inspire them. The method doesn't matter. What matters is to be receptive to your more obscure urges and intuitions, and to follow them even when they don't make sense. There will be time in later drafts to tame the jungle of your pages – those strange, exotic plants and beasts you never imagined could come out of you. For now, just let them flourish and roam.

My most astonishing beast emerged when I was writing my third book (still in Hebrew). It was a novel about a provincial young woman who moves to Tel Aviv to live out her dreams. But one day a new character appeared in my mind. Christina. She lived in pre-revolutionary Russia, was Jewish, unhappily married and in love with a Georgian poetess. In short, she was trapped by her gender, sexuality and ethnicity. A promising setup for a story, perhaps. But I was already in the middle of another tale, set in a different time and place; and it was a bildungsroman, not a midlife crisis. What was I to do?

The logical move was to forget Christina. Or lock her into one of my notebooks for later use, which was what I did. But as I kept writing my novel, images of crystal chandeliers and floor-sweeping ballgowns of the kind you wouldn't see in Tel Aviv kept intruding. Lines of poetry appeared in my mind, speaking of Siberian forests and heady Georgian wine. Of Christina's full, pale thighs. I was getting increasingly distracted.

Eventually, I submitted. I stopped writing my novel, created a new file named 'Christina' and tried to accept that the year I'd spent on the bildungsroman was a waste. I wrote more about Christina and her poetess, for whom she felt she could die (and eventually did). I had no idea where all this was going. Then one day the following passage appeared in my mind:

> Today nobody would guess Christina's charm just from looking at the faded photos of her, which Lora, her great granddaughter, inherited. It was not only the wealth of her parents (thanks to which they had received a permit to live in Moscow despite their Jewishness) that seduced the men. It was the deceptive idleness she exuded. Her ambiguity, her elusiveness and ephemeral nature. These were the qualities

that had turned the daughter of Jewish merchants into a sought-after guest at Moscow's high society salons.

Lora, her great granddaughter . . . Those four words came to me spontaneously. Just slipped out. See, Lora was the protagonist of my bildungsroman! So that was it. That was my novel sorted. Where I'd thought I was writing a linear contemporary story, I ended up with a circular inter-generational saga. Christina's murder by a homophobic priest was the ghost haunting my young heroine, disrupting her own love life. Once I joined the two storylines, my novel deepened, developed internal caves and passages. It's not my best book, but I like it more for Christina's presence. I even named it in her honour: *I Will Love Christina.*

*

Nowadays, I am still anxious when I begin a new work. It still takes me a long time to move into a more coherent writing phase, but at least I am done with feeling guilty about this. Instead of seeing this time as procrastination, I think of it as akin to child's play – both fun and work.

Being more aware of how my creative process works, it is easier for me to enjoy this preparatory phase and I am more willing to let myself be led off course, even to the remotest regions of my brain. I am better at trusting that at some stage, amid all the trial and error, my main themes will become apparent and a storyline will emerge. But not too early, I hope. First, let me linger in this biblical time of darkness, before the form comes along to delineate what is possible. After all, it was at the very beginning, when the earth was still empty, that the Holy Spirit hovered closely above it.

But then God said: 'Let there be a full draft.'

BUILDERS AND RENOVATORS

This morning my children are not at home. Instead of seizing this precious time to write, I water the plants in the front yard. I notice that my favourite flower, a blood-red geranium, needs to be dead-headed, and the golden hibiscus I planted last year is refusing to flower, despite showing no signs of disease – a mystery I am keener to solve than the mystery of how this chapter will unfold. The way I am writing today – in a combination of procrastination, agony and self-deception – is the way I always write my first drafts.

Notetaking may ease my entry into a new work, but not much helps the tedium, Herculean labour and terror of the next phase of writing – when I finally commit to creating the first comprehensive version of my story, which is what I refer to here as 'first draft'. Such a draft might have a messy structure, sloppy prose and gaps to be filled, but the key scenes and/or arguments will be there, however loosely sketched, and it will have a (provisional) start, middle and end.

First drafts stir up all my insecurities – that my imagination is lacking, my voice sucks, that I am not smart enough for my subject or have no stamina to complete a story, that I'll offend my dog with what I write. Alternatively, I can be seized, to the point of paralysis, by the feeling that I have absolutely nothing to say. Sometimes the paralysis is so acute that the work dies an untimely death. Other times, I manage to push past this painful phase to my favourite place, where all the romance of writing resides for me – the redrafting stage.

I don't think it's just me. All seasoned writers I know are clear on whether they belong to the first draft or redrafting camp. There might be some lucky ones who relish both stages, but I don't want to know them! For the rest of us, it's important to be aware of where we belong, then develop strategies to get through the phase we dislike without giving up.

*

A friend once said I am more of a poet than a traditional storyteller. In some way she is right. Like poets, I am most interested in the minutiae of language, how it expresses and affects our thoughts and feelings. I care much more about composing a sentence than composing a scene, about understanding a relationship dynamic than constructing a plot that *shows* these dynamics, about finding a telling detail rather than writing dialogue. That's why I relish the redrafting stage. Soothed by the fact that the story already exists, I enter a mindfulness-like focused state where I revise word-by-word, contemplating such delicious matters as whether describing my protagonist's dress as crimson is more effective than pomegranate-red. At this phase, the sensual pleasures of language compensate for my anxieties about the quality of my work, my prospects of being published, the state of contemporary literature . . .

I also love the macro aspect of redrafting, pondering my already-existing work from a bird's-eye view – its structure, themes and their interrelationships, mood, recurring metaphors. I like adding a window, shifting a staircase to a different corner, planting a gargoyle on the roof. I like all this just as much as I detest the methodical brick-by-brick construction of a narrative where you have to gradually introduce your characters and their problems through carefully constructed scenes. At heart, I am a renovator and interior designer rather than a builder.

The stuff about first drafts that terrifies me – all that emptiness yet to be filled, all those possibilities to choose from – is precisely what excites the builders, writers who love the phase of *creating* the story. They relish the freedom of the unknown, the surprise of what happens next. The blank page is their playground. This is true for memoirists too as they make decisions about what to tell and what to omit, how to order their lives to create enticing scenes and a tense narrative.

I also like surprises, but not those of an unwritten story. My favourite surprises are concealed within the drafted story: hidden meanings and interconnections that I discover as I revise. These also dwell in what I learn about myself as a writer and a person as my understanding of the work deepens.

To put it simpler, builders are more likely to lose interest in further writing once the story itself is told. For renovators, only after the story is told does the fun begin. These differences in preferences might be innate, bound to the shape of our deepest fears and desires; perhaps something to do with how much control we are prepared, or able, to relinquish. Renovators need something, even ruins, as their security blanket; for them, anything is better than nothing. When asked about the most frightening thing he had ever encountered, Hemingway – that bullfight aficionado who fought in the First World War and reported on the Spanish Civil War – replied, 'A blank sheet of paper.' In contrast, builders trust more the twists and turns of their minds and that the words will come. Perhaps they tolerate uncertainty better than I do, have a stronger imagination and are too immersed in living imaginary or reliving real events to be overwhelmed by what has not yet been written. On the flip side, the grandeur of the edifices they erect intimidates them. They are hesitant to retouch the building lest it collapses. Indeed, isn't it frightening to wake up and see our charming dream in the clear light of the day, how shabby and pale it is, how much work it requires to be rendered vivid for others too?

*

Ideally, a writer would spend most of their time inside the phase where they get most joy (or experience the least amount of suffering). For the builders it might be best to compose their stories slowly, deepening and refining them as they go, page by page, until the first draft and redrafting stages blur. In this way, they can still revise their works thoroughly but avoid spending a lot of time improving an already-known story. (Ian McEwan, who works like this, says he pretends that his first draft is also his last one.)

There are different methods to slow down the composition of a first draft through ongoing editing. William Styron perfects 'each paragraph – each sentence, even – as I go along.' Conversely, Stephen King doesn't concern himself with prose in first drafts, but focuses on the big picture, carefully writing and rewriting the major story elements, such as voice, characterisation, motivations and themes. He has even developed a formula that reliably works for him, where he completes a novel in what he calls 'two drafts and a polish'. In his second drafts he deals with smaller issues, such as finetuning his scenes, and the 'polish' stage is where he revises on the sentence level.

If you're a builder by inclination, you can also try some version of what Peter Carey calls 'cantilevering'. His approach to first drafts sits somewhere between Styron's micro-perfectionism and King's macro-focus. Carey begins writing each chapter from 'a poorly typed incorrectly spelled mess of messages and questions to myself', then he goes back to the chapter's start several times, refining it and getting a little further each time before finishing it and moving to the next one. The American novelist Richard Price works similarly, but instead of returning all the way to the chapter's start he might 'write a page, reread it, edit it, write half a page more, and then I'll go back to the very first thing I wrote that morning . . . So, I don't know whether I'm editing, reediting, or writing something new, but it's kind of a creeping, incremental style of writing.' And Joan Didion possibly works the hardest on her first drafts. Not only does she revise them as she creates a story, but she retypes them: 'Every day I go back to page one and just retype what I have. It gets me into a rhythm. Once I get over maybe a hundred pages, I won't go back to page one, but I might go back to page fifty-five, or twenty, even.'

*

In my younger years, when I rarely paused to consider what kind of a writer I was, I thought everyone's first drafts should be as thorough as those of Styron. Not a few of my ideas perished simply because I tried to develop them in this way. But renovators work better when they give themselves permission to figuratively vomit their first drafts, to create the raw material, as messy as it may be, fast. John Steinbeck advises along these lines:

> Write freely and as rapidly as possible . . . Never correct or rewrite until the whole thing is down. Rewrite in process . . . interferes with flow and rhythm which can only come from a kind of unconscious association with the material.

Steinbeck's whirlwind fashion suits me and nowadays I battle my terror of first drafts by attacking the page in fast and furious typing sessions that last anywhere from thirty minutes to two hours.

Despite the rubbish I often produce writing like this, I also see that Steinbeck is right, because I do find sentences, and even longer passages, that express my vision better than if I had written more carefully. The speed – not dissimilarly to notetaking – induces a temporary loss of self-consciousness, unruffling my more conventional patterns of thought, making room for more visceral ways of perception.

In the first weeks or months of laying out the story, I might write messily, dipping in and out of various chapters, or writing passages without quite knowing where they belong. At some point (sometimes from the start) I arrange my material into a provisional structure and then proceed writing chapter by chapter. Even then, I've learned to give myself permission not to write anything I don't feel like writing. Whether the 'undesired' section is essential to the story or not, I skip it and race on so I don't lose the momentum of creating a draft. Once the first draft is complete, I find two things may happen: either I have more energy to write those parts because I no longer stand on the precipice of the blank page, or I realise that what I had been resisting writing is not in fact essential to the story and can be summarised briefly.

I give myself all these freedoms, yet I am no Steinbeck who never stopped to look over his shoulder (he'd have made a better Eurydice). Just as there are many ways to write slowly, there is more than one way to write quickly. Between my stormy typing sessions, I check in with my earlier pages, revising here and there, non-systematically. The purpose of these random edits is not so much to polish my material but to stay in touch with it, so that I can keep creating the story more knowingly. Even more importantly, this helps me to figure out the work's mood and flavour, by trying out various rhythms and incantations until I strike the right note. To get the voice right in the first draft at least occasionally is important to me, because voice shapes the story too (more about this later).

The finished first drafts vary in coherence and structural integrity, depending on the work and the writer. Some look like a scattered jigsaw puzzle – all the pieces are there but it's unclear yet how they fit together. Others are structured chronologically only to be rejigged in later drafts into something more interesting. Yet others already have the final structure and, generally, require little revision. My own first drafts usually have their overarching shape (in the sense that their start and end are final), but their internal structure might change, perhaps even significantly, in later drafts. As well as that, they are at once frivolously oversized *and* miss chunks of research, scenes, even entire chapters. Still, once my unwieldy edifice stands upright – awaiting me to add some bricks, cover its exposed electrical cables and rearrange the internal furnishings – I finally start turning up at my laptop without an internal wail.

WRITING AS LAYERING

In 2009, when I had already been working on *The Dangerous Bride* for a while, the then-director of Varuna, Peter Bishop, invited me to participate in a residential masterclass with the visiting American writer Robin Hemley. During our first session, in front of Varuna's blazing fireplace, Robin asked each student: 'What's your book about?'

We were puzzled. Didn't he already know? Hadn't Peter briefed him about our projects? Still, polite as we were, we recited our usual spiels. 'But what's your book *really* about?' Robin asked. Aha! So, he wanted us to probe deeper into our works. We tried to come up with more interesting answers, but Robin wasn't satisfied. 'What is your book really, *really* about?' he asked. Thinking harder, several writers now headed in new, exciting directions. Yet Robin asked again: 'And what's your book really, really, *really* about?' He added that he wasn't expecting any answers now. He just wanted us to keep this question in mind as we went on writing our books.

That night, no great epiphany about my memoir struck me. But the notion that grasping the heart of your work can be a gradual, even long, process that unfolds throughout redrafting stayed with me. It took some pressure off. It was as if Robin gave me permission to be ignorant, unclear far beyond the phase of notetaking. (Indeed, it would take me another year to realise that I'd used my messy love life to explore the larger conflict in my life – my concurrent desires for adventure and security.)

Later, I came to think of all the aspects of a literary creation as akin to the development of a young brain where, over the years, increasingly intricate pathways between neurons form to make the brain more complex and mature. With this analogy in mind, I adopted a method of redrafting which I call *layering*, as in layering your work incrementally with meaning and craft until all of it is complete. This, too, has taken some pressure off. I'll share my method here.

*

Redrafting is damn hard, even for writers like me who love it. In this phase writers leave their solipsistic dreaming behind and get to the more prosaic task of rendering their dreams enchanting for others. Iris Murdoch calls this phase of work 'thinking that hurts'. And to hurt from everything that a literary work requires – a singular voice, fine characterisation, thematic depth and coherence, sound structure, sense of place and so on – this is a lot of pain!

Conceptualising writing as layering means you spread this pain between many drafts until it becomes manageable. As counter intuitive as this sounds, doing numerous drafts makes work easier, just as allowing yourself to write first drafts quickly and sloppily does. This method soothes the perfectionist in me, because in each draft I concern myself with just a few aspects.

In fact, many writers work like this; they just don't give their process fancy names. How they divide the labour of revision between the drafts varies. My preference is to zoom in – gradually move from solving macro problems to increasingly minor, cosmetic stuff. In my second and third (or subsequent) drafts I attend to such big-picture issues as filling in the gaps, restructuring the narrative, developing my characters or arguments further, finetuning the build-up of narrative tension and its eventual resolution (for example, I check how the work's end corresponds with the opening). Later, I spend several drafts addressing easier stuff, such as clarity of time transitions, pace, and setting and other sensory details.

Line-by-line revision I leave for the final drafts. Then I read my work very slowly, immersing myself in every sentence. I work on making my prose more direct in some places and subtler at others, deleting passages that tell readers how to feel, or that explain the obvious. I comb for cliché, superfluous or imprecise words, mixed metaphor. I read some paragraphs aloud to detect false notes in the rhythm. This is an odd time – the time when a placement of a comma becomes a matter of high importance, the time when I consider the benefits of square versus round brackets and dream about semi-colons.

My description of how I redraft might imply I am very organised. I am not. I don't adhere to a work plan. My zooming in occurs intuitively and layering stages can get mixed. The poet in me is always impatient to move beyond larger concerns and tinker with words and sentences, and sometimes I make concessions to that part of me, fixing some small stuff as I work on the big picture.

In a way, redrafting is also a circular activity, every draft returning me to Robin's question: What is this work reallyreallyreallyreally about? Even in the final drafts, honing my prose sometimes deepens my understanding of themes and characters. This was, for instance, how I discovered a new theme in my second memoir, *Imperfect*, where I tell my story of living with multiple scars. Having revised the opening chapter about my childhood line-by-line, I noticed how frequently words and metaphors related to death appeared there and realised that my early awareness of my mortality was intrinsic to the story of my scars. In turn, that realisation led me to making more structural changes just when I thought I was done with the big picture. And structural discoveries can alter the work's voice. Once I knew what my non-monogamy memoir was *really* about, I modified my prose so that the tension between safety and adventure infused it with language continuously wavering between calm and wild, experimental and traditional registers.

At some point, believe me or not, the work is done. Although, ask any author and they'll tell you that no work is ever really done, only wrenched out of our still-editing hands. Nevertheless, with time writers learn to recognise certain signs (other than an externally imposed deadline) that it's time to stop. Often, it is just an intuitive feeling, a faint voice inside that tells us – enough! But there might be some concrete indicators too. For me, there comes the time when I start reversing many of the changes I just made. Or when I suddenly know that from now on I would rather volunteer at my children's school fair than cast another look at my work.

*

The American poet Marianne Moore once remarked: 'Do the poet and scientist not work analogously? Both are willing to waste effort. To be hard on himself is one of the main strengths of each.' During the redrafting phase, it is imperative to take off the blinkers – those same blinkers essential for completing the first draft – and turn searingly honest about the quality of our work. We must become our own ruthless critics, ready, as Stephen King famously pointed out, to murder our darlings – those metaphors, sentences, scenes, even characters we are particularly attached to but that do not serve the narrative. (We can also enlist external critics and more on this later.)

Effective revision requires bloodshed, especially in the second draft when the work is still so tentative. It's not uncommon for a writer to radically re-imagine and re-do what they just created. Sometimes all the first draft is good for, says the Australian novelist Finola Moorhead, is to pick out of it 'the gems' which in later drafts we 'set in a muted background, which, naturally, makes them shine the brighter.' For her, as for many other writers, the real story unravels only during redrafting. Graham Greene's novel *Brighton Rock*, for example, was initially drafted as a detective story. Greene then discarded this idea and began writing the story again, turning it into a thriller and retaining only fifty pages from the first draft.

I can be as murderous as any writer, but my 'layered approach' reduces the unpleasantness of the task. I kill my darlings in stages. Especially, I don't pressure myself into killing the newly born ones, even if I already know they have to be executed. I let them languish on the page for my private pleasure until in some later draft I am ready to strike.

How do you learn to observe your material coolly, to distance yourself from something you've pulled out of your guts? I asked some Australian literary peers this question. Danielle Clode sometimes prints out her drafts on different coloured paper and in a different font to re-read before and during revision. Rebekah Clarkson also rereads entire drafts, and she does that on buses or in cafés while imagining herself to be one of the strangers surrounding her. Alice Robinson prints her first drafts out, then retypes them into a new file, revising as she goes. I've tried some of these strategies, but what works for me best is simply the passage of time. Even with the strictest of deadlines I'll take a break between drafts, even just a week. When I have no deadline, I wait between drafts for as long as I can – preferably some months – until the latest version of my manuscript stops convulsing and quivering, becoming submissive to my examination.

Goethe believed that creativity requires the ability to move fluidly between the conscious and unconscious states of mind.

I think waiting not only helps me gain a fresher critical perspective on my material but also switches on my unconscious during what is otherwise a hyper-analytical phase, helping me to maintain some poetic sensibility and a deeper connection to the work as I revise. Neuroscientists agree that pausing the creative activity reactivates our unconscious and that this part of our brain has a role in solving creative problems. Guy Claxton calls such intentional postponing 'incubation', arguing it helps us find original solutions:

> It enables you to get out of a rut in which your more deliberate thinking might have been unwittingly trapped . . . It also allows *cogitatio* to occur, reducing the strongly focused . . . desire for a solution, and replacing it with a broader, weaker kind . . . that has the capacity to attract . . . the less obvious material . . . Thus, casual conversation or observation . . . can throw up possible analogies and associations that sometimes offer a different more productive "angle" on the problem.

Some writers use the incubation strategy short-term. When Graham Greene grappled with some narrative problem, he would read the problematic passage just before going to sleep. He would find that in the morning 'the obstacle has nearly always been removed: the solution is there and obvious – perhaps it came in a dream which I have forgotten.'

Incubation helps one re-enter the wilderness, but wilderness is generally never far away from an attentive writer, edging itself around. Even as we strain over our twentieth draft's differently coloured pages with a critic's severe expression on our fatigued face, our work-in-progress potentially remains 'elastic . . . [capable] to accommodate each new thought, every nuance in the writer's mood,' as the American novelist Nicole Krauss writes. It doesn't have to 'harden' until the final draft. I'm witnessing this elasticity in action now, as the COVID-19 pandemic creeps into the pages of this book while I go on redrafting.

*

No matter how my outlook has changed since that Varuna masterclass, I can still despair at the magnitude of effort literary creation requires. At such times, I remind myself that the laborious redrafting that I do isn't a consequence of my initial sloppiness, or compensation for a lack of talent via hard work. Revision *is* the real writing. Writers do not write. We re-write. Sometimes even long after publication – in our fatigued heads. Re-writing is a natural crystallisation of thoughts. Or their excavation.

If even after this self-talk I still feel like drowning myself in a bottle of Campari, I try to take heart at the struggles of the greats, which certainly supersede mine. Isaac Babel would write up to forty drafts of a short story. Sherwood Anderson could take a decade to complete a book. Vladimir Nabokov rewrote his words so much that his 'pencils outlast[ed] their erasers.' Yet Nabokov, and Babel, and Anderson kept going, kept entering their torture chambers, aka their writing desks. How did they find the will to persevere? And how did they manage to complete a book, let alone several, at such a pace?

TAMING THE LION

The American writer Annie Dillard writes in *The Writing Life*: 'A work in progress quickly becomes feral . . . It is a lion you cage in your study . . . a lion growing in strength. You must visit it every day and reassert your mastery over it. If you skip a day, you are, quite rightly, afraid to open the door to its room.' In short, take leave of a book for too long and you may never find your way back. Or if you do, you'll probably get mauled.

The least sexy writing truth is that regular practice makes all the difference between writers who succeed and those who don't (assuming that a baseline of talent is present). Rarely do books get written in spontaneously inspired bursts by an author exhausting themselves in the spur of creation. Even Jack Kerouac is no exception to this prosaic rule. The story of him writing the modern classic, *On the Road*, in a three-week-long binge is one of those writing myths that fool aspiring writers. The more realistic, and lesser known, version of this story is that, prior to that, for seven years Kerouac had struggled writing this same book, producing volumes of notes. By the time those magical three weeks arrived, he'd already written several versions of his novel.

A writing regime made creation possible even for the excruciatingly slow-working Philip Roth. He managed to complete over thirty books in his lifetime. In contrast, in my younger years, despite knowing the obvious – that to be a decent writer you need to *prioritise* writing – I avoided taking my creative work seriously. Artistic success is elusive and I dreaded failure, at least in the sense of not achieving my best. So, I chose to work in demanding non-writerly jobs and acquired more academic degrees than I needed. I partied excessively and had too many friends for whom I cooked elaborate meals. I was always writing but in snatches, as if it was a mere indulgence and as such had to come after everything else. Which was ridiculous, given that those snatched sessions often felt more like torture than pleasure. When you write so irregularly, the lion grows more and more feral. Each time I went into the cage, I had to cajole the beast at length before I could enter. In turn, because I often felt estranged from my work, I kept it as a low priority. I was trapped in this self-perpetuating cycle, completing my works with far greater difficulty than was necessary. To avoid writing, I even enrolled in a PhD in social sciences. Paradoxically, it was this decision that helped me develop better taming habits.

In my mind, academic writing has never been bound with my self-worth the way creative writing is. The PhD was a challenging task to be accomplished – no more and no less. I was nervous at the project's enormity, but I approached it as I would any other day job. First, I prioritised my research time; I was teaching social sciences and writing, so I reduced my teaching load to the necessary minimum. I also cleared the decks: I did my tax return, caught up on my reading diary, re-organised the pantry and even unsubscribed from group emails. I figured the simpler and tidier my life was, the better I'd deal with the chaos of writing a thesis. Then I began working on it, daily.

I noticed that for me, the process of completing a PhD wasn't that different to completing an artwork. Like my books, the thesis began with a vague idea, which grew clearer as I went on researching, thinking and taking notes. Once a story emerged, I set about communicating it to others. Soon I noticed that writing every day made even completing the first draft bearable. If I ended a workday feeing dissatisfied, I didn't despair as I would when writing creatively. I knew I had the next day, and the one after, and the one after that, to keep improving. My usual sense of impending failure was replaced by the more hopeful thought of 'tomorrow I'll make it better'. Daily writing also helped me be more intimate with my work and grasp it clearer as a whole. This, too, lessened my premonitions of failure, so I procrastinated less.

Regular writing, I was learning, doesn't make fear go away, but it makes it more manageable. Two-thirds of the way through my thesis, I decided to apply these learnings to the writing of *The Dangerous Bride*. I took study leave and this time, instead of fitting writing into my life, I re-organised my life around writing and worked on the memoir in the same steady manner I'd had with my thesis. Soon enough, I entered the state of single-mindedness that writing a book requires and finally, after five years of work, finished my memoir. Then I returned to the thesis and finished it too.

*

Today is Saturday and I am having breakfast in a café while my husband is minding our sons. It is a glorious, glossy summer morning; soft jazz is playing. As I eat poached eggs, I am also working on this chapter. I'll do this for exactly two hours and then return home to spend the rest of the weekend with my big and little men. Since completing my PhD, I no longer have a scholarship. Instead, I have small children. Between paid work and parenting, it's difficult to clear a full writing day, so I often write like this – in short sessions.

The good news for the busy and the fearful (and let's face it, writers are usually both) is that as long as you visit your lion frequently, you can tame it even in the little time you have. Kafka held a full-time job in insurance and still became *Kafka*. Don DeLillo, Salman Rushdie and Peter Carey did long stints in the demanding profession of advertising. The prolific Anthony Trollope paid his servant an extra wage to wake him up every weekday just before 5 am with a cup of coffee, so that he could do three hours' writing before going to work as a civil servant. The Australian novelist Natasha Lester has no servants, as far as I know, but she wrote a bestseller per year over four years while raising three children by working every weekday for two hours during her kids' naptime.

Writing in short, frequent sessions can be more productive than doing, say, one long day each week, even if the total number of hours works out the same for both, because of the said hopefulness, intimacy and clarity that emerge from frequent contact with our project. Short spells also make writing time appear more 'sufferable' as well as precious, so you're less likely to procrastinate. Finally, as I suggested in earlier chapters, the lion's share (an intended pun) of creation occurs in the swamp of our unconscious. While we're working on a book, Helen Garner says, 'even when you think you are idle, just walking around gaping at the world, you are actually working quite hard.' Being in touch with our work often, even if briefly, keeps this internal simmering going and the work infiltrates our skin until we dream and daydream it. Then, even if you write just, say, for an hour four times a week, ideas and prose snippets will come your way as you're washing dishes or making love, and the next time you visit the cage, you'll get to the business of writing faster. Of course, none of this happens overnight. It might take weeks, sometimes months, of regular writing before our lion greets us pliably at the door, ready to do our bidding.

Ideally, the writing routine should always be scheduled for the same time, as Anne Lamott recommends in her popular book on writing, *Bird by Bird* – to train the subconscious to kick into action at a particular hour. Hers is good advice but not feasible for me. Given that I raise children as well as teach and mentor writers, I no longer have a regular work schedule or a clear distinction between weekdays and weekends, workdays and holidays. If your life is as unpredictable as mine, or even just if you dislike strict routines, then you might like to try my method, which I call 'flexible discipline'.

This is how it works: once I begin a book, I write five or six days a week, for a minimum of two hours a day. I do this no matter what else is going on – school holidays, overseas visitors, a meteoroid crashing to earth . . . Every Sunday I plan the next week's writing schedule, depending on my other commitments, putting these times in my diary as I would teaching gigs or medical appointments. If I must, I write at 5 am or 10 pm, as I did yesterday when my boys decided sleep was optional. Whenever possible, however, I give my writing the best time of the day, when I am most receptive to my muses. In my youth, it used to be the smoky spell of night. Nowadays I write best first thing in the morning, when the day is perky and full of promise.

*

During my first visit to Varuna, when I was still fruitlessly trying to write the memoir of my Russian childhood, one of the books I found in the library was the Australian author Gail Bell's *The Poison Principle*. It is a powerful true story about a man who poisons his sons, as well as a fascinating history of poison. But what captured my attention the most was one uneventful scene where Bell describes herself writing. The way I recall it, she is about to begin, but something is holding her back. Is she going to drink tea or chai while writing? She cannot make up her mind.

Tea or chai . . . For the rest of that Varuna stay I couldn't get over this. My emotions, already ferocious on account of my failing project, now spun out of control. Tea or chai. I wanted to punch poor Bell and also to get under her skin – be *her*. Tea or chai . . . Oh, Gail, Gail. How fortunate you are. How infuriatingly fortunate you are went the refrain in my mind. If only I had your problems! My problem was that I *never* wanted to begin *any* writing session, no matter what I drank throughout.

Tea or chai . . .

I don't think I've hated or envied a writer so much before or since.

Now that I am no longer blocked, not only am I sympathetic towards Bell's dilemma but I share it. Although I am too lazy to go to the effort of making proper chai – boiling milk, adding spices and grating ginger (and chai from a tea bag just won't do!) My version is: tea or coffee?

I cherish my hard-won luxury of worrying about such a matter, but I've also come to appreciate its significance in the act of taming. It's not enough to visit our lion frequently. Once we are there, how exactly do we reassert control over it? Frequent writing reduces procrastination, but it doesn't eliminate it, especially if, like me, you are a fidgety writer, happy for any excuse to ditch your work. And let me tell you, we are not exceptional. Even if we practically live in the cage, it can be bloody hard to get into a creative headspace. Here is Albert Camus writing to his lover from a secluded house where he'd retreated to complete a book: 'I kick and stamp and gnash my teeth until I take myself by the scruff of my neck and go back to a blank sheet of writing paper. Having lounged about idly for a good half-hour yesterday, I insulted myself aloud.'

John McPhee, one of the pioneers of the creative nonfiction genre, never insulted himself for a half-hour of procrastination since his bouts could last for eight hours:

> It's nine in the morning. All I've got to do is write. But I go hours before I'm able to write a word. I make tea . . . And exercise . . . It's four-thirty and I'm beginning to panic. It's like a coiling spring. I'm really unhappy . . . Five: I start to write. Seven: I go home. That happens over and over and over again. So why don't I work at a bank and then come in at five and start writing? Because I need those seven hours of gonging around.

McPhee accepted procrastination as a part of his process, but he could afford it. Those of us who must work at a bank or have limited time to write for other reasons have to appease their lions faster. One method is to develop a ritualistic association with the writing session's start to activate the creative part of our mind faster. It is there that Bell's dilemma assumes significance.

You may recall Pavlov's dogs – conditioned to associate a ticking metronome with food, they would salivate at its mere sound. Not dissimilarly, the first sip of a certain beverage can trigger our artistic part of the brain into salivating. For the same effect, the American author Gay Talese and the Australian playwright Louis Nowra dress up in suits to begin writing, even though they work at home. The Scottish novelist AL Kennedy plays certain pieces of music. Lamott says a little prayer. And some get their creative saliva flowing by reading over what they've written the previous day, their words luring them into their writing dream.

*

On my longer writing days, I have the luxury of attaching myself to the nipple of my muse at a more leisurely pace. I might begin by reading passages from Marguerite Duras or Joan Didion to immerse myself in the pleasures of prose, or by doing research. My difficulty on such days is sustaining momentum and keeping procrastination at bay throughout the day, so I break the writing into one- or two-hour segments. In between I do administrative tasks or reward myself with a spell of gardening, a walk or more reading.

This approach of 'divide and conquer' – where you break your work into smaller components – is effective both to combat short-term procrastination and more generally to sustain the gigantic effort that a book-long work requires. The American writer A. J. Jacobs writes along these lines on my blog *The Writing Life*: 'If you think of your book as one big chunk of 250 pages, it can send you spiralling into depression and despair. Instead, think of it as 25 chunks of 10 pages linked together.'

Another popular way of breaking down a project is by composing working lists. This can help to 'de-clutter' the mind and free space for creative thinking as well as make the work seem more feasible. Plus ticking items off the list affords some sense of achievement. In the early writing stages, you might like to make a list of scenes or chapters you already know you need to write. You can then write these either in a chronological order or pick whichever chapter or scene appeals to you on any given day. During redrafting, you can make a list of changes you need to implement. The Australian short story writer Vicky Daddo wrote to me that she rates the changes on her revision list according to their difficulty. Then she sets to work at the same time on 'deeply entrenched issues' that might take a while as well as doing 'easy fixes' to feel she is achieving something. The Australian novelist Charlotte Wood prefers eclectic lists for 'any creative tasks'. Her typical list may include 'themes to expand upon, characters to develop, timeframes to resolve. I often don't stick to the list, but it's a calming safety net'.

Lists work well for certain types of personalities, whereas other writers need the opposite – to exorcise the big picture out of their mind, put blinkers on and move along incrementally. When the Australian memoirist Kate Holden writes, she'd rather cast her glance only:

to the end of the chapter, or the next killer line, or the delicious moment of suspense, or the edge of what you've thought so far. This is rather how I live my life too, and it achieves both a dulling of the horror of pre-fatigue, and a sharpening of the sense of cheerful amazement when anything actually happens.

Whether you prefer seeing the big picture (divided up into parts) or just the next step, during the writing of first drafts you may like to break your work down by setting yourself word counts. Trollope used this method strictly: he would write with his watch in front of him, pushing himself to complete 250 words every fifteen minutes. This demanding pace worked for him, but most writers set much lower word counts so as not to feel discouraged by unfulfilled quotas (but encouraged when exceeding them). Hemingway, for example, was satisfied with writing as little as 450 words a day and for motivation kept track of his daily progress on a cardboard chart. (Being Hemingway, he set up his chart under a mounted gazelle's head!)

The main thing is once again to discover which method works for *you* – usually through trial and error. For me, word counts are useless, because I think through writing. I might write many words quickly then discard most of them and leave only a few last sentences. I do make lists sometimes, especially of research tasks, but often I feel they confine my imagination. What I like is breaking my project into micro-deadlines for finishing various drafts, including setting a final finish date. I rarely meet these goals, but having them gives me something to work towards and once again reduces my procrastination. The self-imposed deadlines also help me to visualise my creation as a series of drafts, which renders the process more doable.

*

Now that this chapter is coming to an end, you, dear reader, might feel just as frustrated as I do about having to put all these prosaic admonitions on paper. Cages, diaries, cardboard charts . . . But where, you might exasperatedly wave your lovely arms at the heavens, is the free spirit of creation in all this? To respond to this very reasonable indignation I'll quote Jeanette Winterson's writing advice: 'Turn up for work. Discipline allows creative freedom. No discipline equals no freedom.' In other words, the most reliable pathway into the wilderness of writing reverie runs through a strict regime.

Certain writers take this strictness very seriously. Camus – an enthusiastic dancer and womaniser who often had three or four lovers at once – turned monkish every time he was about to begin a new book, as he described in his diary: 'Before any theoretical enterprise . . . one must strain for a month of asceticism in every sense. Sexual chastity . . . and moral ascetism [whatever he meant by this].' Then once the writing began, he needed 'solitude and frugality . . . So that work is a violence that I do to myself, but a necessary one.' To do this violence, Camus would leave his wife, children and mistresses and go to isolated places to write around the clock, sometimes for months at a time, in monastic conditions. But as we'll see next, a cell isn't a compulsory requirement for writing. And sometimes we don't even need a room, with all due respect to Virginia Woolf.

THE WRITER'S SPACE

At the age of nine, the Israeli novelist Aharon Appelfeld managed to escape a Nazi concentration camp in Romania, the country of his birth, then survived the last three years of the war by moving from one hiding place to another. As an adult, now living in Israel and still haunted by wartime horrors, he couldn't work in confined spaces and wrote his novels in the cafés of Jerusalem and Tel Aviv, as he describes in his memoir, *A Table for One*:

> 'A man who has lost his home as a child will never have a home again'. I don't know where I read this; perhaps it was what I told myself. Years ago, a well-known author invited me to his home. He was wearing a blue dressing gown, he was in slippers, and he was ensconced behind a wide, heavy writing desk. I would have found such 'comfort' suffocating. When I work, I'm at a small café table, surrounded by people, and what I find myself writing there are things that the place evokes in me.

When they have to, writers write anywhere. It is a matter of pragmatics. Jean Genet composed his first novel in jail where he served time for theft and other misdemeanours. Another French literato, Jean-Paul Sartre, jotted drafts of his trilogy, *The Roads to Freedom*, at his meteorological army post during the Second World War. I wrote some of *Imperfect* crouched beside my children in their playroom. Still, where we write matters. It makes a difference to our stamina, focus and even, as in Appelfeld's case, the nature of our work.

The cafés Appelfeld frequented were bubbles where sabras, native Israelis, rarely came. Most of the customers were European refugees who, like Appelfeld, dwelled simultaneously in the past and the present. Among them he found the subject for his fiction – the wounded consciousness of survivors. It was also in cafés that he honed his skills of observation and learned how to translate abstract emotions and ideas into vivid, specific descriptions as he looked 'carefully at the human body, its positions, its movements; a body tells you far more than words like "loneliness" and "sorrow"'.

To do your best as a writer, once the term in jail, army or early parenthood is over you should move the lion to a cage that suits it best. This way, when you enter it the next time neither of you will be in an awfully bad mood. There is nothing universal about such 'suitability'. As with any other aspect of the writing process, it's important to notice where you work best. We are so used to associating the writing space with a desk at home that it's easy to forget that the comfort of slippers isn't for everyone.

The Turkish novelist Orhan Pamuk writes that 'the domestic rituals and details somehow kill the imagination. They kill the demon in me.' So he established his study in an apartment rented just for this purpose and which, he claims, has the best view of Istanbul. For Stephen King, Pamuk's view would be a nuisance, a distraction. His study is a bubble designed to keep reality away from interfering with King's imaginary worlds. The blinds there are always drawn and the stereo blares heavy metal music to further block the world. In a similar vein, Maya Angelou used to set up 'temporary studies' in rented hotel rooms where, to eliminate external stimuli, she'd ask for any artworks to be removed from the walls. This way, she said, 'all my beliefs are suspended'.

*

I am writing this chapter at home, in the study I share with Daryl, my husband. I am sitting in an orange swivel chair at a large desk upholstered with fake leather. Behind me is a red armchair where I read and think. Under my feet is a flowery rug. Sunlight is streaming through the window overlooking our front garden with its rich green of citrus trees, and the purples, pinks, reds and yellows of the geraniums and roses. To my right hangs a painting of two women standing serenely side by side, its palette predominantly olive-green. It is called *My Silent Friend* and was given to me by the Australian writer Virginia Peters. Looking at it makes me think of our friendship that's rooted in a shared passion for the focused (sometimes to the point of self-obliteration) silence of the writing hours.

Unlike King and Angelou, I like being aware of my surroundings when I write. The riot of colour and the presence of meaningful objects in my study energise and inspire me. I am particularly nourished by the view of our many bookshelves. Rows upon rows of fiction in my three languages; my collection of books on writing and literary criticism; Daryl's collection of travel guides and music books; tomes of history, psychology, cultural studies and philosophy; shelves of creative nonfiction, poetry, biographies, art books and plays. These bookshelves are also memories made tangible. Here is the signed book written by my first writing teacher. There is the Russian translation of *The Little Prince* which I bought in New York while visiting my parents. And the many books written by my friends and students. The story of my marriage, too, is written on our bookshelves: Paul Auster's novel *Leviathan* that Daryl and I discussed on our first date; the English translations of Russian and Israeli writers my husband read to learn about my former homelands; the slim volumes of Bernard Malamud's novels he introduced me to; and the many books we've given each other over the years. Books, books, books . . . I use them for teaching and research, but most of all they are my hothouses of inspiration, transporting me back to the times I want to recreate in my works or refuelling me with their melodies on days when there is no poetry in me.

If you are as domestic as I am, then you'll be more productive if you put time and thought into nesting in your writing space, surrounding yourself with objects that cast creative spells on you or are at least practically useful. This can be as simple as burning incense while writing or placing a vase of fresh flowers on your desk. Or as elaborate as Walter Scott's example: he installed a specially designed gigantic desk with two working surfaces in his study, because he always had at least two projects on the go and wanted to keep them separate.

Consider also whether you thrive on mess or order, plenitude or minimalism. I like my study to be stocked with lovely things but not cluttered and I keep my desk as clear as possible. Some writers would find such conditions dispiriting, stifling their imagination. For me, they are essential. The orderliness of my writing space helps me manage the chaos of my inner life, which my writing requires. This need for external order extends to my entire house, especially the kitchen where all my spice jars are labelled and easily accessible despite their great numbers, just like the research materials in my study.

As varied as our nesting preferences are, most twenty-first century writers, I suspect, would be sympathetic to Lee Child's story. He has said his 'productivity breakthrough' came when he disconnected the computer in his study from the Internet. This is something I aspire to but haven't achieved yet in my quest to perfect my writing space.

*

For Appelfeld, as we know, a room, any room – whether overflowing with books or the sounds of Metallica – just won't do. Not a few writers depend on more porous writing spaces, where reality slips in with greater ease, loosening an overworked mind and sometimes seeping into the written words. Louise DeSalvo, for example – that most plan-oriented of writers – likes working in busy public places, be it a library table near a glass wall overlooking greenery, a park bench or a lounge chair at a pool: 'If I only write at my desk, my work becomes too reflective and introspective'. Working away from home encourages her to pay more attention to the outer world on the page too. Not dissimilarly, the Australian writer Beverley Farmer recounts in her book, *A Body of Water*, how, during her writing residency at the Geelong College, the ivy pigeons abundantly around her crept into her fiction.

As far as 'porous writing spaces' go, Appelfeld's preferences are far from unique. Cafés particularly inspire passion in writers. The Norwegian playwright Henrik Ibsen grew so attached to a certain corner table in his favourite Oslo café, Grand Café, that he would scare off any would-be intruders. The Austrian satirist Karl Kraus had even higher expectations from cafés he frequented: 'Sitting alone at a table does not satisfy one's need for solitude. There must be empty chairs standing around. If the waiter moves away a chair that no one is sitting on, I feel a vacuum, and it awakens my gregarious nature. I cannot live without empty chairs.' Such conditions weren't easily achieved and I wonder whether this was the reason for Kraus's fatal heart attack, which took place in the famous Viennese establishment Café Imperial.

The love affair between writers and cafés might be fierce partly on account of the sensual pleasures these places offer. Hemingway's memoir *A Moveable Feast* is possibly the most famous tribute to café hedonism. It describes his time in Paris when he was in his twenties, broke and still happy and excitable, still years away from his bitter retreat to write in his bedroom in Cuba in the vicinity of the gazelle's head. Hemingway spent long writing days in cafés. The legendary Café de Flore and Les Deux Magots were among his favourite haunts. In summer, their bohemian patrons sat on the footpaths, sipping on beer as they tried to change the world. In winter, they moved to terraces heated by large *bracieri* filled with coals, the sparks popping like exploding stars. In any season, Hemingway would work there, focused amid the happy chaos and drinking coffee, or – when he had some money – feasting on oysters and sausages. The wellbeing he experienced in those places fuelled his work – not metaphysically as in Appelfeld's case but physically: 'I ordered a rum St James. This tasted wonderful on the cold day and I kept on writing, feeling very well and feeling the good Martinique rum warm me all through my body and spirit.'

I understand Hemingway. The mere word *café*, so French and soft, makes me feel alive, indulged, as if I am on holiday. Life is beautiful in cafés – bright, creamy, made of poached eggs and croissants. As much as I love writing at home, cafés are indispensable to my work too, particularly during the writing of first drafts when the start of each workday fills me with dread. At such times, I often take my laptop to my local establishments. Once I walk in, I enter a meditative state. I shift my focus from my anticipated failure to the smoky smell of coffee beans, and the buzz of juicers and music. I sip on my latte, gaze through the windows, bask in Melbourne's delightful streets filled with tram rattle and evergreen trees, and pretend I am here solely to enjoy myself.

Even as I begin writing, nothing feels serious. I can always stop, can't I? But really, cafés discipline me. Even in my most despairing hours, when I once again consider retraining as a chef, café magic works itself on me. In this liminal space, where the outer world surrounds you but loosely and things always happen – you notice someone you know, discover a delicious dish or hear a song that takes your breath away – something in my mind clicks, my fingers pounce panther-like onto the keys and the electronic page loses its virginity.

Unlike Appelfeld or Hemingway, however, I cannot spend a full writing day amid the hum of espresso machines, even when the staff don't give me dirty looks for overstaying. Cafés help me to get started but after a while I lose concentration. What I prefer is moving from home to a café and then back. Even at home I often wander – between my study and the couch in the living room. The novelty of each place clears my head and helps me see my work from a new perspective. That's why some writers, when they feel stuck, get away from their usual writing places to work somewhere different, like the beach or a friend's house; somebody I know takes long train rides to write. I like to retreat to writers' residencies, especially during redrafting when I need to be immersed in the work as a whole. It might be, then, more apt to speak not of writer's space but writer's *spaces*, given how mutable our creative needs are. One day you want to write near another café patron, your pal and rival F. Scott Fitzgerald, the next day you prefer the proximity of a taxidermised gazelle . . .

THE WRITER'S BODY

It is about to rain in Melbourne when I begin writing; the sky has been deceptively cloudy since the early morning. I say 'deceptively' because the sun is still finding its way through the fluffy celestial bedding, smudging this summer day with a sandy haze. The heat in the air reminds me how much of Australia is on fire right now.

The house is empty and quiet. Still, I cannot write. I cannot get my mind off my compatriots losing their houses, livestock, memories – often uninsured, un-backed-up. I cannot get my mind off media images of koalas screaming in the trees burning alive, the devastation of the bush, the continent, the planet.

As is always the case with me, lofty concerns mix with domestic anxieties. I am fuming over a recent botched electrical job at our place. I am planning the dinner I'll be making tonight for my stepson and his new girlfriend. I am considering what to pack for our trip to Perth tomorrow and what this family holiday will mean for my book's deadline. I am unable to access the inner stillness writing requires. My husband calls to ask me to fix our gate. I organise the repairs, then switch off my mobile phone. I log out of my emails. Still I don't write. I see hellish visions of smoke and fire. I wonder how the online bidding is going – along with many other writers, I am auctioning my writing services in exchange for donations to the Country Fire Authority. I log in to Twitter and find the bid on the writing workshop I offered has gone up. I log out.

I don't write.

I attempt my usual strategies to enter the writing mode. I read passages from Helen Garner's diaries (for inspiration). I read an online article on memoir writing (for research). The article is good, so I decide I must share it with the world and log into Twitter again. And why not share it on Facebook too? Strategy number three. I copy quotes from a book I've just finished, *Sophie's World*, into my reading journal. This isn't related to my work, but I hope that by engaging with philosophy I'll take my mind off the immediate reality and enter a dreamier space. But on the page I am looking at, Alexandria's library is burning . . . I google 'bushfire updates'.

By now, it is 11 am. My best writing time, morning, is disappearing down the drain. I am feeling hot. I am feeling desperate. Ever since the bushfires began (and to be honest, also since the school holidays began), I've been absent-minded during my writing time, producing little. Despondency takes over and I slump in my chair. Then I make a swift decision. I change into bathers and race to the local pool. I hurry inside, drop my bag, take off my dress and enter the silky water. I stretch and contract and stretch my limbs. I push against the wet elasticity. I begin breathing more steadily.

As I keep swimming, I am still thinking about how to maximise the online bids and what to make for dinner to impress the new girlfriend. But I also feel calmer, less guilty about wasting this precious morning. At least I am working on my body if not on my book. I dive into the warm water. When I come up for breath, feeling the air on my face and the faint ache in my muscles, a serenity descends. Words begin forming in my mind of their own accord. *It is about to rain in Melbourne . . . botched electrical job . . . silky water* . . . The words come and come, fleshy, exerting insistent and pleasurable pressure on me, just like the water as I move through it. Eventually, the pressure grows so powerful I bolt out, dry myself impatiently, sloppily, and race back home, to my laptop.

*

Sometimes when the mind is recalcitrant, nothing but the body can save us. And how lucky is that? If there is one thing all writers have in common is that we happen to have bodies. They are yet another road to our minds. The trick is, as always, to find your individual path: how *your* body can assist *your* work.

Just as I swim in order to empty the mind of mundane concerns and artistic insecurities, centring it on the work to be done, Anne Lamott achieves the same by performing breathing exercises at her desk. But physical exertions of our choice can serve more purposes than just help us get into a creative zone. Studies show physical exercise – not unlike a deliberate break from writing – can temporarily block the habitual pathways of our mind, allowing our stories to emerge less self-consciously, more organically. That's possibly why when American philosopher and writer Daniel Dennett feels creatively stuck, he does physical chores at his farm – cutting wood, harvesting, mowing. Virginia Woolf went on long walks, focusing her mind on the scenery. Woolf then, as her scholar Louise DeSalvo writes, 'entered that receptive, passive, meditative, yet alert state that created the optimum condition for the inspiration for a new work to surface in enormous detail'. And occasionally, like Beverley Farmer's ivy and pigeons, the environment enriched Woolf's pages. In her novel *Jacob's Room*, for example, the protagonist replicates the author's strolls through London. Philip Roth also used to walk, but his version of exercise was less scenic – he paced around the room. He did so with more deliberate goals in mind, to plot his novels; he once claimed he walked half a mile for every page he wrote.

The bestselling novelist Dan Brown is the most acrobatic writer I know. He uses 'inversion therapy', hanging himself upside down while wearing gravity boots. Apparently, this practice, or torture, brings him new ideas by changing his perspective. Fortunately, the treadmill in my gym has the same effect on me, so I don't have to hang. It is there that I often solve the structural problems of my works. This might be no mere coincidence considering how many runners there are among writers. In some ways, running and writing parallel each other: both are done solitarily and afford us a certain feeling of freedom. The measured breathing and the repetitive rhythm make running well-suited to induce the meditative state writers depend on when attention drifts, time disappears and creative thinking flows. Joyce Carol Oates, who runs regularly in between blocks of writing 'through pear and apple orchards, through fields of wind-rustling corn towering over her head, along farmers' lanes and on bluffs', says her cognitive state is cinematic when she runs. She experiences 'an expanded consciousness in which I can envision what I'm writing as a film or a dream', where ideas await her.

Regular running as well as other types of physical exercise also strengthen our discipline, our ability to concentrate on a task and execute it patiently, incrementally, step by step or word by word. Haruki Murakami, a long-distance runner, explores this relationship between physical activity and creativity in his memoir *What I Talk About When I Talk About Running*. He describes how his daily ten-kilometre runs, sometimes coupled with fifteen hundred-metre swims, have helped him to maintain his strict writing routine which begins as early as 4 am. He makes the point that 'talent is nothing without focus and endurance'.

*

When writers become grumpy with their audiences, one of their pet complaints is how often they are asked supposedly ridiculous 'technical' questions, such as whether they write with a pen or a keyboard. But are such questions really foolish?

The impact of exercise on writing practice is well established, but we tend to overlook that the act of writing itself, this flight of spirit and imagination, is also a physical act. Isn't it done with our hands? Writing literally comes from our bodies, even if it is only the mind that gets the accolades. The pulsing sensations, rhythms and aches of hard-working fingers are supposedly at the mind's service, but I believe they also feed it, stamping their tactile music onto our tales.

There is scientific evidence that how we write affects our brain activity. Apparently, cursive writing assists the building of neural pathways important for memory and complex thinking. Perhaps that's why some writers feel more connected to their work when they write by hand, like Paul Auster does. In *The Paris Review* interview he discusses his predilection without getting precious about it: 'A pen is a much more primitive instrument. You feel that the words are coming out of your body and then you dig the words into the page.' But during redrafting Auster uses his old Olympia typewriter, to experience his words differently.

For Robert Stone, another novelist who alternates between handwriting and typing, the deciding factor is speed. He usually uses a computer, but when he faces problems with narrative development he writes by hand to slow the writing down in order 'to be precise. On a typewriter or word processor you can rush something that shouldn't be rushed – you can lose nuance, richness, lucidity'. John Banville also thinks the pace of writing matters. He writes both what we call literary fiction and crime novels – the latter under the pen name Benjamin Black. 'Black' types his books on a computer because the speed affords him 'the kind of spontaneity and risk that crime fiction requires'. Conversely, Banville uses fountain pens for his novels, needing 'the resistance of the nib on the paper'.

I have no knack for racy, plot-driven fiction and yet, like Benjamin Black, I prefer computers. It is not so much their speed that attracts me as the quality of my hands' movement, their fluttering and slapping on the keys that I associate with artistic flair. Typing makes me feel as if I am, although tone-deaf in real life, playing piano. I feel lighter when I type, flightier, more daring, and even grand – as if performing a private recital. It is easier for me then to soar up, up, up towards the residence of muses . . .

*

There is another reason why, scientific findings notwithstanding, I choose computers over the possibly more poetic cursive writing. For me pens hold little poetry, because writing by hand weighs me down, drags me back to earth by wearing me out physically much faster than typing does. Here, too, the body shatters the illusions we hold about writing being merely a delicate business of spirit. As we write, our arms move, often vigorously, and they ache (repetitive strain injury is almost as common among writers as it is among masseurs). Our backs stiffen. Our behinds grow numb.

Sustainable writing practice requires physical self-care. Taking regular intervals during the writing sessions to move around doesn't only keep the mind fresher and more alert but also the body healthier. That's why when Dan Brown isn't hanging upside down, he does hourly stretching exercises. I incorporate bursts of physical activity into my writing routine mostly by doing housework and gardening.

For perseverance as well as health it's also important to notice what posture suits us best while we write. By creating optimal conditions for your body, you send your mind free, so just as there is nothing trivial in debating typing versus handwriting, there is nothing trivial about ensuring our chair is comfortable or the height of the writing desk fits. And let's not march automatically to our desks (or café tables) just because 'that's what writers do'. This is exactly what I used to do until a decade ago when I hurt my back and couldn't sit in my study that day. Instead, I parked myself and my laptop on the couch and four hours later found myself staring at my watch in disbelief. Four hours! An incredible bounty for me who had struggled to stay focused for more than two hours at a time. The reclining position provided me with the comfort I didn't know I needed. It also eased my entry into the luxurious, creative space of daydreaming. (But too long on the couch and my brain goes to mush. That's why, as you know, I now wander between it, the desk and cafés.)

Some writers surpass me in their decadence, composing their books in bed. Truman Capote did that while also indulging in other sensual comforts: 'I can't think unless I'm lying down, either in bed or stretched on a couch and with a cigarette and coffee handy. I've got to be puffing and sipping. As the afternoon wears on, I shift from coffee to mint tea to sherry to martinis.' Nabokov used to be a horizontal writer too until in his later years he decided that to remain productive his body and mind required Spartan discipline. So, he shifted to working while standing by a lectern. In turn, Hemingway, another writer who turned vertical with ageing, placed his typewriter chest-high on top of a bookcase in his bedroom (near the gazelle's head, of course) where he wrote with an open window no matter the season, even with the cold wind blowing in.

At this ascetic image, a question beckons: What did Hemingway have *in* that bookcase on which his typewriter stood? It is the importance of this quandary that I'll consider next.

THE WRITER'S LIBRARY

'To write is to read', the majestic Australian novelist Brian Castro once said from a lectern at the University of Melbourne and I, undertaking a Masters in Creative Writing at the time, wrote his words down. They became my golden writing rule.

Why do these words matter so much to me, a hungry, adventurous reader since childhood? I've read writers from around the globe: Indonesian and Scandinavian mythology; ancient Japanese stories; *The Arabian Nights* as well as the *Mullah Nasreddin Tales*; Russian, French and English classics; the Israeli canon and some Yiddish writers; and all those famous American novelists. I've sampled most genres, even fantasy and science fiction which aren't my thing. From the age of four, I've read every day. I need reading for the same reasons others need meditation or wine – to ground myself, maintain my mental health. The only time I went without reading was the first week of my first child's life. I had the time, but all I wanted was to hold my son and look at him, so rattled was I by his existence. I did, however, read several pages on the day my second son was born, once the drugs wore off.

I did know from early on that to write is to read, just as I knew not to take seriously the anxiety about being influenced, which some budding writers cite as an excuse for not reading. When we read a great variety of books, we are unlikely to copy one particular voice. Instead, I like imagining books inside our conscious as well as unconscious memory as organic matter, slowly breaking down to blend into a rich compost that nurtures the seedlings of our own works. I don't think of the writings of E. M. Forster when I write, but having read him, I believe something of his sensibilities have remained in the back of my mind, expanding my horizons. It is ignorance rather than familiarity with literature that leads to conventional, clichéd writing.

Then, and forgive me for sounding pompous, not to read is simply unprofessional. Serious writers read constantly. As Philip Roth puts it, for a writer reading is a 'way of keeping the circuits open. It's a way of thinking of my *line* of work . . . It helps inasmuch as it fuels the overall obsession'. Elena Ferrante is sterner on the topic: a writer 'has a duty . . . to have a vast literary culture.' Or forget duty. Reading can, and should, make us 'drunk with ecstasy', Henry Miller writes in his bibliomemoir (written before bibliomemoirs were invented), *The Books in My Life*. Apparently, after reading a good book he returns to his own work 'revivified' (what a great word!). Whatever the reading reasons for an individual writer are, Paul Auster's account of his reading as a young writer in his memoir *Hand to Mouth* is more typical of dedicated writers than exceptional. He 'drank them [books] up in staggering numbers, consumed entire countries and continents . . . I read as if my brain had caught fire, as if my very survival was at stake'.

Even an obsession with one particular writer or book is unlikely to turn us into copycats, as long as we read other books too. Consider this instead as training under a master. Many original writers proudly admit that certain authors or works have shaped their internal landscapes, linguistic sensibilities, artistic visions. For Ian McEwan, Philip Larkin's poems are 'part of my mental furniture'. Reading the Austrian writer Peter Handke inspired the younger Helen Garner to be more honest in her work. Isabel Allende says *One Hundred Years of Solitude* was instrumental in launching her career: 'I wrote my first novel, *The House of the Spirits*, with the same freedom, magic and insanity that I thought Márquez had called upon in his own writing.' In all these ways, as the American fantasy writer and literary critic Lev Grossman puts it, some books can become writers' 'fixed stars to navigate by'. That's why whenever Joan Didion begins a new novel, she re-reads Joseph Conrad's *Victory*, as it 'opens up the possibilities of a novel. It makes it seem worth doing.'

My own writerly soul, despite the many different books it has absorbed, is essentially Russian. The theatrical, sometimes hysterical, sensibilities of this country's classics imprinted themselves on my younger self and I've never succeeded in trampling the romantic out of my pages. Luckily, there were also Chekhov and Gogol to temper all that drama, to instruct me in the art of irony and shadows. But above all, one book looms – Mikhail Bulgakov's novel *The Master and Margarita*, which shaped me both as a writer and a person.

This masterpiece, often compared to Goethe's *Faust*, is set during one Easter, when the Devil and his crew of demons decide to visit the aggressively atheistic Stalinist Moscow, wreaking there merry havoc. The visit is the main plot, but the book has a labyrinthine structure, teeming with sub-plots, characters and themes. More so, the novel moves between different genres: it is at once a wild political satire, fantasy, romance, historical fiction and philosophical tract.

I read *Master and Margarita* first when I was ten, while still living under the Soviet dictatorship, and it taught me all I needed to know about the power of laughter in the face of the despicable. Since then, I've re-read this novel many times, in all my three languages, with a writer's eye too, appreciating how Bulgakov stretched the form to its limits, breaking most rules sternly laid down in various writing courses. Most notably, he gets away with the overload that his book is by remaining highly entertaining throughout. His example encourages me, as a writer, to trust readers' stamina and adventurousness, instead of trying to fit into their (imagined by me) comfort zones. It is as if Bulgakov says, the only rule in writing is Express Your Vision. As if he gives me licence to be bold, daring. The way he continuously navigates between the past and the present is also fundamental to how I see life and describe it. Bulgakov may even be responsible for my tragicomic worldview, which I try to express when I write.

So, reading for me has always been symbiotic with writing, and yet . . . I needed to hear Castro's words. Sadly, I needed an external affirmation that my reading habits weren't an extravagance, a guilty indulgence that ate at my writing time, but constituted the very core of my creative life. The way I interpreted what Castro said was that the best thing a writer can do is not enrol in a Masters in Creative Writing but bury themselves in a library, allocating at least half of their writing time to reading. Unwittingly, Castro encouraged me to take my reading more seriously, more deliberately – not just as a pleasure but as artistic practice. This changing of gears increased my awareness of the extent to which others' books affect my own words and I began taking active charge of my reading to improve my writing. In short, I began reading *like a writer.*

*

To read like a writer is foremost to steal. Yes, it is to read for inspiration, to be absorbed in a literary atmosphere, but also to uncover other writers' tricks of craft and adapt them to our needs. Then, let's be honest, sometimes the theft is more direct. I know no writer who didn't, even once, steal something or other from the authors they love, be it a (paraphrased) sentence or some narrative twist.

Writers read analytically; they read slower and more attentively than they would when reading just for the pleasure of it. They notice how other writers structure their sentences, what overt and covert information their syntax conveys, what mood they create. They are more alert to structural ebbs and flows: at which point of the story the narrative begins, what happens mid-book and how the central tension is resolved at the end. They pay attention to common storytelling techniques, such as foreshadowing and flashbacks, to the amount and quality of dialogue, and how time transitions are flagged.

There is so much to note that it can be useful to re-read books that leave a strong impression on you, digging deeper for their secrets. Proust went as far as making a career out of translating and annotating the English writer John Ruskin, doing so for twelve years! Some writers find it useful to copy passages from the books they love. David Sedaris is one, hoping his 'fingers might learn what excellence feels like'. And legend has it that in order to write his autobiographical novel, *Fear and Loathing in Las Vegas*, Hunter S. Thompson copied the entire *The Great Gatsby.*

Such deliberate reading is hard work and an art in itself. In the second part of this book we'll practise this, examining examples of emotionally honest prose. But in this chapter, where our concern is still with the writing process, I'll keep the focus on how to match what we read to our writing projects.

*

I notice a curious angst among teachers of writing, themselves often writers and ambitious readers, about coming across as elitist when they discuss reading in their classes. While they might complain to peers about how little their students read, in the same breath they often say it doesn't matter what students read as long as they read something, and it is not a teacher's role to pass judgement on their choices.

Such an attitude might benefit the teachers, render them more likeable in a classroom. However, it doesn't benefit their students. Reading choices are not a trivial matter. Reading is our most important means of honing our art, but not every kind of reading makes us grow.

For the record, Hitler was an avid reader. His private library contained more than sixteen thousand books and he'd often finish a book in a day. Yet, as much as some scientific studies stress (just as certain teachers do) that *any* book you read is good for you and will supposedly make you wiser and more empathic, you'll probably agree that neither wisdom nor empathy were Hitler's strongest points. He chose his books through the prism of his views: Henry Ford's anti-Semitic book, *The International Jew*, for example, was among Hitler's favourites. He read for affirmation rather than enquiry.

Hitler is an extreme example but he, too, was a writer of sorts, even if it's a stretch to class propaganda as literature. My point is that to improve our art (as well as personhood) we're better off challenging ourselves by reading not just books that confirm our views but also those that introduce difference. This was why recently I read Steven Pinker's *The Blank Slate*, even though evolutionary psychology, with which Pinker is aligned, is a discipline I view with suspicion. I am glad I did. Firstly, I found Pinker to be a fine writer and thinker. Secondly, while I wasn't convinced by all his arguments, he made me reflect deeper on one of my writerly preoccupations – the gaps between our moral convictions and instincts. Then, reading this book also helped me better understand what it is about evolutionary psychology that goes against my grain.

Writers, I believe, should also read *up*, reach for the best of the best. It is easy to get caught in the desire to 'stay up to date', focus on the latest literary sensations. Such books can sometimes be very good – absorbing, thoughtful works to learn from. However, how many of them prove to be masterpieces? On their own they aren't enough to make us better writers. If you are serious about your art, you need to familiarise yourself with as many masters as possible, do the kind of reading that Karl Ove Knausgaard and Amos Oz did since their young adulthood, spending long hours devouring Faulkner, Nietzsche, Dickinson, Dostoyevsky, Kierkegaard, Sophocles, Melville, Seneca. Virginia Woolf even set herself a 'reading program' and kept a journal where she took stock of what she learned.

Reading up can be a tough job. At least for me it is, as it requires all of my brainpower to stretch my reflective faculties to the maximum. Still I do this – to find my own fixed stars to navigate by. To open myself to the strangeness, the wilderness, of human existence as shown vividly by the greats.

Chekhov doesn't just paint a portrait of pre-revolutionary Russia's middle and lower classes, he also shows how, in any class, despair can edge out even the greatest of happiness, lurking in the most ordinary of spaces – a kitchen, a nursery room. E. M. Forster layers every square metre of the ground on which his novels are set with history, illustrating (not unlike Bulgakov) how the past always underlies the present. And I haven't looked at cats in the same way since reading how Nabokov's character in *The Gift* 'nearly tripped over the tiger stripes which had not kept up with the cat as it jumped aside'.

The difficulty with reading masterpieces, I am sorry to say, extends beyond intellectual exertion. Such reading wounds fragile writerly egos. Nabokov injures me greatly. I'll never be capable of writing a sentence as good as the one above or the following one: 'Sleep is the most moronic fraternity in the world, with the heaviest dues and the crudest rituals.' Even if I were to read Nabokov every day, his erudition, wit and originality are impossible for me to match. Still, I keep reading his works, because the higher the quality of the organic matter I absorb, the better my writing gets fertilised. I do hope that some specks of Nabokov's greatness might rub off onto my pages. This is why whenever I start feeling I can write just as well as, or even better than, the author I am currently reading, I take it as a sign for me not to feel smug but to pick a different book: the kind of book that is likely to leave me feeling like putting a bullet through my skull, or at the very least finally wanting to retrain as a chef.

*

The other side of the reading coin – the one certain teachers of writing might deny – is that reading can also cause harm. As much as some books take our writing to the next level, others bring it down. I am speaking from experience here, for although I began my 'reading career' with flair, somewhere in my mid-twenties I lost my intellectual stamina.

For several years I was mostly a body. I smoked and drank and fell in lust all the time. I danced until dawn. I kept bad company. This is a crude summary of an intense, and in many ways vital, period in my life. Even back then I read every day, and I still read the occasional classic. But, in sync with my overall mood, most of my reading was the latest popular literature, untested by time – books that traded in linguistic, emotional and moral banalities (the three, I think, go hand in hand). Unsurprisingly, my own writing came to smack of nonesty.

There is no diplomatic way of saying this: poor reading choices dumb our writing down. If we mostly read the kind of books that simplify human nature then our words are likely to turn more simplistic too. This is not to say writers should never read ordinary books. I, too, occasionally consume and enjoy them; I just no longer make them my main meal. Such books give me a break from my more ambitious reading, and they, too, aren't without their educational value, mind you. As Stephen King writes, sometimes reading 'the mediocre and the outright rotten . . . helps us to recognize those things when they begin to creep into our own work'. King himself is a quite sophisticated reader as are most commercial writers at the top of their game. They are there precisely because they know that to read great literature in a systematic, sustained fashion is their best training.

*

Reading like a writer is a hungry, colossal act. It is reading until a cacophony of voices sounds in our heads, until our minds become kaleidoscopes and our sense of possibilities for syntax greatly expands. And yet. Sometimes, particularly in the early stages of composing a book-long work, a part of the writer's job is actually to (temporarily) narrow down their reading. To ensure the books they read are the ones to best nurture the new work.

I think of the reading choices we make during such times as keeping a 'reading diet' and it's a known fact that people's dietary needs differ. Certain writers don't read at all while they write. They produce books in between reading, in bursts of intense work. They are usually well-read, but while they work reading only distracts them from the enormous effort of creating something good so fast.

Still, most writers read while writing, at the very least for research. (The Israeli novelist David Grossman goes as far as reading only whatever is relevant to his topic for the entire creation of a book, even if it takes him years to complete it.) Writers may research facts or see how others compose works similar to theirs in subject or genre. When I was working on *The Dangerous Bride*, I found reading another creative nonfiction work, *Stasiland* by the Australian writer Anna Funder, immensely useful in finding a form for my book. The narrative of *Stasiland* is driven by Funder's quest to interview former Stasi officers and informers. Reading her book, it occurred to me I could also weave my story around my search for people who had been in non-monogamous relationships, given that I was having difficulties finding interviewees. Non-monogamists appeared to be almost as secretive and difficult to find as those Funder was after, unwittingly providing me with a richness of narrative obstacles, crises and resolutions.

Some writers, however, find reading books on a similar subject or in the same genre to theirs dispiriting because this prompts them to compare their works-in-progress to already finished works. Preventing harm from coming our way through reading while we write is just as important as seeking books to learn from. That's why, as much as I love them, I avoid Jonathan Franzen's novels while writing. Franzen's fiction is thick on dialogue and thin on poetry, whereas my ratio is the reverse. Franzen's powerful voice, speaking an entirely different language, can easily silence my own when I am at my most fragile. Structurally, too, my works are looser, more circular and dreamier than his; against the sharp outlines and polished surfaces of Franzen's books my writing can appear like a puddle of mud. So, while I write I'm careful of choosing books that don't discourage me.

The purpose of a reading diet can also be to get into the right headspace. That's why Ferrante limits her reading while writing to re-reading certain fiction she loves, calling it 'books of encouragement'. Salman Rushdie reads poetry while composing his stylish prose: 'When you're writing a novel, it's so easy to have odd bits of laziness slip in. Poetry is a way of reminding myself to pay attention to language.' I also read for language, seeking writers whose voices remind me of the tone I want to achieve on my pages. I gravitate towards extravagant writers in whose cascading sentences I can drown or whose words I want to eat – Didion, Fitzgerald, Duras . . . And funny, playful writers in love with ideas, such as Robert Dessaix, Geoff Dyer and Elif Batuman.

Putting ourselves on a reading diet is a skill that requires sustained reflection about our needs, which might shift with every new work.

It also requires discipline, which can be a struggle. I enjoy reading the most (as I do food) when I am free to pick my next book (meal) according to my current mood, interests or other whimsies (and never according to latest prize lists). That's why I rarely read books as soon as I buy them. Instead, I shelve them like some shelve wine – to open when the right moment arrives. Just recently I read a biography of Marc Chagall, which I'd purchased twenty years ago, because I finally felt like indulging my interest in modernist art. And that is the wonderful thing about writing this book – because it's all about literature, I can read anything and still nurture this work. But most works-in-progress, unfortunately, require a stricter regime.

THE WRITER'S DREAD

Writer's block – not a specific creative problem needing to be solved but sustained difficulty in writing – is a common, and commonly debilitating, phenomenon. Yet there is little agreement among writers not only about the reasons and remedies for this affliction but even about its existence. The prolific American novelist Ann Patchett, for example, thinks writer's block is a myth, an excuse for lazy writers, as in 'writer's block is out of our control, like a blocked kidney. We are not responsible.' Another fertile writer, Philip Pullman, does believe in the existence of writer's block, but he is as judgemental as Patchett. According to him, it is 'a condition that affects amateurs and people who aren't serious about writing'. However, many serious, and brilliant, writers have endured this affliction; among them Mark Twain, Anne Lamott and, of course, Fitzgerald, whose frequent bouts of writer's block are forever imprinted on the history of modern literature.

To my mind, Patchett and Pullman's attitudes come from the sheer luck of having never suffered writer's block. From bitter experience, I have learned that the difficulties associated with this condition are much greater than an inability to work out a feasible writing schedule or to tear yourself away from Instagram. When they are in the grips of writer's block, some writers, like Geoff Dyer, cannot write at all, even if they have hours and hours at their disposal; others write, but with enormous difficulty and often with limited results. I am among the latter. During my four years of being blocked, I wrote for just as many hours as I do in happier times; I even produced some publishable short works. But I hated everything I wrote and most of what I started I never finished.

After my writer's block ended, I reviewed the unfinished material and found that while some of it was rubbish indeed, other pieces weren't that bad and I wove them into subsequent works. I see now that one symptom of my writer's block was that I lost a valuable artistic asset – the ability to evaluate my own work. During those years, I grew convinced that something about the soul, the essence, of writing had eluded me. Writing had become a secret I was incapable of uncovering. My writer's block wasn't procrastination but an existential crisis where I lost my most fundamental identity. From what I've seen, it is so for many other 'blocked' writers. Perhaps what gets blocked in a writer isn't so much their access to ideas and language but access to the truth of our writing self – artistic vision, voice, creative needs. And I doubt it's possible to find a way back to ourselves without first understanding the causes of this enigmatic, and devastating, condition.

*

Circumstantial reasons for writer's block vary. Some common ones are: shame about our subject, a sense of having nothing to say, misguided or overblown ambitions, sheer fatigue or even some consuming personal problems. Often there are multiple causes, and these combine into a rather murky medley – of the kind plumbers find in the underbellies of our homes. This was my case too.

My writer's block began not long after I settled in Australia. I lost my Israeli readership and was struggling writing in a new language for new audiences. With more ambition than insight, I chose the wrong writing subject. On top of all that, my then-marriage was in trouble. However, what underpinned everything, and what I now think is at the root of any writer's block, was fear – no, dread. A dread of discovering I wasn't good enough. A dread of criticism, humiliation, failure. (For some, this can look like its opposite – the dread of success.) My hunch now is that if writers choose to watch Netflix instead of writing, or drink themselves to death while straining to write, as Fitzgerald did, it's not because they are lazy or amateur, but because there is something deep inside them that is petrified of their creativity.

My semi-educated guess has some support with researchers who have studied the phenomenon of writer's block. So far tentative, but still, evidence is emerging that writer's block is as real as mental illness, linking writer's block to changes in brain activity associated with fear. Apparently, under particularly strenuous professional or personal circumstances the parts of our brains associated with creativity may become disrupted, shifting to produce symptoms of anxiety. These changes can be lasting, resulting in a serious psychological affliction or even, some scientists suggest, a form of depression.

Whether fear is an underlying cause or an effect, it was surely bound with my experience of writer's block. My anxiety about writing was so pervasive and enduring that it overshadowed most of my waking hours. I would party or go to theatre or have drinks with friends, but at the back of my mind my worries that I might never be able to produce another book continuously played their sombre tunes, distracting me from whatever goodness came my way. And surely it was no coincidence that my writer's block unfolded during the years of my struggles as a new migrant and a wife.

The good news, according to scientists, is these changes are reversible. My recovery was a gradual, subtle process, but I am confident the turning point was when I finally recognised that neither the book I was writing nor my marriage were working. Soon after I let go of both and was making first steps with *The Dangerous Bride*, I met my current husband, Daryl. During the first year of our romance, I – already the equivalent of a Woody Allen character – was seized by so great an anxiety about what I realised was my first real love that it superseded any creative fears. Writing was no longer everything. With my dread of hypothetical failure redirected onto my beloved, the pressure I felt when I wrote lessened. Not only that, but unwittingly Daryl helped me to reconnect to my writer's voice, an experience I will describe later in the book. My point isn't that finding love is the antidote to writer's block (although it can be . . .) but that unblocking takes time and may involve implementing all sorts of life changes. Just as it's difficult to imagine someone ending a depressive episode while they remain in a crippling relationship or job, so it is with ending writer's block. Solving personal problems helps. At the same time, we should also try writing-specific remedies.

*

It has been thirteen years since my writer's block ended. I believe I emerged out of that dreadful time more in touch with how my creative process works. Above all, I am now attuned to my reasons for writing and more ruthless about abandoning a work that feels wrong. Possibly, for some of us the experience of writer's block is essential for growing artistically – a sort of baptism by fire. Possibly, this was how it had to be for me. But I am certain it didn't need to grow as severe and last as long as it did.

One frequently suggested remedy is establishing a writing routine. However, this targets symptoms (the inability to produce new, or good, work) rather than cause (fear). Writing routines are most effective *after* we've acknowledged and treated the dread. They are far less likely to help a writer paralysed by fear. A better starting point would be to do some soul searching (alone or with professional help) – to examine our deepest anxieties as well as creative circumstances and priorities. What do I really, really want as a writer and am I doing everything I can to achieve it? Is there something I fear to such an extent as to sabotage myself? Am I too scared to pay the price of living as a writer? Once you know what it is you dread, you can try writing about, and around, it until, hopefully, it'll be written out of your system. And sometimes such writing gives rise to a new work, as happened to Geoff Dyer whose superb memoir, *Out of Sheer Rage*, is above all a description of his creative blockage.

In fact, the best thing a writer can do is to identify the early signs of writer's block to prevent it from becoming a crisis. Nowadays, I am watchful for such signals as excessive procrastination, anxiety at the mere thought of approaching my laptop, a feeling of disconnect from or overwhelm by what I am writing and, most commonly, acutely detesting the sound of my own voice. When any of this happens, it's important to act fast. Let's look at some common strategies, so that you can build your own arsenal in case you need it one day.

Hunter S. Thompson was fond of remarking: 'I hate to advocate drugs, alcohol, violence or insanity to anyone, but they've always worked for me.' He wasn't the only one. Fitzgerald, as we know, consumed alcohol liberally to quiet his fears – gin was his favourite medicine, but it is also possible that his drinking caused much of his blockage, especially during his final years. However, moderate amounts of booze or any other mood changer work well for some writers I know.

For more wholesome methods, there is the advice of Hilary Mantel, who thinks solitude is crucial during vulnerable times. Her suggestion is: 'Don't make telephone calls or go to a party; if you do, other people's words will pour in where your lost words should be. Open a gap for them, create a space.' She also suggests you engage in such 'mindless' activities as baking, meditating or sleeping. Then, not a few writers resort to such 'mindful' methods as immersing themselves in non-literary arts – cinema, ballet, paintings . . .

In my experience, any of these methods can be effective as long as we use them early enough, before our dread hardens into creative paralysis. When I was deep in my writer's block, no amount of drinking, lonesome baking or reading helped me.

Anne Lamott believes less in a writing routine and more in loose, even very short but daily, writing. It can be anything: 'memories or dreams or stream of consciousness on how much they hate writing – just for the hell of it, just to keep . . . fingers from becoming too arthritic'. A similar, and often cited, suggestion for combating writer's block is to keep a regular personal journal. For many writers these strategies work, but here is a word of caution: as with any other method, no matter how common, this isn't going to work for everyone. It didn't work for me. When I was blocked, I found myself journaling *instead* of writing creatively. I guess I'm one of those writers who have limited writing energy. Writing doesn't generate more writing for me, as it does for some. So nowadays I am more mindful of how I spend my creative mojo, saving it for my artistic projects.

These differences among writers bring me back to the crucial role of emotional honesty, in the sense of reflective capacity, in the writing process. In other words, it helps us tune into our singularities. These days, when I start feeling writer's block clawing into my skin, the first thing I do is I reassess the project I'm working on. Is this the right one? Am I still passionate about it? If the answers are in the affirmative, then I remind myself that writing is a slow, gradual accumulation of words and meaning; this helps me to lower my expectations about the quality and quantity of words I should be producing.

Once I resume writing, I try to hypnotise myself into self-belief by doing a self-talk I've developed. I begin by telling myself that there is no formula for good writing, that simply transporting the constellations and rhythms of words from my mind onto the page might suffice to constitute decent prose. If this doesn't help, I launch into a mantra that goes something like this: 'Remember how tough it was writing your previous book? And the one before that? And the rest of them? You thought you couldn't do it, but, hell yeah, you did. And remember how you hated most of your sentences in your first drafts, but then had another go and made them better? You curse the day you chose to be a writer whenever you write anything, but perhaps this is just your lot, girl – to write like this. So off you go, and write your crap again, and turn it again into something less crappy!'

Usually this works. But this doesn't mean that occasionally my dread doesn't materialise. In other words, sometimes the crap just doesn't get less crappy. And then what? How are we to keep going in the face of failure?

FAIL BETTER

Recently I came across a quote by the American visual artist William Bailey: 'Every painter is in a state of continual failure.' At first, I was puzzled, particularly given that Bailey's art is a great success, residing in various major museums. But the more I contemplated his words the more I agreed with him. Isn't making art all about trial and error, groping in the dark? And once it is made, we put our creations, ourselves really, out to public judgement, with little if any control over the reception. (Is it a wonder, then, that writer's block is so common?)

Even if you are excruciatingly successful and the public cannot get enough of you, in committing to your art you are dooming yourself to a lifetime in the shadow of failure, or at least the possibility of it. Lives of many prominent writers are characterised by wild swings between highs and lows, creative joy and profound self-doubt – the perpetual fear of falling short of if not public expectations then their own. Midway into composing his masterpiece, *The Stranger*, Camus wrote to his wife-to-be: 'I've just re-read all that I've written of my novel. I was seized with disgust and it seemed to me a failure from the ground up.' Helen Garner's diaries are another vivid proof of how persistent the sense of failure can be, weaving its thorny way through writer's psyche. Not long after her debut novel *Monkey Grip* came out to accolades from readers and critics alike, Garner's difficulties with writing her next book led her to conclude that 'maybe I'm a one-book woman'. Five years and two more successful books later, she expressed the following sentiment about her work: 'Grief is not too strong a word for what one feels before one's own weakness and mediocrity.' Perhaps the myth of the tortured artist is no myth after all . . .

Even when I am not blocked, the possibility of failure is my background melody, frequently making me a miserable person who snaps at her family and ignores sunshine and cuddly dogs. In the face of creative problems, my default response is defeatism. When I was drafting *Imperfect*, for example, at first I couldn't figure why I wanted to write about extreme body modification. This uncertainty led me to deduce that my months of research into this topic were a waste of time and I should throw this material out. And if I couldn't work out (in that same book) how to describe my years in Tel Aviv? I must throw *the whole book* out . . . I usually end up clawing my way out of such far-fetched conclusions (in the end, *Imperfect* was not only completed, it included two chapters on body modification), but it takes me a long while to stop the panic as well as stop pushing away cuddly dogs.

Some writers are better than others at tolerating the feelings of frustration and inadequacy that are our occupational hazards. Think of V. S. Naipaul who for the first nine months of writing his novel, *A House for Mister Biswas*, couldn't get the work to come alive. Still, he persisted, trying different approaches until one day something clicked and the work began to breathe.

How Naipaul managed to convince himself he hadn't failed with the novel, that it was worth persevering, I don't know. I do know what helps me: to remind myself that the writing process is more than mysterious machinations of sexy Olympic muses. It is also a pragmatic endeavour of ongoing problem solving. Getting stuck in some quandary is the norm rather than proof of outstanding failure – even if sometimes this 'stuckness' can last for a long time, like in Naipaul's case. Being patient and understanding that failed attempts do not necessarily equal an aborted work are other keys to unlocking the door of self-belief.

But what about those failures that are not anticipated but real? Those failed works that were never meant to be. Every writer I know of has a closet with skeletons of discarded works in it. How do we not take these deaths as evidence of our artistic ineptitude?

I say, let's not recoil at the sight of the corpse. Let's brace ourselves for the stench and face it before relegating it to the closet. A failed work can teach us stuff, provided we are honest and humble enough (as well as not overly squeamish) to receive its lessons. A failure can teach us who we are creatively and who we are not. As much as my discarded books, including that 'murdered novel' hurt, they also taught me valuable lessons about how my creative process works. For example, I now know not to do a lot of research before and during the writing of my first drafts, so as not to get overwhelmed by my material as well as not to inhibit this intuitive phase of creation with too much *knowing*.

But I am nowhere near as resourceful as Michael Chabon. Chabon managed to use the dead bones of a novel he'd discarded to create a living work. This happened in the aftermath of the publication of his debut novel, *The Mysteries of Pittsburgh*, which did well critically and commercially. This success set Chabon up for the dreaded Second Book Syndrome. Eager to repeat or even surpass his accomplishment, Chabon's ambitions for his second novel were sky-high. Five years and fifteen hundred pages later, he conceded his unwieldy beast was never going to be tamed. But what might have driven another writer towards excessive drinking or an alternative career in bank robberies didn't stop Chabon. He channelled the despair of those years into the protagonist of his next completed and acclaimed novel, *Wonder Boys*. That character turned out to be – surprise, surprise – a failed writer.

Feelings of inadequacy in the face of creative difficulties, as tough as they are, are only one problem in the multitudes of what can make writers, these delicate creatures, feel like a failure. You may recall, for example, how in the years I was working on *The Dangerous Bride* I found myself constantly, meekly, apologising for my choice of subject. I felt I was failing people who believed in me, as well as my potential readers. And I was failing people I was writing about by portraying them inadequately or 'too honestly', or just by writing about them. Yet there was also something vital about my despair then, something that spurred me on. The more I felt I had failed, the more I felt as if I was writing against everyone, as if my book and I were comrades in our struggle against the Big Bad World. I felt the heat of inspiration at the tips of my typing fingers, even if my hands were unsteady with fear. The tension generated made the book feel even more urgent, and possibly some of that urgency seeped into the writing itself. In any case, my suffering made the way I approached my work healthier. It kept me on my toes, made me dig deeper into my story, made me more vigilant.

Perhaps we shouldn't just tolerate but actually cultivate our feelings of inadequacy – as long as they are not so mighty as to block us creatively. They can be useful (in the same unpleasant way that fish oil is) to foster a healthy measure of self-criticism. Rilke writes along these lines in *Letters to a Young Poet*:

> Your doubt can become a good quality if you train it. It must become *aware*, it must become criticism. Ask it, whenever it wants to spoil something for you, *why* something is ugly,

> demand proofs from it, test it, and you will perhaps find it helpless and nonplussed, perhaps also aggressive. But do not give way, demand arguments . . . and the day will dawn when it will become, instead of a subverter, one of your best workmen . . .

Whether we like it or not, a measure of failure is intrinsic to gaining a measure of success. Perhaps this was what Beckett had in mind when he advised writers to fail again, and to fail better.

'I hope you suffer prettily in Paris,' somebody said to the American writer Djuna Barnes upon her arrival in that city. This anecdote reminds me yet again that there is suffering and there is suffering. Creative catastrophes – actual or anticipated – can produce great beauty. So, as we approach the next part of the book, which focuses on the actual words we put on the page, I wish you the same – to suffer prettily as you keep writing.

PART TWO:

HONESTY ON THE PAGE

'Honesty in story-telling makes up for a great many stylistic faults.'

– Stephen King

In the Soviet Union, where I grew up, writers were revered, and at the same time closely monitored by the state. A writer, Stalin decreed, is the engineer of the human soul – a lofty task indeed. The engineers, pardon – writers of whom the state approved, received handsome salaries. In return, they were expected to write in the genre of socialist realism: to describe the world not how it was but how the Soviet dictatorship wished it to be. There were no food or housing shortages in those books nor any restrictions on personal liberty. The state officials were kind and noble (unless they were corrupt and eventually punished for this). The 'working masses' were always right and the 'individualists', as the people who thought for themselves were called, were always wrong. Ironically, the only writers who were able to say something true about their time and place without being censored were the fantasy and science fiction ones. These brave souls disguised their critique of the Soviet regime with dragon fire and spacesuits, not fooling anyone but the kind and noble state officials.

The Iron Curtain crumbled a long time ago, and it never existed in the West. Yet a form of socialist realism is alive and thriving in some (published and unpublished) Western texts I have encountered over the years. Such works don't necessarily glorify communism but their essence is the same – they describe the world as the writers wish it to be, or as they are habituated to see it through the lens of various received wisdoms and ideologies. Naturally, such stories are simplistic and their heroes (which may or may not be the authors) might make mistakes but never touch the darkness, while the villains can do nothing right.

Writing of this kind is partly a result of various external pressures writers are vulnerable to, and some of these I discuss in the third part of the book. Yet I don't believe the socialist realism impulse is a sociocultural matter only. It also belongs to human psychology. We all wear the blinkers of our experience and bias, our predilections and fears. We all have, albeit to varying degrees, nostalgic and sentimental urges to perceive certain people, places, events and periods as monochromatic. When I write about my childhood, for example, I find it difficult to reconcile the ample anti-Semitism I experienced in Russia with some other, profoundly wonderful, experiences I had there, like building snow houses into which I could fit or going to the opera. So I have to fight my impulse to choose one or the other, to either idealise or demonise my place of birth, depending on my mood at the time.

Karl Ove Knausgaard says that 'the duty of literature is to fight fiction.' He isn't suggesting we should only write nonfiction but that writers must battle the fiction of the delusions, illusions and outright lies that are a part of every society's fabric. Whatever genre they write in, the writer's job is to capture real life's mixture of wisdom and folly, justice and injustice, comedy and tragedy; to show that light and darkness are more tangled than separate. In worthy literature, 'good' people are susceptible to shadowy desires and deeds; 'bad' people can at times be sympathetic. Most humans would be better described as 'complicated', not to mention that not all the concepts of 'good' and 'bad' are universally agreed upon.

It's not easy for a writer to discard their fears and illusions, given that both these things protect us from the discomforts of reality. And it is difficult to write with fairness about something that goes against our beliefs. Or to master courage to cast a look at life's many atrocities. If you do all that, you might come to feel like David Grossman, for whom writing means 'dismantling my personality. All my defence mechanisms, everything settled and functioning, all the things concealed in life break into pieces, because I need to go to the place within me that is cracked, that is fragile, that is not taken for granted.' But, he concludes, 'this is how books should be written.'

In this second part, I invite you to follow in the footsteps of Grossman (and Knausgaard) and foster the art of deep observation to reach towards the dark, the complex, the paradoxical, the tense, the raw, and towards the truths of the stories we tell. For such purposes, the writer's starting point should be themselves, no matter what genre they work in, because our self is the prism through which we create art. Artistic writing begins with self-awareness of, and honesty about, our psychological landscape – all those messy emotions, thoughts and memories that make us who we are.

Once you grasped some of your fundamental truths, hopefully you'll be capable of seeing more clearly the outer world and understand what stories you can tell about it. The next challenge will be to find the best words to express what it is that you found, the kind of words that will imbue your pages with boldness, vividness and precision. This latter task, too, is the concern of this part of the book.

VOICE IS YOU

To talk about the elusive concept we call writer's voice, I'll first go back to 2002 – the time when I lost mine.

'Yeah . . .' sighed Simon (in Russian). 'And what does *this* mean?' He looked at the pages I'd given him and quoted from my story in English: 'The Art Deco lamb winked at us from a distance.'

'You know, lamb,' I responded in a frivolous mixture of English and Russian coloured by my heavy Israeli accent. 'Like the one I have in my room . . . Oops! I meant, lamp. Art Deco lamp.'

'Aha . . . And what do you mean by *winked*?'

'That's not a mistake.' I defended myself. 'The lamb . . . sorry, the winking lamp is my voice.'

Simon, an accomplished poet, looked at me uncertainly but said nothing. For a while he kept reading my work in silence, then pointed at the words *nekudat hashaka* and asked with a now-pronounced despair: 'What's *that*?'

'I couldn't find the English translation of this term,' I said, 'so I wrote it down in Hebrew.' After a heated discussion we discovered in English it meant *point of contact* (in geometry).

Simon, I should tell you before this gets utterly confusing, was my friend who had immigrated to Australia from Russia twenty years earlier and had a great command of English. I was, at that time, brand new to this country and its language. Simon offered to help me learn writing in English, but his generosity was costing him his nerves.

Those were strange days. I would write something in Hebrew, translate it into bad English and then discuss it with Simon in Russian as he helped me improve the English version. If this sounds confounding, it was! I also studied English on my own. I spent all my money on dictionaries, thesauruses and books on idiom. I read books in English as if my life depended on it, painstakingly checking the meaning of each unfamiliar word. In the process, I learned that certain English words sneak into the Russian dictionary while being absent from the Hebrew one, or vice versa. I also learned that when Australians say *bigwig* they don't mean a drag queen or Marie Antoinette.

Eventually, I got to the point where I no longer needed to torture Simon but could write directly in English. (This is probably why we're still friends.) Yet my lamps continued to wink from a distance, which is to say my metaphors, and generally my prose, were often clumsy. I had lost my voice.

*

The English writer A. Alvarez argues in *The Writer's Voice* that 'literature is about listening to a voice . . . neither the medium nor the message is the point. The point is that the voice is unlike any other voice you have ever heard and it is speaking directly to you.' I also think that an honest, bold voice is the magical wand that turns narratives into artworks. If you've got it right, the rest of the story elements, like plot and characters, are likely to come together eventually. Without the voice, nothing is going to work. But what exactly do we speak of when we speak of the writer's voice?

A common assumption is that a writer's voice stands for a unique writing style, and it does. But this is not the entire story. The style is the 'micro part' of voice, which I discuss in the following chapter. Here I am talking about the very foundations of voice, about what the accomplishment of a distinct style stands for – a precisely expressed singular consciousness with its unique psychology. Our voice emerges when *how* we say something fits the contours of our mind. Another way to describe writer's voice is as the *weather* in which our stories dwell. Or as Raymond Carver puts it, it is 'a unique and exact way of looking at things . . . There is another world according to Flannery O'Connor, and others according to William Faulkner and Ernest Hemingway . . . [voice] is the writer's particular and unmistakable signature on everything he writes'.

To forge a singular voice, then, a writer needs to know who they are. We all are singular, even those of us who present a perfectly polished 'average Joe' exterior. Underneath it, everyone is running an inner monologue, with its particular quirks, anxieties, desires, prejudices and curiosities; a monologue informed by our genes and upbringing and everything else that makes us unrepeatable. This is what writers need to tap into: the part of us that we often keep to ourselves, and sometimes hide even from ourselves. It is this part that needs to show on the page. Our foremost task is to describe the world as it appears through the prism of our person, without holding back. Isaac Bashevis Singer says, along these lines, that:

> Writers who are truly original do not set out to fabricate new forms of expression, or to invent themes merely for the sake of appearing new. They attain their originality through extraordinary sincerity, by daring to give everything of themselves, their most secret thoughts and idiosyncrasies.

All of the above doesn't mean a work with a powerful voice is a transcript of the writer's stream of consciousness, nor do our books have to have protagonists 'just like us'. Once again, a voice is the *climate* of our story. It is something amorphous, diffuse, yet deeply felt. You know you're reading somebody talented when you get the sense that only this writer could have written this piece; when you feel a distinct sensibility behind the work. Can you imagine the sharp, sardonic Joan Didion, a writer who battles her terror of disorder through her writing, composing her essays with the unrestrained, hungry, drug-fuelled romanticism of Kerouac?

Or take this brief passage from Geoff Dyer's memoir *Out of Sheer Rage*:

> I drove back to Cheltenham, glad of the motorways that had ruined the countryside, glad of the car that smudged the air, back to my parents' house on the semi-detached estate on the edge of the town that had played its part in ruining the Cotswolds.

Dyer doesn't just tell us where and how he travels. His prose conveys his neuroses as exemplified here in the unresolved tension between his environmental concerns and his enjoyment of the comfort of driving. This brief passage also shows Dyer's dry sense of humour, and humour – be it absurd, slapstick, sarcastic, dark or gently ironic – is a crucial element of a writer's voice. Mel Brooks once remarked that humour is the conscience of mankind. Indeed, it helps us see through received wisdoms, the gaslighting and racket of the social world. I've never read a wise (and compelling) work that was utterly humourless. But any of our other psychological features, be they an inclination to superstition or a penchant for socially unpalatable desires, are key elements of voice as well.

Once you get into the habit of writing through the prism of your uniqueness, you can weave compelling stories out of the most mundane material, because you're capable of doing what the Russian literary critic Viktor Shklovsky famously suggested to be a key aim of literature: to render 'the familiar strange so that it can be freshly perceived'. To do so you need to relearn to look at everything – a sandpit or a woman in an evening gown on your television screen – as if you were still a child (or a visiting alien) with little pre-existing knowledge of how things are *supposed* to be. Then everything can acquire a fresh, even disorientating, aura. In mediocre books, the air is always cool, the birds are singing and the sun is yellow. But is this so, or is this how we are programmed to think? Today I looked up at the sky and the sun was green, I swear.

And here is an ordinary visit to a Melbourne market, dominated by Asian vendors and customers, turned into a hilarious, riveting tale by the Australian writer, Alice Pung, in her memoir *Unpolished Gem*. Filtered through Pung's darkly humorous mind, the market is 'swarming with fat pigs and thin people' and is saturated with 'piss and other filthy drips'. To be understood there, Pung tells us, customers must not only speak but also perform 'much movement of hands and contortion of face'.

*

It is not only the writer's psychological makeup that shapes their voice but also their worldview (although the two are, of course, closely related). Elena Ferrante puts it this way: 'there is no story that doesn't have roots in the feeling that the writer has about life. The more that feeling filters into the story, into the characters, the more distinctly the page gives form to an incisive effect of truth.' Think of Dostoyevsky, whose oeuvre is imbued with spiritual, quasi-hysterical anguish.

Do you see the human condition as essentially dark? Or unjust, or wonderful, or mysterious, or tragicomic? Is your view of the world anthropocentric or misanthropic? Are you a romantic? Whatever your perception of the world, it needs to inform how you write. The same can be said about your passions, things that matter to you deeply. If you are a lover of nature, for example, capitalise on this in your work, no matter what your main subject is, whether by imbuing your settings with fine details of weather and landscape, or drawing your metaphors from nature or giving your passion to one of your characters, or in any other way.

The fact that works with strong voice are infused with the author's deepest and dearest held obsessions and convictions might be more apparent in creative nonfiction where the voice telling the story – with all its inherent metaphors and neuroses – always belongs to the author. Yet writers' worldviews and preoccupations inform fictional works and the questions they explore just as well, only more subtly.

When a fiction writer has a powerful voice, their whole oeuvre is infused with their person even if at first sight their works might appear thematically, and sometimes stylistically, different. The novels of the Czech-French novelist Milan Kundera, a refugee from communism, vary in many aspects, including their degree of realism, yet their protagonists are usually lone individuals armed with their courage and their words, standing in opposition to the big bad world with its big bad problems, like dictatorships and institutional hypocrisy. In the stories of Jorge Luis Borges, who saw life as a metaphysical enigma, the world is often a puzzle which his characters attempt to solve. Whereas the detective novels of Raymond Chandler are imbued with Chandler's poetic melancholy. Take this sentence from *The Big Sleep*: 'Under the thinning fog the surf curled and creamed, almost without sound, like a thought trying to form itself on the edge of consciousness.'

But is this Chandler or his narrator Philip Marlowe speaking?

This is the kind of question I am frequently asked when I teach writing. In fiction, stories are often narrated by characters. So where does the writer's voice end and the character's begin? The answer is complicated, because the two are tangled; the language and the views often belong to both. But what does this actually mean?

The way I see it, the writer's voice is the foundation, the common ground from which the voices of different characters sprout. How this works in practice is difficult to grasp unless we think of specific examples. Hemingway's male narrators come from different backgrounds, have different personalities and distinct speaking voices, yet they share certain sensibilities that fit Hemingway's vision – toughness, secretiveness, sensuality, linguistic sparseness. They pay close attention to the outer world of rivers, forests, noisy cafés and cold beer; they think little of themselves. In contrast, William Faulkner's narrators are caught within torrential streams of their internal existences. Fragmented and bewildered, they at once straddle past and present or move between the two temporalities erratically.

Hemingway and Faulkner wrote books grounded in reality but even Stephen King, whose fictional worlds are often fantastical, writes 'every character you create is partly you'. However different our protagonists might be from us, they still arise from the depths of our minds – our quirks, passions, anxieties, the lives we've lived. Even writers writing about aliens work within these confines, and I see these boundaries as a good thing for they make our works singular. In this vein, King advises: 'write what you like, then . . . make it unique by blending in your own personal knowledge of life, friendship, relationships, sex and work'.

*

The problem with following King's excellent advice is that being ourselves on the page doesn't always come naturally, just as we often struggle being ourselves in the social world. We live and write under the daily assault of platitudes and social regulations, and so, Knausgaard points out in *The End*, 'that is what we do, all the time, deny the reality we have experienced in favor of the reality we have learned'.

Perhaps it was to counter such denial that Saul Bellow, one of the finest American stylists, felt, that to write well he first needed to 'prepare the ground' for what he described as 'a primitive prompter or commentator within, who from earliest years has been advising us, telling us what the real world is . . . From this source come words, phrases, syllables.' And what a tough and risky job it is to cajole that commentator out, to shake ourselves free of received wisdoms and the anxiety of making impressions, to make ourselves vulnerable – for what we find inside ourselves often defies good manners, self-protective lies, the zeitgeist.

However, the risks are worth it if your commitment is to making art. A unique voice, Knausgaard continues, goes 'down . . . beneath the ideologies, which you can only stand up to by insisting on your own experience of reality.' His is a good reminder of the high stakes in having an original voice, that it is not just the aesthetic but also moral basis of our work. To forge a voice is to take a stand.

As a young writer, it took me years to take an authentic stand on anything on the page, even though I began writing for publication at sixteen, when I was accepted into the Young Reporter program run by an Israeli national youth magazine. In that job, which lasted until I turned eighteen and began my compulsory army service, I wrote prolifically and, by literary standards, badly. Later, journalistic clichés seeped into my first book, a novel published when I was just twenty years old, and which sold poorly and went critically unnoticed. My prose was mostly functional, describing people, places and emotions, but without conveying who *I* was. Many others could have written the sentences I did. That was because I wrote that book while looking outward, with journalistic-like aim of providing easily digestible information rather than expressing myself. No wonder I failed.

In the aftermath of that failure, I was so demoralised I stopped writing for a year. But I didn't stop reading. In fact, I read more than ever and more selectively: Camus, Marquez, Amos Oz, Iris Murdoch . . . This may sound odd, but I read those books primarily to exorcise my writing disease. I masochistically inflicted those delectable punishments upon myself to remind myself how great literature was and how implausible it was that I might find my own tiny space within it.

Yet the opposite happened. On reflection, I see that intense reading as my version of preparing ground for my internal commentator; the more I read, the more I noticed what captivated me most, namely the author's voice. I began pondering what my own voice might sound like. When I eventually resumed writing (How could I not? Who was I kidding?), I was no longer interested in following well-trodden paths. I wanted to venture into the jungle inside me. I wrote short stories and I wrote them bitterly, painfully, with far more struggle than I'd ever experienced before.

Several years later, my second book came out, a collection of those stories. It received some critical recognition, including one review which described my writing as the work of an observant outsider who peeps into everyone's secret chambers, wide-eyed and excited. And this was exactly who I was at the time. I was a provincial migrant who had left her family's traditional bosom for the big smoke of Tel Aviv only to remain on its edges, unnerved by that sophisticated city, and by my own desire and curiosity.

I took that review as an indication that I'd managed to convey something of myself across my otherwise different stories, where protagonists ranged from criminals to academics. I felt I'd found a place within myself from which to write. But then, in my mid-twenties, I moved to Australia and – even though I was still the excited outsider skulking at the margins – my voice was gone.

*

For me, the most difficult part about changing the language in which I wrote wasn't acquiring English vocabulary or memorising local idioms. That was hard. But even harder was to know who I was on the page. Syntax, phonetics, all that verbal arsenal that differs from language to language shapes our psyches – how we process the world. The gulf between Hebrew and English is vast as these languages belong to separate linguistic families: Canaanite and Germanic respectively. In Hebrew, my voice was fairly tough and bold, at ease with obscenities and colourfully colloquial; it didn't translate well into the softer, more elegant English with its longer words. What's more, I had no affinity with Australian street-speak. In Israel I spent my youth in difficult, sometimes dangerous, places, absorbing the rough poetry spoken by drug dealers and nightclub bouncers into my skin. In Australia I had been mostly moving in the hyper-educated circles of artists and academics. Gradually, I did get to know people from other social milieus and their turns of phrase, but it wasn't the visceral knowing I had in Israel.

There was also that: my new language and new life rearranged my internal furnishings. I hadn't become a different person, but rather had undergone a certain synthesis. The ultra-bookish and dreamy Russian child that I'd suppressed after arriving in Israel so as to fit in there resurfaced in Australia. Perhaps it was English that prompted her appearance. Although English also significantly differs from Slavic languages, its versatile syntax is closer to my mother tongue than Hebrew. Soon after my arrival here, the dreamy child and the young woman from the tough places merged in some odd ways, creating an Australian-flavoured self. The rhythms of my thoughts, my sense of humour, my views hadn't entirely changed, but they weren't the same either. I was no longer certain who I was.

Perhaps nostalgia is so popular among migrants precisely because of this, because of how a new geography, with its different grammar, music and logic, remoulds us. In this confused state, it is tempting to cling to the past. But how can you write while refusing to face the changes in you? Where is the honesty in that?

I think these questions are relevant for any writer, not only of the migrant variety. Everyone undergoes life changes at some point, be they even as obvious as having children or simply getting older. Such changes can shift your perspective, your worldview, and therefore affect your writing. The writer's voice is you and so, just like you, it is a continuous work-in-progress. Which is to say, once you've found your voice, it doesn't mean you'll always 'have' it. Time may come when this voice will no longer feel authentic, as it happened to me during my second migration. Many writers keep honing their voices throughout their lives, whether they change their writing language or not.

To forge, and maintain, honest and authentic voice, writers need to remain vigilant, sensitive to the changes outside and inside them, and work with them rather than against them. But back in my early years in Australia, rather than trying to understand who I'd become, I once again looked outward – towards other writers as well as hypothetical readers, trying to endear myself to local audiences. I alternated between artless imitations of some of my favorite authors and stilted sentences, such as 'The story of how my parents met strikes me as a perfect example of the tight connection between personal and political that characterised the Soviet Union.' This prose, meant to convey my 'genius', came from a place of deep insecurity. When writing, I often felt as if I were a gladiator, fighting for my life in front of a bloodthirsty crowd of readers who only wished for my death and for it to be as gruesome as possible. So I protected myself with an armour of quasi-intellectualism, guarding my soft spots so tightly that the essence of me didn't flow into my prose and – coupled with a wrong choice of writing subject – I entered the writer's block I'd described.

*

I wrote earlier that several factors combined to help me rediscover my voice and end the writer's block. One was my decision to abandon the book I wasn't meant to write. Another was meeting Daryl. Not long into our budding romance, he left Australia for a four-month sabbatical he'd arranged long before we met. This was unfortunate timing for falling in love, yet – as I discovered – fortunate for my writing.

During our separation, we wrote to each other daily. I felt pressure to impress Daryl, who is an intelligent, well-read man. Yet the pressure was different to the one I felt when doing my creative work. I wasn't writing for some imaginary audience ready to pounce on my smallest misstep, but for one real person who thought warmly of me and was curious about what I had to say. I was too focused on eliciting that wry smile of his or conjuring up turns of phrase I knew he'd appreciate to have the space for the generalised paranoia I felt during my creative writing. I tried to bring the best out of myself rather than pretend I was someone smarter than I was. I looked inward again, tapping into my interior monologue in my emails to him:

> I finally met X. He was charming and chatty and everything I hoped he would be. But also sicker than I imagined him to be . . . We had a great conversation about such matters as polyglotism and Siberian architecture, until his friend arrived to pick him up. I watched them walking away, X leaning onto her heavily. That sight was the saddest thing I'd seen in a while. This wonderful, decadent, so-alive man literally collapsing onto someone else's body. He looked so thin. He turned back to say goodbye and I could see death at the edges of his smile.

There was something else about our correspondence that helped me re-establish the line to my gut. We emailed each other every day, but I didn't always have newsworthy events to discuss. I thought of Rilke who advised an aspiring writer: 'If your everyday life seems poor to you, do not accuse it; accuse yourself, tell yourself you are not poet enough to summon up ts riches'. So to keep seducing my new man with my words and to please Rilke (and Shklovsky), I took a magnifying glass to the minutiae of my days – the songs on my car stereo, the food I cooked, the rain I smelled; I considered what thoughts, emotions or memories they evoked in me beyond the immediate, cliché responses.

> It's Saturday night now, my neighbourhood is unusually quiet. I'm reading Y's book-in-progress; the first essay there is about his uneasy relationship with his father. This made me think of my own father, how his inner world is a mystery to me and yet it is my mother, more known to me, whom I am always chasing in my writing, always trying to pinpoint her yet failing . . .

As time passed, I increasingly liked the trail I left behind on my electronic pages. Sometimes I re-read my emails, listening carefully to my new sound. It was a version of my Hebrew voice – still desirous and excitable, still darkly humorous. However, in English I was less susceptible to grand statements, more pensive and hesitant. I think it was because my sensibility was now rooted even more than before in uncertainty, in a state of never quite trusting myself, of being more of an observer than an inhabitant. As painful as it was to be so untethered, my tenuous relationship with my new language helped me write more vigilantly, or to use Hemingway's words – hone my 'built-in bullshit detector'. At some point, the melody of my emails permeated my creative work too.

What I learned about the writing process from that time was that if a writer struggles with discovering or finetuning their voice, the most important thing to do is to find a way to take the pressure down. One strategy for that is to imagine that you're addressing your story to one particular reader – someone who knows and cares about you, and won't judge you, but also won't let you get away with bullshit. Or you can try to write daily for some period about whatever happens to you and do this reflectively, lingering on each detail to unpick what it means for you. Do you find the ritual of teeth brushing irritatingly wholesome? Does the sight of a fruit bowl with blood plums fill you with vitality? Both methods are variations on what spontaneously unfolded during my correspondence with Daryl.

Or you might like to follow the Pulitzer Prize–winning author Carol Shields's example. With every sentence she writes, she asks herself: 'Is this what I really mean?' Hers is a useful tool to cultivate a healthy dose of self-doubt essential to forging an honest voice – just enough to deepen writing, but not enough to stop writing altogether. I implement this sometimes too, especially when I feel my words are slipping out with more ease than they should, because writer's voice is us, but it shouldn't be a verbatim transcription of us. Rather, as we'll see next, it is an edited and artfully refined version of whatever it is we find within ourselves.

VOICE IS STYLE

My favourite writers are not so much writers as seducers, shamans, tricksters. I cannot explain my excitement about Marguerite Duras, for instance, in intellectual terms, cannot say I love her work for her characters or plots or even themes, though these are good and matter to me. Many other writers have compelling characters and plots, yet I am not obsessed with them like I am with Duras. Her prose affects me on a gut level. It washes over me in tidal ebbs and flows, leaving me dazed, unnerved. Take this passage from the novel *The Lover*:

> In the daylight I was less afraid, and death seemed less important. But it haunted me all the time. I wanted to kill – my elder brother, I wanted to kill him, to get the better of him for once, just once, and see him die.

It is difficult to overestimate the impact that the texture of prose, the linguistic embroidery of the story, has on readers. It affects us as music does by creating a mood and by speaking to something in us that eludes language. So just as certain pieces of music speak to certain listeners, many readers are (consciously or unconsciously) drawn to particular writers because of the way their prose affects their senses. That's why careful word choices, and attentive rendering of syntax and rhythm are the very basics of good writing. Taken together, these elements become style, which in turn creates the atmosphere of the work, its soundtrack.

Elena Ferrante writes: 'Literary truth is the truth released exclusively by words used well . . . It is directly proportional to the energy that one is able to impress on the sentence.' A well-honed style also expresses the work's emotional truth, as is evident in Duras's example above, where the protagonist's fear and hatred of her abusive brother are conveyed through a repetitive, drawn-out incantation.

On the deepest level, style is the most concrete manifestation of the writer's voice – their singularity. Or as Proust puts it: 'style for the writer, no less than colour for the painter, is a question not of technique but of vision.' It shows a particular way of looking at the world. The incantatory voice of Duras across her novels expresses the pain of her narrators but also her own dark feelings about life, including her anguished sensuality – it fits the content of her fiction *and* her.

Some writers have more varied styles across their works, but this usually means their works express different parts of them. My voice in *The Dangerous Bride*, for example, is bewildered and erotically charged, fitting the subject of desire. Conversely, in *Imperfect*, which delves into my bodily anguish, the mood is still neurotic but more philosophical. And yet both books bear my 'signature' (or so I hope), particularly as far as my sense of humour is concerned, just as some of Matisse's paintings might be predominantly red and others predominantly green, yet it's easy to see they all come from the same artist's palette, reflecting his vivid, dramatic vision of the world. But on a practical level, how do we stamp our prose with our signature, while also matching its colours to the particular stories we tell?

*

At the most basic level, style is the outcome of countless word choices we make all the time. Words which are then strung into sentences, sentences which are then strung into paragraphs. But first come the words. They make us feel things. You may agree that 'she *walked* into the room' affects us differently than 'she *sashayed* into the room'. The choice you'll make will depend on the story you're describing. To keep with Proust's painterly analogy, we can think of words as the colours on the palette that impact the viewer's experience. Interestingly, Flaubert visualised what he wanted to achieve in his fiction precisely in these terms. Flaubert's contemporaries, the French writers Goncourt Brothers, report him as saying: 'When I write a novel I aim at rendering a colour, a shade. For instance, in my Carthaginian novel, I want to do something purple . . . In *Madame Bovary*, all I wanted to do was to render a grey colour, the mouldy colour of a wood-louse's existence.'

Well-chosen words also reveal something about the author. Helen Garner's lyrical as well as sharply ironic prose is an outcome of the particular selections she makes in each sentence, selections that other writers wouldn't necessarily make, like in this passage from her short nonfiction work, 'Tower Diary':

> An expensive couple in a Bondi café. She's in her twenties, glossy, slim, grittily determined. He's pushing sixty and his grey hair is receding, but money is oozing from his pores and she is soaking it up – on her terms.

Imagine Garner had written this instead:

> A couple was sitting in a Bondi café. The man, in his late fifties, looked rich and powerful in his expensive suit. His

companion, thin and pampered, twenty-something, was probably a gold-digger.

While the information in the second version is essentially the same, how much more vivid yet subtle is the first description? How much more *Garner* is it too? In the second version, we get neither Garner's spiritedness and wit nor her genuine fascination (as opposed to judgement) with her subjects. Garner's passage conveys both the content and the author.

To hone a style, being attuned to the subtleties of words' meanings is only a starting point. We also need to cultivate a sensual relationship with them, not unlike the kabbalists who perceive words as multidimensional. We should notice their flavours, shapes and phonetics, like the swishy sound of *witch*. (Phonetics particularly matter to me; I even chose my children's names solely on the strength of their soft, lulling music – Luca, Ollie.) We should pay attention to the mystery of words: how 'sandwich' contains sand, and 'serendipity' is a serpentine word. And to the fact that words have a texture and flavor in our very mouths. Say it aloud and you'll notice how *chocolate truffles* melt in the mouth, how *ophthalmologist* resists the tongue . . .

Just as important is to observe which words are most delicious to *you*, or most naturally fit with your personality. I am, for example, as you may have noticed by now, linguistically extravagant, in complete opposition to purists like Hemingway. I love long, dramatic words; each one and its own melody – strawberries, picaresque, sophisticated, gigantic. If I can get away with writing 'metamorphosis', I won't write 'change'. My vocabulary is consistent with who I am – a sensualist and a romantic. It expresses my predilection for weaving myths out of daily happenings, for elevating reality.

Words . . . The pleasure of them, the velvet of them. But also the torture of them. The torture of endless alternatives. As E. B. White writes, 'When you consider that there are a thousand ways to express even the simplest idea, it is no wonder writers are under a great strain.' Slim or thin. To shit or to defecate . . . This resentment I sometimes feel, since even in a short story there are hundreds of choices to make, more choosing than I do in any other area of my life . . .

*

The building blocks of style are words, but how they are woven together is just as important. In an accomplished work, the length, syntax, punctuation, repetition, alliteration, even grammatical 'errors' of the sentences are crafted with intent.

For an example of syntax significance, let's consider how the meaning of the sentence *They began dancing and he noticed she had cornflower-blue eyes* changes once we rephrase it as *It was only when they began dancing that he noticed she had cornflower-blue eyes.* The former is flat writing: joining two simple sentences with 'and' makes for generic, tedious storytelling in the style of reportage – 'this happened and then that happened'. Whereas in the second version, the syntactic emphasis on the discovery of eye colour creates tension, drama, energy. The noticing is no longer a mere fact reported within a sequence of other actions but a promise of something to come. Those eyes, they must have some meaning for the man who notices them. Why? And what is he going to do about it? Now the sentence isn't just informative. It also elicits emotion.

Another thing to consider is that often the most affecting sentences aren't the grammatically correct ones, but those where the writer *disrupts* language. Garner's *An expensive couple in a Bondi café* lacks a verb. It's the 'incorrectness' of this sentence that makes it expressive, makes readers stumble and notice that this is an important moment, the moment where they are invited into a story – a story of money, power and eros set in a fittingly expensive and sexy place.

Effective sentences, just like effective words, work on two levels: they express the content and the writer. When the voice is strong, the shape of sentences reflects the writer's natural rhythms of thinking, speaking and relating to written language. Do you love or detest semi-colons? (In either case, you *must* have strong feelings on the matter . . .) Do you fancy using ellipses? If you are a lover of adverbs, forget those stern admonitions you must have heard in writing workshops and use them where it works. Or if you are like me – think and speak in complex syntax, with multiple clauses and qualifications – structure your sentences on the page accordingly.

If you have trouble connecting to your natural melody, you can try doing free-flow writing. This popular strategy, which encourages us to write without editing or self-censoring, can help to access our internal monologue. My version of it isn't entirely 'free', but I find it works best for the said purpose. I set a timer for seven minutes (less than this isn't enough; more than this I find exhausting) and write without stopping. If you need a prompt to get started, my favourite is 'Yesterday I . . .' Prompts or not, the main thing is not to worry about creating beautiful or 'correct' prose, and not to try and tell a story. Instead, record your thoughts exactly as they occur. If you're thinking about not wanting to write, write that down. If your next thought is 'I need to buy milk', write that. Don't fight your mind. Submit to it. The content isn't as important as the vocabulary and the shape of sentences that emerge. You may need to repeat this exercise over some days to excavate your internal monologue.

As far as expressing content goes, a satisfactory sentence, the English novelist Anthony Burgess tells us, 'fits the subject so closely that we have the impression of living skin rather than a glove.' Readers are more likely to feel something if a sentence lingers when the character is tormented by indecision, wavers like the slur of a drunk, echoes the thunder or the rush of desire at hand. The prose in the following excerpt from Kerouac's *On the Road* does just that.

It expresses the protagonist's passion for jazz and also *becomes* jazz – an intense, unpredictable music. Notice the erratic, passionate tempo, syntax and punctuation.

> Then here came a gang of young bop musicians carrying their instruments out of cars. They piled right into a saloon and we followed them. They set themselves up and started blowin. There we were! The leader was a slender, drooping, curly-haired, pursy-mouthed tenorman, thin of shoulder, draped loose in a sports shirt, cool in the warm night, self-indulgence written in his eyes, who picked up his horn and frowned in it and blew cool and complex and was dainty stamping his foot to catch ideas . . .

Kerouac's sentences mirror the sassy emotions and happenings of this scene. They are also flavoured with the unmistakable Kerouacian voice, already influenced by jazz. As Kerouac said in an interview for *The Paris Review*, when he writes he aspires to follow

> the raciness and freedom and humour of jazz instead of all that dreary analysis and things, like, James entered the room and lit a cigarette . . . [I am like] a tenor man drawing a breath and blowing a phrase on his saxophone till he runs out of breath, and when he does, his sentence, his statement's been made . . . That's how I therefore separate my sentences, as breath separations of the mind . . .

(In fact, throughout that entire interview, Kerouac's spoken sentences resemble his written ones. But that's *his* way of being a writer. The direct speech of many others is tonally different, and most likely inferior, to how they write.)

Striking the right balance between 'the writer' and 'the content' can be difficult. That's why, during revision, the American writer

Christopher Beha continuously asks: 'What do I need this sentence to do?' and 'What role does the sentence play in its scene?' Similar questions can be applied when we consider the sentence length. On one hand, most writers would have a predilection. Orhan Pamuk, for example, prefers long sentences, because they allow him to 'prepare the reader for something and then I surprise him.' But sentence length should also reflect the story's events, so sometimes Pamuk shortens his sentences, especially in dramatic passages. Occasional length variations also prevent the rhythm from becoming monotonous. That's why it's important, during revision, to ask yourself questions along the lines of 'What does the length of this sentence *do*? Does it express something significant to the story?'

The Australian writer Mandy Sayer skilfully manipulates the length of her sentences, and the other elements of her prose, in the opening of her memoir *Dreamtime Alice*, which describes Sayer's year-long sojourn in America with her estranged father. There they made a living by performing music and tap dancing:

> In the evenings we pushed our red shopping stroller along the five-minute walk from our hotel to Columbus Avenue, where crowded dining tables spilled out onto open terraces and tall mannequins in tight black dresses stared down at us through plate glass and neon. It was in New York, I decided, that we would be successful. It was there that we would work every evening until the crowds drifted away after midnight. It was there that we would have lots of glorious fun and return home with bags of money. There that we would live out the long, warm nights that would later complete the repertoire of my father's stories, a repertoire of which I longed to be a part.

The first sentence – long, meandering, loaded with detail – doesn't just tell readers but invites them to experience what it's like to be a newcomer to New York, feel the city's energy and sensory overload. Sayer then expresses her youthful determination, her hopeful bravado of those days, by moving on to shorter sentences that echo each other like footsteps in a military march (It was . . . It was there . . . It was there . . .). The final sentence of this paragraph, while initially resembles the preceding ones (There . . .), soon takes on a life of its own, lengthens and uncoils, leading us to its striking finale, to the heart of the memoir, the author's vulnerability and her emotional truth as to why she embarked on that trip: 'a repertoire of which I longed to be a part.'

In this example, like in every passage of fine prose, each sentence has its sound. Taken together, however, paragraph by paragraph, sentences constitute a distinct melody of the work, which is of utmost importance not only in the reading but also the writing experience. We know we write well when we can hear our melody. Paul Auster's books even originate in what he calls 'a buzz in the head . . . Most of the effort involved in writing a novel for me is trying to remain faithful to that buzz, that rhythm.'

The good thing about this buzz, or whatever else you'd like to call it, is that the longer I write, the more often my natural voice – with its word choices, turn of phrase and rhythm – appears in my first drafts. The way I write these drafts – fast, attacking the page before my inner censor attacks me, not focusing on shaping my thoughts and emotions but on laying them bare – helps to extract the mad, wild prose out of me, the kind of prose that carries the truth ignored, or suppressed, in my everyday. I still need to make many stylistic choices when I redraft, but not as many as I once did. It is as if the essence of me is now closer to the surface; as if by practice I've established a more reliable connection to my guts. So perhaps, with time, style can become less stylised – be more a matter of intuition than selection.

INVITATION ISSUED

Many literary works don't begin at the start of the story. A powerful opening isn't a chronological reportage but a seduction. Or perhaps it does report something – the work's emotional truth. In this sense, effective beginnings are enticing invitations to enter a particular universe, with its own moods, images and impressions; they set an (explicit or implicit) contract with the readers about what is on offer.

There are so many different ways to issue an invitation to readers that the best I can do is present the more common types of beginnings. But first let's consider what is best avoided. Many dull openings that I see in contemporary unpublished and published works have to do with the current fashion (influenced by film, it seems) to begin stories mid-scene, where characters are *doing* something. This can be effective, especially if you are writing a fast-paced thriller or some other suspenseful story. But generally speaking, action lends itself to banality. Far too many stories start with someone staring out of the window, or running for their lives, or tracing something with their finger. It's easier to get away with clichéd descriptions in the middle of a story, but to initially lure readers in we need to work harder, crystallise the stakes.

Having said this, one of my preferred ways to start a story is with what I call 'a revelatory event' – a scene that captures the question, the quest, at the heart of the work. There the action isn't just for the thrill of it but to illuminate some emotional truth. My memoir *Imperfect* opens in this spirit:

> And then there was that afternoon in summer, with the mango-yellow light filtering through the blinds, when my lover – his long, slender body moist against my skin – asked me, 'What happened to your leg?'

The question my lover posed when he finally noticed my scars was more revelatory for me than for him, I think. It made me realise how skilled I became over the years at manipulating my body, to the extent that I could even hide my scars during sex. Concealment became such a natural part of me, I no longer noticed I was doing it. The seed of *Imperfect* was sown at that moment, which sparked my desire to understand how my scars had shaped my life. By beginning my memoir at that point, I hoped to get readers thinking about their bodies, too; to turn my quest also into their quests.

There are plenty of ways to seduce readers that do not lean on action. Take the opening of *The Great Gatsby*, hailed by some critics as the perfect novel:

> In my younger and more vulnerable years my father gave me some advice that I've been turning over in my mind ever since. 'Whenever you feel like criticizing anyone,' he told me, 'just remember that all the people in this world haven't had the advantages that you've had.'

Instead of inviting us into the action of characters we don't yet know and care about, this start establishes intimacy with readers by plunging us into the mind of the narrator, Nick Carraway – into his thoughtful, measured sharing of an important personal memory. While not as dramatic as running for your life, this opening creates tension by raising questions. Why does Nick begin his story with this memory? Is it because someone he cares for 'misbehaved', leaving him torn between the temptation to judge and to empathise? Who is this person and what did they do? What choice will Nick make? Not only we are curious, we're also getting the sense that this story's stakes are high and that it deals with moral dilemmas. And the novel's emotional truth infuses this enticing opening, as it hints at the humble origins of the 'misbehaving' Gatsby, and that these count in what is about to unfold.

*

In *The Great Gatsby*, Fitzgerald hooks arms with his readers, inviting them for an intimate stroll through his tale. Other openings bewitch with what the legendary American editor Gordon Lish calls 'magical utterances' – visceral passages that transmit the author's desire for their subject to the readers. To enact such magic, Lish advises writers not to 'think in terms of communication but in terms of what enchants'. The siren call of Nabokov's first line in *Lolita* comes to mind:

> Lolita, light of my life, fire of my loins. My sin, my soul. Lo-lee-ta . . .

There is no clear communication of meaning in this opening. It is closer to music than to literature, speaking directly to our viscera, setting us on fire too. We aren't told any facts yet, but already we sense the novel's emotional truth in Humbert Humbert's maddening wail of yearning and guilt. Alight, we follow the narrator, tormented by love for an adolescent girl, no matter what (moral) dangers lie ahead.

Or consider the magical utterances of Arundhati Roy in the opening of *The God of Small Things*:

> May in Ayemenem is a hot, brooding month. The days are long and humid. The river shrinks and black crows gorge on bright mangoes in still, dustgreen trees. Red bananas ripen. Jackfruits burst. Dissolute bluebottles hum vacuously in the fruity air. Then they stun themselves against clear window-panes and die, fatly baffled in the sun.

This sensual start is suffused with another complicated longing – for a beautiful yet dangerous place where Roy's tale of love, prejudice and betrayal unfolds. The desire is palpable in the rhythm, and the choice of words and images: brooding, gorge, dustgreen, dissolute bluebottles, fatly baffled in the sun . . . As well as being unbearably vivid, this opening establishes the themes intrinsic to the book. Pleasure and menace; sex and death; change and inertia – all these contrasts are locked in an impossible embrace within this first paragraph, seductively hinting at destructive passions and the pleasant yet suffocating, traditional, circular way of life that is at the centre of this story.

*

You can lay your honey trap more directly. In his novel *Something to Tell You*, the English writer Hanif Kureishi comes across as a skilful salesman:

> Secrets are my currency: I deal in them for a living. The secrets of desire, of what people really want, and of what they fear the most. The secrets of why love is difficult, sex complicated, living painful and death so close and yet placed far away.

In the book's first two sentences, the narrator, a therapist, shamelessly lures us in by declaring himself to be the depository of secrets. What could be a cheap shot at the hands of a lesser storyteller is redeemed in the subsequent sentence, which is more specific and nuanced, and equally enticing. Who wouldn't want to find out 'why love is difficult' or how death can be 'so close and yet placed far away'? This opening also hints at the heart of this novel: the narrator's life, too, is shrouded in painful, weighty mystery to do with love and death. While we don't know this yet, we do get the sense that the universe we're about to enter is duplicitous as well as Freudian in nature.

Kureishi seduces us in the manner of Salome, veiled transparently but veiled nonetheless. Annie Dillard advises writers to opt for the explicit appeal of nakedness – declare the highest stakes at once by placing all the 'deaths, accidents and diseases . . . at the beginning'. This is what Paul Auster does in the opening of his novel *Leviathan*:

> Six days ago, a man blew himself up by the side of a road in northern Wisconsin. There were no witnesses, but it appears that he was sitting on the grass next to his parked car when the bomb he was building accidentally went off . . . no one seems to have any idea who the dead man was . . . As far as I am concerned, the longer it takes them [to identify him] the better. The story I have to tell is rather complicated . . .

The ingredients in this opening are just right. It begins with a dry yet intriguing report of the death of a mysterious, dubiously intentioned man. Who was he and what was he after? Soon, the 'I' of a narrator emerges, someone who has a stake in the case, personalising the news item and creating even more tension. The narrator knows more than anyone else about what has happened and doesn't want the mystery to be solved. How is he related to the deceased? Why is it in his interests to delay the identification of the body? The answers, we are told, are going to be complicated. And how delicious is that! Then, the emotional centre of the story – the wounded friendship between these men – is already there, hinted at.

An effective opening is likely to resonate throughout the entire reading experience. It can even utterly shape it, as it does the short story 'My Brother and the Girl from Surat Thani' by the Israeli author Lior Ofek. It begins in the fashion Dillard likes, foreshadowing death:

> A month before my younger brother enlisted into the army as a paratrooper and eight months before he met his death in a clash with terrorists on the northern border, he came to visit me in Bangkok.

The rest of the story is predominantly amusing, describing various (mis)adventures of the two brothers in Bangkok's glaring nightlife. Yet the knowledge of the imminent death of an eighteen-year-old boy renders every trivial event – a leisurely boat trip, a casual kiss, brotherly banter – poignant, at times almost unbearable, and always meaningful. You are on edge throughout the story. You smile with your eyes moist.

*

Another effective way to start a story is with summary – the kind of summary that encapsulates the truth of the work. This is how Bruce Chatwin's novel *On the Black Hill* begins:

> For forty-two years, Lewis and Benjamin Jones slept side by side, in their parents' bed, at their farm which was known as 'The Vision'.

On a superficial level, Chatwin – like Auster in *Leviathan* – begins by merely stating facts, albeit remarkable ones. But Chatwin's facts are also likely to induce certain emotions in readers: claustrophobia, repulsion at the image of adult siblings sharing a parental bed (as well as at a hint of potential incest), sadness at unrealised lives, and of course curiosity. How did these brothers end up in such a symbiotic relationship? Why the *parental* bed? Why would someone call a farm The Vision?

Soon after this puzzling start, Chatwin moves back in time to the very source of the brothers' story – the courtship of their parents. The rest of the novel unfolds chronologically, progressing towards the time of the opening, and whatever events unfold, we always read them as we read Ofek's story, in the light of what we already know about the brothers' strange and sad fate of forty-two years of conjugal-style sleeping.

*

Often a powerful opening imbues the story with urgency. Yet a narrative can also begin in calmer waters and still be enticing – as long as it is true to the work. We can win over readers by starting with the familiar, the relatable, like Jeffrey Eugenides does in *The Marriage Plot*:

> To start with, look at all the books. There were her Edith Wharton novels, arranged not by title but date of publication; there was the complete Modern Library set of Henry James, a gift from her father on her twenty-first birthday; there were the dog-eared paperbacks assigned in her college courses, a lot of Dickens, a smidgen of Trollope, along with good helpings of Austen, George Eliot, and the redoubtable Brontë sisters.

The chant-like recitation of canonical writers coupled with such cosy details as a present from a father, the Modern Library set and dog-eared pages is likely to induce a feeling of contentment in readers – probably themselves bookish people who feel snug in the world of books. And when we relate, we read actively, developing an intimate relationship with the story. I am, for example, always interested in what others read. As I read this opening, I enjoyed comparing the protagonist's literary and cataloguing preferences to my own. Then, this seemingly straightforward introduction of the protagonist through her library reveals something of the novel's essence. It tells us we are about to enter a story influenced by the life of the mind and shows the main character's romantic, somewhat old-fashioned mindset which is also the flaw that underpins the book's central conflict.

Similarly, there is nothing particularly dramatic about the opening lines of *The Master and Margarita*:

> At the sunset hour of one warm spring day two men were to be seen at Patriarch's Ponds. The first of them – aged about forty, dressed in a greyish summer suit – was short, dark-haired, well-fed and bald . . . his neatly shaved face was embellished by black horn-rimmed spectacles of preternatural dimensions. The other, a broad-shouldered young man with curly reddish hair . . . The first was . . . [an] editor of a highbrow literary magazine . . . his young companion was the poet Ivan . . . Reaching the shade of the budding lime trees, the two writers went straight to a gaily-painted kiosk labelled 'Beer and Minerals'.

The charm of this mild opening works on a rather subliminal level: it stamps Bulgakov's storytelling authority in a fashion that goes far back to the archaic allure of 'Once upon a time'. While you could say this novel begins with action, it doesn't open mid-scene. Rather than feeling disoriented, the readers are leisurely grounded in place, time, season and the appearance of the story's characters. The relaxed omniscient narration induces some primal sense of comfort and trust. It's as if Bulgakov tells us: relax and listen, for I've got a good tale to spin. We trust that this seemingly ordinary meeting of two literary fellows is going to be worthy of our attention. Indeed, soon one of them would lose his head, and in very odd circumstances.

Had Bulgakov begun with the beheading, the opening might have been more alluring for some readers. Yet, in my view, the choice he made fits better his story's essence with its largely improbable events, which at the same time are firmly grounded within the oppressive Soviet reality. The mundane start eases us into Bulgakov's fantastical world, establishing a realistic, vivid platform for the magic that ensues. It is also spiced with humour, forecasting the novel's wildly satirical atmosphere: the well-fed man with his preternatural glasses, the intellectuals meeting to discuss the lofty matters of poetry but firstly heading to buy some cheap beer.

There are plenty more ways to begin a story. As long as the start expresses your tale's truth, you are unlikely to go wrong. More so, in my experience, finding a true start is also immensely helpful in the writing process. I can never begin steadily drafting something until I have the first sentence or paragraph in mind. Sometimes it takes me a long time to find this crystallising opening, but wait I must. My writing tends to be digressive, a style which can enrich a work but also obscure its heart, so my beginnings become my beacons. They are there to remind me why I am writing what I am writing whenever I depart too far from the shore and get lost among subthemes, backstory or secondary characters. At such times, I re-read my opening to shine light onto the dark sea of my work-in-progress, to reorient and bring me back to myself.

AUTHENTIC CHARACTERS

Once I mentored a writer who was working on a novel set in seventeenth-century Spain. It was about a young aristocratic woman torn between her love for her fiancé and her wish to become a nun at a time when convent life was the main means for women to achieve some independence. Despite the dramatic premise, interesting narrative twists and some vivid descriptions, the book wasn't working. The protagonist left me cold. Her thoughts and feelings were predictable and generic. She'd 'blush with excitement' upon seeing her fiancé. She 'delighted' at her sister's 'lovely' singing. She thought it was 'wrong' to persecute people in the name of God. I could continue, but you see my point.

I asked the writer how she'd conjured up her protagonist. Had she modelled her on someone she knew? On a mix of people perhaps? Or did the character contain certain aspects of her? I asked all that, because I believe it's almost impossible to create a living, breathing character with no foot in reality. Protagonists especially come to life if a writer inserts something of themselves into them. This doesn't mean protagonists must be our stand-ins. Our selves are multidimensional. We can be, say, controlled overachievers as well as dreamers as well as amateur ornithologists and conflicted lovers, all at the same time – enough to inspire multitudes of characters who are *seemingly* not us. Take William Styron's oeuvre: his protagonists range across epochs, genders and races. Still, Styron says, they 'are not much more than sort of projected facets of myself'. Or a writer can blend themselves with other people they know. The male narrator of my novella from my second book, for instance, is as innocent and easily satisfied as my high school boyfriend, and resembles him physically, but his intellectual pursuits and tastes are mine.

The writer listened to my questions, then said it was nothing like that. She'd researched the situation of upper-class women in Renaissance Spain and had tried to make her character 'authentic', by which she meant authentic for that society. She admitted that although she 'knew' her character – the clothes she wore, the number of her siblings, the prayers she recited – she didn't actually *feel* her.

The malady that afflicted that novel makes me think of Fitzgerald's famous suggestion that if a writer creates a character by beginning with an individual, they may end up also saying something of importance about the character's sociocultural milieu – their 'type'. But if they begin with a type (as my mentee had), they end up with nothing. Fitzgerald spoke of fiction, but I think the same applies to creative nonfiction. Writers can kill a work if they describe real people so as to represent something or other, turning them into a case study, say, of a 'typical miner' or 'typical Frenchwoman', rather than emphasising their unique qualities.

There is no truth in case-study characters, for we are always more than our class, ethnicity, gender or any other demographic factors. The self is shaped by such factors, yet only to *some* extent. A sign of poor writing is when a character processes everything via the prism of their demographics. ('She has a gorgeous thorax,' a doctor might remark about his beloved in a bad book . . .) Nobody is that reductive. Our internal architecture is made of much more – life events, temperament, secret desires, eccentricities, superstitions and so on. Detailed portraiture is the key to creating authentic characters. But detailed in which ways? And to what extent?

*

A skilled portrait painter knows that to convey singularity of their subject they should emphasise their unique aspects – an unusual beauty spot, a posturing mannerism. Writers, similarly, highlight what is unique about their characters and downplay their more pedestrian aspects. We know Sherlock Holmes played the violin. But do we know what side of the bed he slept on? We cannot, and should not, tell *everything* about our characters. The self is too vast to be exhaustively captured between the pages. And how exhausting would it be for our readers if we could?

Selective representation of the person's aspects might seem dishonest, but actually the features that set us apart from others are usually our most vivid and memorable qualities, and most revealing too. Here is one of the instances where Paul Auster sketches in Benjamin Sachs, the man whose death opens *Leviathan*:

> He was a great one for turning facts into metaphors, and since he always had an abundance of facts at his disposal, he could bombard you with a never-ending supply of strange historical connections, yoking together the most far-flung people and events.

Sachs's erudition surely sets him apart, and *how* he uses it tells us something essential about him. Sachs is creative and original as well as manipulative, someone nursing a large ego, brilliant and self-absorbed. These qualities are crucial in understanding his later metamorphosis from famous author into terrorist. If Auster hadn't been selective about what aspects of Sachs to emphasise, we could have overlooked this important information within the avalanche of his other traits and behaviours. The writer's job isn't only to make their characters come alive on the page, but to also ensure that the parts of them that illuminate their story's emotional truth take centre stage.

It is possible Conan Doyle did know what side of the bed Holmes favoured. We need to know more about our characters than our work describes, as per Hemingway's famous 'principle of the iceberg'. According to Hemingway, in his fiction 'there is seven-eights of [iceberg] underwater for every part that shows'. Time after time I see in my classes how this principle works as my students usually do their best exercise writing when they describe a family member or a lover, their brief sketches being the tips of icebergs of intimate knowledge. And notice how detailed and probing are Helen Garner's notes on Dexter, the protagonist of her novel *The Children's Bach*:

> He commandeers other people's experience, remembers their dreams, tells the story always in the same words . . . He hates modern things: postcodes, people write '7 April' instead of 'April 7th' . . . He was the sort of person who'd put on Ravel's Bolero first thing in the morning.

To write emotionally honest (real or fictional) characters, we must know not just a lot about them but know them deeply. This is a crude generalisation, but every person has at least three dimensions to them (although each of the three can be split into many finer ones): the public persona we show at work or other relatively formal situations, the private one we use with people close to us and, finally, our secretive parts we show to no one.

This last dimension is the one that fine writers focus on the most. What is our character's greatest disappointment to date? Their sexual hang-ups? Which celebrity do they secretly worship? You'd think memoirists are exempt from such copious homework, since they write about themselves and people they know. Not exactly. They write at their best when they penetrate deeper and deeper, gathering a wealth of knowledge not readily available: What are my greatest flaws? How did my mother's upbringing shape her? Did the fact of me being the oldest sibling in my family impact my behaviour in romantic relationships?

*

There was another problem with the Spanish protagonist. Outside of her dilemma of choosing between love and independence, nothing else motivated the woman. She had no other desires or grievances. I sinned similarly in that novel I once killed, defining each of its characters by *one* internal struggle:

> Marina, the singer, drinks because she overstayed her visa and has no certainty in her life. Lora has a good career in academy, but she also has this deep wound – the loss of her mother – and her consequent fear of true love leads her to a succession of unsuitable relationships. Misha is continuously tortured by his fear of death.

At first glance, there is nothing wrong with my notes. Almost all literary narratives are basically about characters wanting something and struggling to get it. In a good story, the main struggle would be two-fold: internal and external. The external struggle is the action – what the protagonist *does* to get what they want, be this getting ahead at work or getting away from pursuers. The internal struggle is psychological; it may be the source of external struggle or it may complicate it, or do both. Emma, the protagonist of Flaubert's *Madame Bovary*, for example, struggles to find and retain love. Her restlessness and unceasing need for heightened emotion is her internal struggle, which at once generates her desperate search for love in all the wrong places *and* blinds her to her lovers' dubious motives.

Even the most complex stories are usually built around such twin struggles, because if you have too many main conflicts the narrative is likely to get muddled. *The Master and Margarita* – a work so structurally and thematically intricate that the American critic Andrew Barratt called it 'a puzzle novel' – nevertheless can be boiled down to the external struggle of the Master to keep writing with integrity in the face of Soviet censorship and his internal struggle to believe in his work's worth.

The notes for my novel were sound starting points, but the key word here is 'starting'. One of the reasons that book failed was that I couldn't see beyond them. Pinpointing the most fundamental struggle of a character isn't enough to make them flesh and blood. In reality, nobody's life trajectory diligently follows One Central Conflict. Why would readers believe that Lora got into bad relationships *only* because she'd lost her mother? There must be some other factors at play too – say impatience or unrealistic ideas about love.

Human motivations are tangled. Literature cannot replicate this complexity precisely, but it should reflect it to some extent. In good works, the main problem is at the narrative's forefront but the edges around it teem with other complications. What if, say, that Spanish protagonist also nursed a grievance about her pockmarked skin?

But how could such vanity coexist with her monastic aspirations, you may wonder. Perfectly, that's how. Aren't we all steeped in incongruities? Isn't it possible, say, to be a vocal supporter of animal rights while occasionally, guiltily, indulging in a juicy steak? I think holding contradictory views, desires and motivations is far more common than bulletproof integrity. Good writing acknowledges and explores such paradoxes, rather than ignoring or artificially reconciling them. *They* make characters authentic. Notice how the greatest of writers – Flaubert, Tolstoy, Proust – make human inconsistency the very heart of their writing.

*

I'll return to the seventeenth-century lady for the last time. Unfortunately, my prognosis for her isn't promising. Even if we endowed her with some peculiarities (She enjoys picking her nose in public? Wears only star-shaped jewellery?), and added more conflicts and wounds, there would still be the problem with how she carries herself in the world. She is infinitely *nice*. Always trying to do 'the right thing'. This for a character, particularly if they are the protagonist, is a fatal illness – such a character is unrealistic, dishonest. I have often seen – particularly in my work in mental health and more recently as a writing mentor, which is also a type of counselling – how, given the opportunity for safe disclosure, even the loveliest people reveal problematic thoughts and instincts. All too often, so-called ordinary people divulge internal dramas worthy of a Shakespearean play. No human is exclusively governed by benevolent, altruistic impulses; not even Gandhi, if you believe his biographers.

Still, some writers exhibit a failure of imagination to see the human animal for what it is. Others assume that any shade darker than cream in their protagonists will repel prospective readers. Whatever the underlying reasons, the result on the page is supposedly 'relatable' characters of the perfectly sensible, sometimes heroic, kind. They help children cross the road and feed stray cats. If they have flaws, these are carefully calculated and in the long term would render them only more honourable. They might snap at their grandmother, then spend the rest of the book feeling terribly ashamed. Such characters are meant to represent the story's moral compass. They are meant to be good for us (in the way spinach is). But are they?

Joyce Carol Oates suggests that 'the more complexity we acknowledge in others, the more dignity we grant them'. This resonates with my view that representations of uncomplicatedly 'good' humans are not only tedious but irresponsible. In nonfiction, such character portrayals are unfair towards real people. And in any genre, simplistic representations of goodness set impossible ideals for the more impressionable readers, making them feel inadequate, wanting. Conversely, describing people's emotional tangles honestly is a gesture of generosity towards readers. In this way, we let them know they are not alone in their emotional 'imperfection'. What any of us might imagine as our private, freakish shortcomings is usually shared by many. We all possess inner demons, so please give us a break.

Even if you aren't into altruism, you are still better off not bleaching your protagonists. Compelling characters are not to be confused with the kind of people we would like to have over for dinner. To be likeable is a useful asset in daily life but not in writing. Our writing compels not when we court agreement, but when we create characters so singular, so alive in all their flawed glory, that readers can't help but care about what happens to them, even if they dislike them or certain aspects of them. Such writing affords dignity not only to our protagonists but also to readers – shows trust in them not to be simple-minded idealists.

Then, perfection isn't relatable but flaws are. The misanthropy, restlessness and indecisiveness of Geoff Dyer's persona in *Out of Sheer Rage* repels some readers and can drive even his biggest fans bonkers. Still, even his most controversial lines resonate with many, since they strike a sincere note, expressing the kind of things we think but don't say. When I read the following statement: 'I hate children and I hate parents of children', it surely occurred to me that I belong to Dyer's category of hated people. Yet I was also exhilarated by his unabashed admission of something I, too, feel sometimes, especially after spending time at my children's school events. Besides Dyer's provoacations, whether I agree with them or not, make me laugh out loud. Reading him feels like having a conversation with someone with no pretences or reservations. I may not like this human sometimes, but here he is in front of me – unguarded. And that is precious.

Then, let's not forget also that darkness – literal and metaphoric – has fascinated humans since our very beginnings, long before electricity was invented, when at night we found ourselves at the mercy of stars. Even the darkest of protagonists compel if they are rendered skilfully, if their darkness is complicated rather than relentlessly monstrous, and therefore is real, authentic. *Lolita*, for instance, is one of the most widely read modern novels notwithstanding the fact its narrator is Humbert Humbert, the paedophile professor. Listen to him relate his tale.

> I grew, a happy, healthy child in a bright world of illustrated books, clean sand, orange trees, friendly dogs, sea vistas and smiling faces. Around me the splendid Hotel Mirana revolved as a kind of private universe, a whitewashed cosmos within the blue greater one that blazed outside. From the aproned pot-scrubber to the flanneled potentate, everybody liked me, everybody petted me. Elderly American ladies leaning on their canes listed toward me like towers of Pisa. Ruined Russian princesses who could not pay my father bought me expensive bonbons.

Humbert Humbert is repulsive in many ways, but he is also an extraordinarily seductive storyteller. Nobody sees the world like he does, with his blazing blue universe and ladies listing like the Pisa tower. It is to experience life through his eyes, not to approve of his deeds, that we follow his tale.

The fragrant bouquet of Humbert Humbert's old-fashioned charm, erudition, linguistic fireworks, gentle irony and hypnotic rhythms not only sugarcoats the evil of his intentions but also complicates them. The fact that the 'good' and the 'bad' are inextricably entwined in him is intrinsic to why we are compelled, fascinated. And our however faint, however fleeting, susceptibility to Humbert Humbert's allure makes us question our own morals and motives, involving us even more in his tale, reminding us what is always worth remembering – that (surprise, surprise . . .) we aren't morally perfect.

*

The necessity to know our characters deeply, with all their peculiarities – so as to make them complex, real, compelling – is something I emphasise in my teaching. But when put in practice, sometimes my own advice leads me astray. In my notes for that failed novel I dutifully recorded the following intentions: 'Must ensure all my characters have some curious interests. Lora collects objects with elephants. Tamara is obsessed with Jesus, and also with Jews.' I implemented all that, yet it did my work no good.

The problem wasn't with the advice itself, but with how I used it – not as a loose framework but diligently, as if I were following a recipe:

1. List the character's demographics and personal history.
2. Identify their major desire and ensure it is sufficiently conflicted.
3. Add equal quantities of strengths and flaws to the mixture.
4. Sprinkle the character with spicy idiosyncrasies.
5. Bake them in a moderately hot oven for 3 drafts or until they are ready for consumption.

The risk in developing characters in such a thorough yet compartmentalised way is that this can impede the complex, partly intuitive, process of grasping them in their singular totality. Perhaps it is due to the popularity of writing advice like mine that today's readers have to endure so many lonely, hard drinking yet basically decent detectives who do yoga in 38-degree heat.

Speaking of detectives, John Banville, who writes both literary and crime fiction, says that he crafts characters for the latter books 'consciously', but his literary characters 'sort of drift out' of him. Banville's distinction between the conscious mind and the instinctual impulse is illuminating. Merely assigning qualities to our characters runs the risk of objectifying them, making them if not a 'type' then some sort of 'sub-type'. Just as different people can fit the same demographics, different people can fit under the umbrellas of certain quirky habits and flaws. Characters, fictional or real, become authentic when we *feel* them. When we can imagine the chaotic, pulsing space of their mind – all those minute confusions, associations, memories, impulses – and see the world through their eyes. It is surely from such deep perception that Humbert Humbert's blazing blue universe arises.

To illustrate further, let's imagine you and I are looking at the same river at the same moment in time. I am certain we would have different internal responses, based on our life experiences and personality (and, yes, demographics too). You might have once almost drowned and now fear water. I might be an urban princess and find nature boring. Perhaps we both are stunned by the river's beauty, but you notice what is distinct about this particular one, whereas in my mind any river's charm is forever bound with Waterhouse's anguished painting of the Lady of Shalott sailing towards her death, and now I am also trying to remember where I last saw that artwork . . .

Once the 'character dream' takes hold, one of the best ways I know of making it palpable is by transcribing their internal monologue on the page – the content and rhythms of the ongoing inner chatter in response to small and big events (such as seeing a river); obsessions that come and go; and the constant low- and high-minded battles with themself and others that take place in their heads. Look at the singular fashion in which Hannah, the mentally unravelling protagonist of Amos Oz's novel *My Michael*, responds to the graffiti inscription visible from her window, *Judaea fell in blood and fire, in blood and fire will Judaea rise*:

> It is not the idea in this slogan that appeals to me, but a certain symmetry. A kind of disciplined balance which I cannot explain, but which is also present with me at night, when the street-lights print the shadow of the window-bars on the wall opposite and everything seems to be doubled.

The most authentic descriptions of internal monologue capture the serpentine, disordered movement of the human consciousness: how thoughts and emotions veer, clash, slink away and reappear. Such writing hums like the flow of blood, and feels warm and elastic like flesh, as it conveys the essence of being human, being alive. Albert Camus does this in his novel *The Fall*, where his protagonist's observations of a busy bar follow their own logic rather than that of the outer world's happenings, moving inwards to reveal his loneliness and restlessness.

> All these people, eh? Out so late despite this rain which hasn't let up for days. Fortunately, there is gin, the sole glimmer of light in this darkness . . . I like walking through the city of an evening in the warmth of gin. I walk for nights on end, I dream or talk to myself interminably.

To inhabit these far subtler individual differences requires spending considerable time with our characters outside of the writing hours – mulling them over in our minds until they are lodged in our cells. David Grossman finds it useful to write letters to his protagonists, asking: 'What's the difficulty? . . . What is preventing me from understanding you?' Peter Carey journals in a stream-of-consciousness fashion, as in these excerpted notes about one of *Oscar and Lucinda*'s characters:

> The indulgent streak in him too, in his appetite for food, not a glutton but a sensualist, his love of wine, smells, cigarettes, something to happen. A nervous energy, a love of life, so that for all his Christianity he WANTED MORE. MORE MORE. He would holler, MORE his voice comical, his face a sight.

I find doing free-flow writing, in the fashion I mentioned earlier, useful even when my characters aren't based on me. Recording the movements of my consciousness teaches me invaluable lessons about the nature of the inner life. But capturing internal monologue, in all its messy glory, isn't the only way to breathe life into our characters, to make them live on our pages, as we'll see in the next five chapters.

WRITING EMOTIONS

Years ago, I ran a writing therapy group in a mental health organisation. Several of the participants had a diagnosis of clinical depression. Yet, even though they shared many symptoms, their descriptions of illness differed. One person, for example, wrote that being depressed felt like being smothered by a heavy blanket and struggling to breathe. Another described it as seeing the world through a grey, flattening prism. The word 'depression' applied to all, yet every person experienced it differently.

The same can be said about ordinary sadness. Moreover, what we call sadness comes in many shades for each person. Recently, I re-watched a Soviet film I loved as a child. I bawled my eyes out at its protagonist's thwarted hopes for love. I cried also because of some complicated longing I felt for my country of birth, which has sort of vanished since *glasnost* and *perestroika*. And I cried with joy, as the film brought me closer to the child I once was. My sadness was genuine but also delicious – rich, indulgent – like hot chocolate. It feels inadequate to be using the same word for this experience *and* for what I felt when my recent grant application was rejected. There was nothing delicious about the latter sadness! Its taste was bitter with failure and some vague anger.

The writer's job is not to lean on such blanket words as sadness, love or anger – words which are supposed to brim with meaning but contain little of it at closer inspection. Rather, it is to express the truth of a feeling without taming it, without marching it along well-trodden linguistic paths. We ought to face the enormous variety of human emotions and try to articulate it. What a mighty task.

Describing feelings with precision is difficult also because casting a closer look at them can be confronting. Emotions are often mixed, ambiguous. Do I really want to admit that it is possible to love someone and at the same time resent them? That my anger might contain a measure of self-righteousness, even when it feels completely justified? Maybe that's why many choose to believe in emotional purity. Feeling pure fury is liberating, isn't it? (In a self-righteous kind of way . . .) Honest examination of real or fictional characters' emotions compromises our, or their, supposed 'goodness' or 'evilness'. This, as I discussed earlier, can be difficult to digest, especially if we are susceptible to idealism or are fearful of challenging conventions.

Yet without precise descriptions of feelings, we have no authentic, singular characters. Everyone can generically describe a teenager in love, but not everyone can do so with the precision of the American writer Emily Gould, who articulates her adolescent infatuation in her personal essay 'Flower'. Hers was 'the complicated constellation of gratification feelings clustered around sex that, because I was a girl, I had taught myself to call "love"'. This sentence tells me not only how Gould felt but also something about who she was in her youth.

Gould succeeds where others fail because she situates her feelings within the broader cultural context. Linking an emotion to something concrete can also render it specific and vivid. For example, we might do so by showing a character's response to a place: a sad person is more likely to notice the unpleasant aspects of their surroundings or *perceive* certain aspects as unpleasant. In her personal essay 'Close to the Bone', the Australian writer Georgia Blain describes visiting the apartment of her father-in-law just after his death:

> The terrace faced north, the full glare of the sun bouncing off the white walls behind me as I looked across a mass of pot plants, all of different shapes and sizes, a profusion of brightly coloured flowers wilting in the heat. The sharpness of the light, the whiteness of the walls and brilliance of the blooms made the glare unbearable. It seemed there was no shade in which I could shelter.

Imagine how different this paragraph would have been if Blain was feeling happy. She might have delighted in the sunshine and in the perfumes of *ripe*, not *wilting*, flowers. She might not have yearned for a shelter.

It is equally possible to show emotions through actions. In my short story 'Floating Above The Village', which describes a mother visiting her estranged daughter, one of the ways I show the daughter's mixed feelings towards her mother – anger, revulsion, pity, love – is by making her act out of character: 'Since her arrival, I've started breaking things. The frame of my newly mounted painting. Daniel's glasses. I trod on my palette, flooding the carpet with sparkling gold. I can't work anymore.'

Similarly, emotions can be conveyed through objects or images. The Australian novelist Mireille Juchau describes the breakup of her protagonist with his girlfriend in *The World Without Us* in this fashion. It happens in a café, where he looks through the window, noticing 'the ocean, seagulls passing . . . a parade of tourist brides, stuffing their white skirts into limousines . . . The tuxedoed men behind them, drowned by tulle and chiffon. Was this what she wanted?' Taken together, these striking images capture the man's complex emotional cocktail of disappointment, contempt, fascination and relief.

A word of caution. All too often writers resort to concrete yet clichéd bodily symptoms to describe emotional states. I come across endless variations on such sentences as 'She felt nauseous as her husband walked away.' Or 'His throat tightened once he realised the robber was his brother.' These descriptions are just another application of blanket words. 'She felt nauseous' doesn't tell us anything specific about the woman's marriage and response to abandonment. Did she feel diminished? Or perhaps both scared and relieved?

If you instead describe character's inner monologue, you have another precise way of unpacking a feeling. *What a bastard*, our abandoned wife might think, *he just beat me to it! I should have left him first.* Or you can combine physical sensations *and* thoughts, which is how Alice Munro conveys her character's bereavement in her short story 'Leaving Maverley': 'What he carried with him, all he carried with him, was a lack, something like a lack of air, of proper behavior in his lungs, a difficulty that he supposed would go on forever.' Or here is Jane's love for Mr Rochester in *Jane Eyre*, marvellously captured by Charlotte Brontë through body and cognition: 'I believe he is of mine [kind] – I am sure he is – I feel akin to him, – I understand the language of his countenance and movements . . . I have something in my brain and heart, in my blood and veins, that assimilates me mentally to him.'

*

Perhaps an even tougher job for a writer is to pinpoint emotional states we have no words to describe: various vague feelings, fleeting sensations, vivid-yet-fragmented flashes of emotion. For me this can be the anticipation of adventure, oddly combined with a profound cosiness, which I experience during thunderstorms. Or the myriad powerful emotions that course through my body when I watch the works of the late choreographer Pina Bausch.

As much as such experiences are integral to our inner lives, we often ignore their existence precisely because we have no language for them. So when you next feel some undefined but powerful feeling, I suggest you pull out your notebook and pin that fast-disappearing exotic butterfly to your page to use later.

The challenge of finding words to articulate such experiences is the opposite of refining blanket words, the opposite of Shklovsky's famous 'rendering the familiar strange'. Here we are faced not with the banal, the overused, but with nameless emotional miasma for which we hope there might be some German words. (And sometimes there are, like *weltschmerz*, which describes the feeling of having the weight of the world on your shoulders, or *fremdscham* – the embarrassment we experience on someone else's behalf.) Here the writer *familiarises* people with their strangeness, fills gaps in language.

Flaubert excels in capturing such experiences clearly and vividly, like in this passage from *Madame Bovary*, which expresses the protagonist's intense need for drama:

> Accustomed to the peaceful, she turned in reaction to the picturesque. She loved the sea only for its storms, green foliage only when it was scattered amid ruins. It was necessary for her to derive a sort of personal profit from things, she rejected as useless whatever did not minister to her heart's immediate fulfilment – being of a sentimental rather than an artistic temperament, in search of emotions, not of scenery.

To make his psychological insights palpable, Flaubert attaches abstract feelings to concrete images – the sea, the foliage, the ruins.

No doubt it is difficult to write so inventively and precisely, and Flaubert's ample correspondences are full of his complaints about how difficult writing is. But how much satisfaction there must have been when he succeeded!

*

There is another category of emotions that challenges writers – the feelings we are describing while they are still burning in us, be this with torment or pleasure. As a rule, we would better wait until we 'exhaust the emotion', as Truman Capote suggests, 'feel clinical enough to analyze and project it'. But sometimes, for whatever reason, we cannot wait or are unable to put this particular fire out (other than by writing it, perhaps). In such instances, it might be best to at least keep cool on the page.

Readers don't want to be passive audiences for authors venting their (literal or fictionalised) passions, self-pity or fury. While it is debatable to what extent expressing anger in life might be liberating or therapeutic, for a writer it is a counterproductive emotion, as it interferes with our capacity for introspection and ability to see other viewpoints. Readers want a story that has been thought through with some distance, so they may decide for themselves how to feel about what's going on. With this in mind, I recently wrote a personal essay 'Bruised', about a brief yet traumatic relationship I had in my younger years.

It took me two decades before I was ready to write this tale and even then, when I finally had enough distance to recall our good moments and find some compassion towards my ex-boyfriend, I still wasn't 'cool' enough to describe the feral fear I felt when, after I broke up with the man, he held me captive for some hours, threatening murder. To bring the temperature in that scene down, I chose not to use emotive words like 'shock' or 'pain'. Instead, I focused on what I recalled myself thinking and observing at the time. I also used metaphor. My hope was that these details would convey my terror without putting the readers off with melodrama (the mention of pirates references my ex-boyfriend's looks):

> I'd read somewhere that pirates took no prisoners. They either sold them into slavery or buried them at sea. I watched the systematic steps of this man, the man who had held me at night at my most vulnerable, the man whom I'd held night and day, and pictured him digging a grave with the same care he'd used for cooking fettuccini. Whenever I tried to get up, he touched me. He touched me and dark flowers bloomed on my skin.

Irony is another effective way to turn down the heat and it is certainly one of my favourite tools. Here is another example from my work, this time *The Dangerous Bride*. I use some gentle irony to describe the mixture of anxiety and denial that was a part of my daily life in Israel: 'Even in the magical bubble of Tel Aviv, reality occasionally intruded into the chic of our cafés and the drumbeat of our music, particularly when buses and people would burst into flames. Then we would remember we lived on borrowed time.'

While I like writing 'coolly', I don't think this is the only way to describe still-fierce emotions. Sometimes 'hot' writing conveys the experience just as well, as long as it's not a self-indulgent, literal rant (I hurt! I hurt!) but 'artful heat', as it is in the following excerpt from Amos Oz's *A Tale of Love and Darkness*. Oz expresses his anger at losing his mother to suicide by likening the suicidal urge to a seducer:

> For many years now I have been trailing this old murderer, this cunning ancient seducer, this revolting old rake, deformed by old age yet disguising himself time and again as a youthful

> prince charming. This crafty hunter of the broken-hearted, this vampire wooer with a voice as bittersweet as that of a cello on a lonely night, a subtle, velvety charlatan, a master of stratagems, a magic piper who draws the desperate and lonely into the folds of his silken cloak. The ancient serial killer of disappointed souls.

The language ripples with the magnitude of Oz's feelings, the potent mixture of rage and longing, anguish and regret, revulsion and fascination. The heat is on, but it is a controlled heat. And Oz uses hot writing sparingly. His memoir is rich in pain yet only seldom scorching in its language. Too much heat and we risk our story burning down.

While there are many ways to write emotions – hot or cold, rooted in place and time, described metaphorically or through setting and action, or the thoughts they trigger – I do propose one rule. I propose that we always view any feeling through a microscope so as to uncover its minutest nuances, so as to grasp and depict it as fully as possible. While it is impossible to copy precisely the texture of our emotions, I believe writers can, and should, strive towards description that at least *feels* (to them and to their readers) authentic.

TO TELL YOU THE TRUTH

In one of my writers' residencies, my duties included attending a weekly writers' group to offer advice on the regular instalments that the members read from their novels-in-progress. On my first visit, one writer said she was about to read a scene that introduces a pivotal plot twist – a revelation of a pregnancy at a family dinner. But it took two group meetings for the announcement to be made in the story. In the meantime, the dinner went on and on. We heard conversations about football and weather as well as numerous requests to pass around a variety of nutritional items. By the time the pregnancy was disclosed, we no longer cared.

Gordon Lish used to say to his students, 'Never be sincere – sincerity is the death of writing'. He didn't mean writers shouldn't be honest. He meant our job isn't to dutifully copy reality, but to pick and choose what is worth telling, what illuminates the story's emotional truth. This is true of any narrative elements, and it is why effective dialogue is more concentrated and dramatic than our typical daily conversations. It distils the essence of the scene as well as of the characters. Good dialogue captures the most idiosyncratic, dramatic, funniest or most revealing parts of conversation.

When the protagonists of 'The Feeder', the Australian author Glenys Osborne's short story about doomed love, first meet in a café, we get just a few glimpses into their conversation. The sparsity enhances the impact of everything they say. Take the male character's pick-up line: 'I hope you don't mind, but I've been sitting here like a man on a desert island'. The poetry and sadness of these words conveys the story's mood. Had Osborne included the inevitable prosaic lines of most first encounters, like 'Can I have your phone number?' it would have weakened the atmosphere. Instead, she followed a popular, and very practical, piece of advice for writing tight conversation, which is to come into dialogue as late as possible and leave as soon as you can. And my own rule whenever I write conversation is to ask myself: If I overheard this, would I keep eavesdropping? If the answer is 'no', I usually delete it.

Dialogue is actually *optional* in literature. How much, if any at all, direct speech writers employ depends on their tastes and abilities. Most importantly, it should depend on what each work requires. The more realistic a novel's tone (think Jonathan Franzen or Zadie Smith) the more its characters converse. In contrast, the magic of more poetic, dreamy stories, like the ones Marguerite Duras writes, would be diluted by too much direct speech.

Unfortunately, rather than following artistic considerations as to how much direct speech to put in their story, many beginning writers – like the author of the never-ending dinner – overuse dialogue. My sense is this happens because, increasingly, writers (especially young ones) are influenced by film, where dialogue is usually the main device for revealing characters' personalities and backstories. Then there is also the unhelpful ubiquity of the categorical 'show don't tell' writing advice, and dialogue is one of the main means of showing. For these, and maybe other reasons, some writers lean on dialogue when they need to convey information. They get characters to lecture in order to reveal what they think or make them say things they have no particular reason for saying, other than to provide exposition. Imagine a woman asking her husband: 'Darling, do you know where our children, the two-year-old Ben and the five-year-old Mila, are?' You may think my parody is crude, but I come across many variations of such 'information dumping'.

If writers 'showed' everything, books would be thick enough to be used as tabourets. There is nothing wrong with simply giving your readers the basic information they need to follow a story (like the ages and names of characters' children). Writers have many more opportunities than filmmakers to invite their audiences into their characters' minds and we should make use of these wonderful possibilities. Both telling and showing have their place in literature and both should be respected. It's all a matter of finding the balance between the two.

The 'telling' summary technique is one common way to avoid the tedium of excessive showing (through dialogue and also through other action descriptions), while still conveying the gist of a scene and moving the story along. Here is an example from Zadie Smith's novel *On Beauty*. When one of its protagonists, Levi, makes friends with a musician called Carl, Smith gets them talking a little on the page to 'show' the new character, then summarises the rest of their interaction, including the logistics of how they'd stay in touch:

> They talked . . . about hip-hop generally, and then about recent shows in the Boston area. How few and far they were. Levi asked question after question, sometimes answering himself as Carl opened his mouth to reply . . . Levi suggested they swap cell numbers and they did so by an oak tree.

Similarly, the novelist I met at that writers' residency would have done better by writing something like: 'At the dinner table they talked of nothing but the Bulldogs and the recent rains, until X interrupted Y's weather complaints to say, "I'm pregnant."'

*

Even when dialogue flows naturally and is compelling, there is the risk that works heavy on direct speech might turn out somewhat pedestrian, more anecdotal than artful, because what we think is usually far more interesting, and truthful, than what we say. Works dominated by dialogue risk remaining on the shallower level of 'what happens' at the expense of 'why this happens', which is the heart of any worthwhile literature.

Filmmakers have visuals and sound at their disposal to complement direct speech, to create mood and depth. The literary equivalent of this is to embroider conversation with description of place, body language and other sensory detail, and of what is going on in characters' minds as they interact with others. In particular, skilled writers capitalise on any disparities between what their characters say and think, which are a common occurrence in real life. In this other snippet from *On Beauty*, Smith's descriptive and reflective narration imbues her characters' mundane dialogue with emotional meaning:

> 'LaShonda, hey, girl.'
> Lashonda waved her talons in a swift, economical move, like the spreading of a fan, each nail clicking off the next. She grinned at him. 'Hey, Levi, baby. How you doing?'
> 'Oh. I'm cool . . . You know, hustling, doing my thung.'
> 'You do it well, baby, you do it *well.*'
> Levi tried hard to hold the gaze of this incredible woman but failed, as ever. LaShonda hadn't yet cottoned on to the fact

> that Levi was only sixteen . . . and therefore not really a viable stand-in father for her three small children.
>
> 'Hey, LaShonda, can I speak to you for a minute?'

Because of the talons spreading like a fan, because of LaShonda's misplaced romantic hopes, in Smith's capable hands the grey of 'how you doing' and 'I'm cool' turns to silver.

*

Having made all these cautionary remarks, I do think dialogue is an invaluable tool when used discerningly. It enhances readability without compromising the work's depth by providing breaks between chunks of denser prose. It is also effective in conveying drama. Being real-time-action, dialogue can create a sense of urgency and immediacy – but only if it is employed in the right measure, because, as we saw earlier, excessive dialogue actually slows the narrative down. (For good examples of dramatic dialogue use I suggest Raymond Chandler's novels.)

I also use dialogue to inject humour, as it lends itself to comedy. The discrepancy between what we say and what we think is often amusing; and our daily conversations, when frozen on the page, can suddenly appear very funny, like in this excerpt from Philip Roth's novella *Goodbye, Columbus*:

> I forked a potato in half and ate it, while Aunt Gladys, who had seated herself across from me, watched. 'You don't want bread,' she said, 'I wouldn't cut it, it should go stale.'
>
> 'I *want* bread,' I said.
>
> 'You don't like it with seeds, do you?'
>
> I tore a piece of bread in half and ate it.
>
> 'How's the meat?' she said.
>
> 'Okay. Good.'

> 'You'll fill yourself with potatoes and bread, the meat you'll leave over I'll have to throw it out.'

Most importantly, dialogue brings characters to life. Well-chosen, specific turns of phrase (or it might be a barrage of clichés – this is also telling!), distinct vocabularies, idioms and rhythms of speech can say so much about a person. It can show their demographics, such as age, cultural background and education. (Emily Brontë's *Wuthering Heights* is an excellent example of capturing class differences through direct speech.) But good dialogue goes deeper than that. It reveals a character's singularity, such as their temperament, private obsessions, past hurts. That's why in *The Dangerous Bride* I chose to introduce my ex-partner, J, through one stark remark he made when we first met: '"I can prove to you that God exists, and also that he doesn't," J told me, perching uncomfortably on the couch.' I think this snippet shows J's swagger and pretension, while his body language complicates his words, hinting at the insecurities lurking beneath his confident façade.

Dialogue also reveals the relationships between characters. The English novelist Monica Ali expertly uses it for such a dual purpose throughout *Brick Lane*, as in the following interaction between a Bangladeshi couple living in London:

> 'Why should you go out?' said Chanu. 'If you go out, ten people will say, "I saw her walking on the street." And I will look like a fool. Personally, I don't mind if you go out but these people are so ignorant. What can you do?'
>
> She never said anything to this.
>
> 'Besides, I get everything for you that you need from the shops. Anything you want, you only have to ask.'
>
> She never said anything to this.
>
> 'I don't stop you from doing anything. I am westernized now.

It is lucky for you that you married an educated man. That was a stroke of luck.'

She carried on with her chores.

In dialogue, silences carry almost as much weight as words. The wife's silence is telling both about her marriage and about who she is, just as Chanu's verbose, one-sided conversation does. Chanu's self-delusion, how he fancies himself as far more liberal than his fellow migrant men, is evident here just as his anxieties, aspirations and insecurities are. His speech reveals his paradoxes, his selfishness and desire to impress mixed with a measure of kindness and guilt, and how conflicted he is about his behaviour towards his wife.

*

Certain lucky writers have a knack for dialogue, others have to work hard at developing this skill. In the last decade, I have inadvertently improved my dialogue writing as I interviewed dozens of people with very different personalities and backgrounds for my books, and then listened back to our conversations, slowly, while transcribing them. That experience sharpened my awareness of the quirks, pauses, ramblings, repetitions, changes in tone and so-called fillers, such as 'hmmm' or 'like', characteristic of human speech. A great part of our conversations is composed of incomplete, sometimes semi-coherent sentences. For a writer, it can be easy to follow the urge to 'tidy up' dialogue, but my lengthy immersion in those recorded conversations reminded me that to do so would interfere with authenticity in writing.

While literary dialogue isn't a faithful record of real conversations, it has to convey the awkwardness and fragmentation of daily speech, as it does in this excerpt from *On Beauty*, where a chairman at a conference is fumbling for the right words to respond to a speaker's inappropriate remarks: '"Is that . . .?" queried Jack, "That's the meat of your . . . so, I suppose we must turn to the Professor and . . . Professor Kipps, could you possibly . . .''' What an apt way to capture Jack's inaptitude at dealing with curveballs.

Interviewing is one way of mastering dialogue, but really all a writer needs is to open their ears wide. Temperamentally, writers are voyeurs anyway, always looking for opportunities to spy on others. This isn't terribly ethical of us, but it helps to notice how real people speak as well as to 'borrow' idiosyncratic, juicy snippets to use in our works. I regularly eavesdrop in cinema queues, trams, playgrounds, recording in my notebook any memorable lines that come my way, like the following conversation I witnessed at a party:

> A Russian-born psychiatrist shares his insights into the 'Russian Soul' with me, Rita and Melanie: 'All Russians are anti-Semites deep down, in two ways. The intelligentsia is jealous of Jews, whereas the others are still upset about them killing Christ.'
>
> Melanie, after the psychiatrist leaves the room: 'What's his ethnicity?'
>
> Rita: 'He's a quarter Lithuanian, quarter Jewish, quarter gypsy and another quarter I don't remember.'
>
> Melanie: 'In that case, I believe him.'

Or here is an older, born-again Christian excitedly describing the moment of his epiphany:

> I was driving and listening to some inspirational music when it suddenly came to me, this euphoria. This joy. I suddenly realised that God loves us as we are and accepts us exactly as we are. I realised that if God accepts me, then I can also accept myself . . . It was, the feeling was like having hundreds of orgasms at the same time!

Ethics-shmethics. How could I possibly let this go?

Stephen King writes, 'if you *are* honest about the words coming out of your characters' mouth, you'll find that you've let yourself in for a fair amount of criticism'. Certainly, the more we listen to how people speak the less it is possible to ignore the fact that they say a lot of stuff that is risky to put on the page – obscenities, casual racist remarks, some other problematic opinions. There is always the possibility that readers might confuse what characters say with the author's views, or at the very least not like when a non-villain character says something upsetting or controversial. King himself has been receiving protest letters for years on account of what his characters say. Yet, he writes, if he wasn't prepared to bear the consequences, there wouldn't be any point in writing. So he cops it and goes on.

CARESS THE DETAILS

'Caress the details, the divine details,' Nabokov famously used to say to his students. If only I could have been in his lecture hall to watch that grumpy, misanthropic genius in action. Did he pace as he spoke? Did he wave his grumpy, misanthropic finger? And what exactly did he mean by those mysterious (and lewd?) directives?

To ponder the last question, I'll first share with you some details of my own: *When I was a child, on Fridays my grandmother cooked soup for me.* Did you find this information interesting? Do you care to hear more?

When I tell this story in my writing classes, an occasional kind student, unwilling to hurt my feelings, answers in the affirmative. Most, though, admit that it's boring, that they couldn't care less. So, I take another chance at telling it.

When I was a child, on Fridays my grandmother cooked borscht for me.

I've only changed one word, yet this time many students say their interest has been piqued. A lively conversation ensues. Someone might mention their interest in Russia. Another might say it's time to harvest the beetroots growing in their garden. Somebody else might announce they hate borscht, while yet another might ask what borscht is. But what about those who still don't care for my story? I have another go at telling it.

When I was a child, on Fridays my grandmother cooked borscht for me. She'd smoke as she cooked, the ashes falling into the pot.

I am no gifted performer, but however I tell this third version it elicits emotional reactions from my captive audiences. Some laugh; others screw their faces in mock disgust; somebody might share a similar memory or exclaim, 'I'd like to meet your grandmother!' It is at this point that I admit my story is fiction. (My late grandmothers did have their charming quirks, including swimming in Russia's wintry sea and cultivating not insignificant moustaches, but neither of them smoked. Albeit both made a mean borscht.)

The point of my fictional anecdote is to illustrate the following paradox: the more specific our writing is, the more universal its appeal. I think this was what Nabokov meant. Details turn the page lifelike, brilliantly vivid. As illustrated, they attract a *response* – opinion, memory, feeling, or at least curiosity – where generic 'soup' doesn't. And when readers feel, remember, consider our words – they are engaged.

Abstract writing is not only boring, it also smacks of dishonesty, because the real world is specific. 'Soup' as such doesn't exist – we always eat *a type of soup*. We wear specific underwear: each with its own colors and textures, its own degree of wear-and-tear. Reducing descriptions to 'soup' or 'underwear' doesn't reflect reality, which is – Coles and Sportsgirl notwithstanding – incredibly diverse. That's why details can never be too specific and why sometimes I stipulate what cigarettes my fictional babushka smoked: surely a grandmother fond of Marlboro Lights would be quite different from the one who is into joints. Yet none of this means *every* detail is divine and deserves caressing.

As with dialogue and characterisation, the quantity of details doesn't stand in direct proportion to its quality. Comprehensive lists of a character's handbag contents, features of their street or their jewellery collection are likely to be just as boring as my generic soup, even if the items they describe are specific. On the other hand, a few well-chosen details make a description memorable while allowing readers to fill in the rest themselves. The principles of emotional honesty can guide us to see through the jumble of details that constitutes life to identify the *divine* details, the ones we must caress.

*

To begin with, I believe writers should be true to their sensibilities in whatever they describe rather than strain to notice what is antithetical for them. If I tried to wax lyrical about the moon, something I don't give much thought to in reality, I wouldn't do a good job. This doesn't mean I can never describe the moon, or other natural features, but my works won't have as fine landscape depictions as, say, Virginia Woolf's whose passion for the natural world is well known. My description of a moon would be brief and more emotional than realistic – the equivalent of how I experience it off the page. I would, however, naturally be drawn to painstakingly describing somebody's kitchen.

Such an approach to writing might appear limiting, but details we are drawn to are a component of our uniqueness, our voice; I believe descriptive prose should come from this place. When readers prefer certain authors, they also respond to the types of detail in their works. Admirers of Hemingway react to the plenitude and precision of his 'trivial' daily details. Fans of Raymond Chandler relish the extravagant richness of his descriptions of urban environments and their residents, like in the following line from *The Big Sleep*: 'She was in oyster-white lounging pyjamas trimmed with white fur, cut as flowingly as a summer sea frothing on the beach of some small and exclusive island.'

To be yourself in your choice of details, however, is just the first step. We observe things selectively yet still aplenty, so what particulars should live on in our stories? One answer is that we need to develop, and the emphasis here is on practice, an eye for picking the most evocative specifics, like the following memorable detail from *The Tale of Love and Darkness*: 'She carefully retracted her red dog's erection of a lipstick into its sheath.'

Often the most vivid details are also the most idiosyncratic. Borscht, as you may recall, elicits responses, but not as powerfully as my sloppily smoking babushka does. A divine detail can render a work unforgettable, sometimes entirely identifiable by this one specific and the feelings it evokes. 'Goodbye to All That', Joan Didion's seminal essay about living in New York, for example, is irrevocably linked in my mind to the author's striking yet bothersome curtains:

> All I ever did to that apartment was hang fifty yards of yellow theatrical silk across the bedroom windows, because I had some idea that the gold light would make me feel better, but I did not bother to weight the curtains correctly and all that summer the long panels of transparent golden silk would blow out the windows and get tangled and drenched in afternoon thunderstorms.

There is an art not only to noticing and choosing evocative details but also to what we *do* with them. James Wood's distinction between 'passive' and 'mobile' details in his book on writing, *How Fiction Works*, is useful. Mobile details are active, increasing the energy and vividness of prose. Consider the following 'mobile' character description from Kate Grenville's novel *Lilian's Story*: 'There was a tinkling and a continual tiny chiming around her from so many necklaces and shivering earrings . . . Her hair at the back was slithering out of its combs.' Had Grenville instead written something like, 'she wore several necklaces and a pair of earrings; her hairdo had loose ends sticking out', the character would have seemed less intriguing, less alive.

*

All this tinkling and chiming and shivering and slithering in Grenville's masterful description makes the character cinematically vivid. It also says something about her interior – hinting at a flamboyant, excitable, energetic personality. It is in such psychologically revealing details that the greatest divinity resides. Those details, as the American writer Francine Prose writes in *Reading Like a Writer*, tell 'more about a character – his social and economic status, his hopes and dreams, his vision of himself – than a long explanatory passage.' It is possible, for example, to show someone in-depth by describing what they pack for travel (say, plenty of anti-bacterial sprays, sunscreen and painkillers) as well as by what they *don't* pack (books or spare underwear).

Thomas Hardy writes that the writer's job is to create 'a disproportioning . . . of realities, which, if merely copied or reported inventorially, might possibly be observed, but would more probably be overlooked.' He means writers should zoom in on the page on what best illuminates the emotional truth of a character. They should show such details in their full potential, because were they mentioned on equal footing with all else, they'd likely go unnoticed. Seen in this light, the golden glow of Didion's impractical curtains illuminates not only her apartment but also her glamorous yet mismatched, unsatisfying life in New York.

Marguerite Duras emphasises the clothes of the fifteen-year-old narrator of *The Lover* in this 'disproportioning' way, as a way of introducing her situation and the story's themes.

> I'm wearing a dress of real silk, but it's threadbare, almost transparent. It used to belong to my mother. One day she decided the colour was too bright for her and she gave it to me. It's a sleeveless dress with a very low neck. It's the sepia colour real silk takes on with wear . . . I think it suits me. I'm wearing a leather belt with it, perhaps a belt belonging to one of my brothers.

The dress reveals the complex socioeconomic position of the girl's family of impoverished French colonisers living in Indochina. Just as they barely have enough money to eat, yet employ local servants, so does the mother pass an expensive dress to her daughter but has no money to buy her a new one. The 'sleeveless dress with a very low neck' also suggests the widowed mother's encouragement of her daughter's budding sexuality, which she's about to exploit in order to improve the family's financial situation. The incongruous leather belt is another sign of poverty, the making do with whatever there is. It is also a menacing hint at the beltings to which the narrator is subjected by her mother and older brother.

*

There is more to be said about putting our faith in details: sometimes *they* might offer us their divine caresses, guiding our hand towards the truth of our tales. This is how my short story 'At the Russian Restaurant' emerged. I'd wanted to write about my brush with the Russian-Australian community during my first years in Australia, but I didn't have a narrative to hang this on, nor did I understand why I was drawn to the subject. One day I randomly jotted down some details that had stuck with me from my visits to Russian restaurants in Melbourne:

> Most of the women . . . were natural-born ball dames – with long elaborate garments that had openings and slits in utterly

unexpected locations. Their heels were long, and their legs were longer, and even the youngest seemed older than their years and so sophisticated, with spray-designed hair and miniature artworks on their sharp nails. I was intimidated – the only one with no evening bag and with loose, knotted hair – and so I settled for the food.

As I kept writing, it occurred to me that when I'd visited those restaurants I hadn't been much older than my mother was when she'd broken off her engagement to a man from Russia's south (before she met my father). That story, too, haunted me and I wrote down some of the details I knew or imagined about it, which also happened to involve restaurants:

My mother wrote in her diary that when she was young, on university holidays she and her girlfriends flocked to Sokhumi's restaurants to dance through the summer nights to the sounds of a moustachioed band. The wine there was yellow like Caucasian cherries. Harcho, the fatty, spicy soup of lamb, rice and garlic, was served in clay pots with pastries layered in cheeses.

Writing those passages affected me emotionally and triggered more memories, which I kept writing down until I better understood why I sought the company of Russian migrants. Somehow, through them I wanted to get closer to my mother, to the younger version of her I'd never known. I wrote down that realisation too: 'I wanted to catch her just then, when she still wore short dresses, just before she met the god she fell hopelessly in love with.'

I still had no narrative, but now I had a hope that if I kept stringing together random details which enchanted me for reasons I didn't always grasp, if I kept following Ariadne's thread, they would lead me towards the emotional truth of what I was doing. So, I described watermelons, chandeliers, Russian songs and so on, until I knew that my (fictionalised) story was about the narrator's relationship with her mother, which had grown more complex since her metamorphosis from a communist to an Orthodox Jew. Learning about the reasons for which the mother broke her engagement with her non-Jewish fiancé helped her to understand her mother's later choices. This was the heart of my story and the details led me to it.

This experience taught me to trust my appetite for certain details, and to trust my memory. I have come to believe that if I remember something seemingly insignificant vividly it is for a good reason and I should write about it until I work out the emotional meaning of those specifics. Fortunately, a life is an ocean of details, so I always have something to write about. In particular, geographical and bodily specifics are potent sources of inspiration. In the following two chapters I'll zoom in on them to explore how they can illuminate our stories and inject them with emotional honesty.

LANDSCAPES OF OUR MINDS

The artist Mark Chagall, a Russian-born Jew like myself, fled the Soviet revolution when he was thirty-five and lived the rest of his long life in France (apart from several years in America during the Second World War). Yet his art remained haunted by Vitebsk, the town where he was born, spent his formative years, and met Bella, his first wife and muse. Vitebsk's cows and roosters, violinists and rabbis, wedding processions and lopsided houses dominate Chagall's canvases. Even in his depiction of the Eiffel Tower, Chagall's iconic floating lovers, having made their way from Vitebsk to Paris, hover above France's most famous structure.

Not once was Chagall criticised for his preoccupation with his past. But, as he wrote in his recollections, he simply couldn't help himself, and I applaud him for that, for remaining true to the subject that possessed him. Geography can arouse passions, or hatreds, strong enough to power an artist's oeuvre. In literature, think of Elena Ferrante's Naples, Lawrence Durrell's Alexandria, Tim Winton's Western Australian coast.

Geography has been my muse too, though I am not faithful to

just one location, probably because of my Wandering Jew history. When I am not moving countries or cities, I move neighbourhoods. Perhaps it is because place for me has always been conditional, impermanent, that the geography of my past has congealed into a myth in my mind, and personal mythology makes for a powerful writing subject. So here I go, writing and writing about Siberian towns choked with coal and snow. About Odessa smouldering with lilac and roasted chestnuts. About the beaches of Ashdod littered with joint butts and beauties. About Tel Aviv the dancing queen, and the blue shadows and spiderwebs of the Australian bush, and the chic of Melbourne's jazz clubs, bookshops and trams.

Even when place isn't the subject, in powerful literary works it usually has a strong presence. At the very least, it is the frame that contains the story, giving context to its events and grounding characters in specificity. It contributes to the atmosphere of the narrative, imbuing it with certain cadences. A love story would have a different feel to it depending on whether it is set in a desert or on the coast. The Australian philosopher Raimond Gaita describes, in this vein, the crucial role of place in the writing of *Romulus, My Father*, his memoir of his childhood in rural Victoria:

> If the landscape had not been important to me, if I did not love it as I still do, I could not have written the book that I did . . . The entire tone and mood of the book would have been different, even, I think, the rhythm of its sentences . . . I hoped that the events and the characters . . . would be bathed in the light and colours of that landscape . . . The colours of the summer landscape were also the colours of our lives.

*

Writing imbued with the colours and light of a certain place immerses the reader by engaging their senses. However, even most vividly detailed descriptions risk being flat, or 'ornamental', in the words of Hilary Mantel, if they are written in a neutral fashion. Place writing, Mantel argues, 'works best if it has a human element . . . if it comes from an implied viewpoint'. This viewpoint can belong to a character or an omniscient narrator; it doesn't matter as long as place description is layered with some feeling and/or opinion. Elena Ferrante, for example, describes Naples as 'a city of sudden quarrels, of blows, of easy tears, of minor arguments that ended in curses, unrepeatable obscenities, and irreparable breaks, of emotions so extreme as to become intolerably false. My Naples is the "vulgar" Naples'. She always feels at risk there, Ferrante tells us.

Ferrante's depictions of Naples are not only vividly dramatic, they are also psychologically revealing. What we notice about our surroundings, or don't, and how we articulate what we see, says as much about our personality, history, desires and fears as it does about the place itself. As Ferrante reminds us, what she describes is *her* Naples, even though in the process she also conveys something about the city's spirit. When done well, subjective description of place gives away those fine psychological differences between people I discussed earlier in the book. Paris of the 1920s appears differently when viewed through the prisms of Hemingway or Henry Miller's stand-in protagonist, even though on a superficial level the two narrators are similar, both being young white male American writers.

Here is Paris in Miller's autobiographical novel *Nexus*:

> I couldn't help observing how many streets were named after writers. Alone I would spread the map and trace the streets named after the famous ones: Rabelais, Dante, Balzac . . . The philosophers, the historians, the scientists, the painters, the musicians – and finally the great warriors . . . What an education, I thought to myself, merely to take a stroll in such a city!

Miller's Paris is cerebral, sophisticated and didactic, a grand and ambitious city. Whereas in Hemingway's memoir *A Moveable Feast* it is a sensual, hedonistic place – a city of cafés, clip-clopping horses, winds and braziers; a city moveable and also constantly moving, where everything shivers, whistles, crackles, eats or is being eaten.

Neither of these narrators is wrong about Paris. They just chose to describe those facets of the city that mean something to them, and by doing so they pinpoint something of the essence of the place and also something of themselves – something that conveys them with far more precision than their demographics.

Even reportage, or at least literary reportage, is more powerful when the facts are filtered through the journalist's viewpoint (as long as it is a self-aware one). The choices Joan Didion makes when describing a certain Californian region in her essay 'Some Dreamers of the Golden Dream' tell as much about her values as they do about the values of the place: 'This is the California where it is possible to live and die without ever eating an artichoke, without ever meeting a Catholic or a Jew. This is the California where it is easy to Dial-A-Devotion, but hard to buy a book'. From this description we know who reports the story; we read the reportage in a certain light.

*

Place writing can capture the human condition even deeper if it considers the impact places have on human psychology and behaviour. Think as far back as to early civilisations: those rich cultures emerged predominantly because of their locations – the fertility of their soil and proximity to fresh water. On a smaller scale, the particular smells, curves of the roads, quality of air and song of local birds (or its absence) all these shape us. I know this just as I know that the snow of my childhood still flows in my veins, making me dream; and that the salty sea air I have breathed in most of the cities I've lived in has infected me with certain restlessness.

Many writers pay attention to this relationship between place and psyche. The Russian-American poet Joseph Brodsky observes in *Watermark*, a memoir about his connection to Venice, that 'because of the scarcity of space people exist here in cellular proximity to one another, and life evolves with the immanent logic of gossip'. Albert Camus thinks temperature matters: 'an extreme climate, whether hot or cold, is nature's way of encouraging people to excess'. Perhaps this is why in Joan Didion's novels, as the American critic John Leonard suggests, 'over and over again . . . wounded women make strange choices in hot places with calamitous consequences'. And here is Didion herself, pondering the impact of environment on humans in her essay 'Los Angeles Notebook':

> Los Angeles weather is the weather of catastrophe, of apocalypse, and, just as the reliably long and bitter winters of New England determine the way life is lived there, so the violence and the unpredictability of the Santa Ana affect the entire quality of life in Los Angeles, accentuate its impermanence, its unreliability. The wind shows us how close to the edge we are.

Many writers describe different geographical regions as having distinct personalities. Lorrie Moore observes wryly in her short story 'Joy' that 'pleasantness was the machismo of the Midwest. There was something athletic about it'. In his essay 'The Grand Illusion', Robert Dessaix makes the following witty distinctions between Australian cities: 'Byron Bay is desperate to be loved. Sydney, big-bosomed and brassy, is not: love me, she says, hate me, I don't give a stuff. Melbourne, being a trifle tonier and knowing she's got a class, sniffs: if you don't love me, then you simply have no taste'. By considering the personality of your story's setting, you can provide social commentary as well as tell something important about specific characters, how they are affected by their location. In my case, Tel Aviv's vanities and zesty energy have never completely left me, although more recently Melbourne has been moulding me in its own, mellower image, slowing me down.

Places exert pressure on our mind, and by extension on our actions and narratives. No wonder then that the narrator of *The Great Gatsby* towards the end concludes:

> I see now that this has been a story of the West, after all – Tom and Gatsby, Daisy and Jordan and I, were all Westerners, and perhaps we possessed some deficiency in common which made us subtly unadaptable to Eastern life.

The Great Gatsby is one among countless literary stories premised on a protagonist arriving in a new place. Considering the ubiquity of such plots, the famous suggestion by the British nature writer Robert Macfarlane might be as useful to writers as it is to travellers. Macfarlane proposes that upon encountering a powerful landscape, you should ask yourself two questions: What do I know when I'm in this place that I can know nowhere else? What does this place know of me that I cannot know of myself? For new places don't only offer us new perspectives, they also bring out new facets of our personalities (think of the sense of impermanence Didion discovered in LA). Then, I find Macfarlane's questions just as useful when I write characters in their habitual places. What can this place tell me about how life is lived? What can it tell me about my characters?

*

So far I focused on geography, but any space we inhabit, even briefly, can potentially affect our being-in-the-world. In airplanes, we touch elbows with strangers, suffer panic attacks and overdose on Hollywood movies while possibly getting a new perspective on the world as seen from above. In the smoky, fluorescent darkness of nightclubs we might imagine ourselves as freer or altogether somebody else. How much privacy a family house affords, or not, affects relationship dynamics. And let's not forget the importance of lavatories, where Henry Miller's characters spend many fulfilling hours dissecting Dostoyevsky's novels and current affairs.

Writers should make use of the fact that the spaces people inhabit – homes, gardens, work stations – reveal them, both through how they express themselves there and unintentionally. Such places can be understood as spatial representations of their inhabitants' interiors. They divulge what matters to them (Are the walls decorated with family photos or artworks?), the vulnerabilities they hide (those stacks of old newspapers in a bedroom), what makes them happy (the garden overflowing with flowers). In the following excerpt from the novel *Late in the Day*, the British writer Tessa Hadley effectively uses the house of her protagonists to show differences in their personalities as well as their marital tensions.

> It was clear two forces were at odds in the tiny house, pitted against each other. On the female side there were jars of lentils and pasta with gaily printed lids, the child's drawings stuck on the fridge, the Indian embroideries on velvet, plants everywhere . . . Ranged against this female brightness and optimism were the books in their plain covers on the shelves in Alex's study . . . piled punishingly high and thick with dust. The electric typewriter, the desk with its brimming ashtray, the broken dirty venetian blind hanging at a slant . . . all these were deliberately ugly, modern, an austere exhibition of the life of the mind.

To practise visualising a complicated human soul through their place, consider your own home – how it is organised and maintained, what it contains or doesn't. Is your television in a living room or bedroom? How healthy are your plants? What colour is your couch? How much physical space do your mementos (if you even have any) occupy? What do you keep in your pantry? Consider that, then consider what your answers reveal about your personality, desires, values, fears.

*

We can write place to reveal the truths of our characters. We can also write it so as to shed light on the emotional truth of a scene or the entire story. The opening of the Jewish-Russian writer Isaac Babel's short story 'Crossing the River Zbrucz', for example, foreshadows the violence at its heart through the landscape in which the story is set: 'The orange sun is rolling across the sky like a severed head . . . The stench of yesterday's blood and slaughtered horses drips into the evening chill.' And Raymond Chandler's quirky, dark novel, *The Big Sleep*, unfolds within idiosyncratically gloomy locations, like the following building:

> A single drop light burned far back, beyond an open, once-gilt elevator. There was a tarnished and well-missed spittoon on a gnawed rubber mat. A case of false teeth hung on the mustard-colored wall . . . [I] looked at the building directory . . . Painless dentists, shyster detective agencies, small sick businesses that had crawled there to die . . . [it was] a nasty building. A building in which the smell of stale cigar butts would be the cleanest odour.

In both examples, the place is at once a physical reality and a metaphor for the work's truth.

I am one of those writers naturally drawn to writing place as metaphor. This usually happens unintentionally. I'd describe the location of my story the way I see it, but on re-reading my description I'd often notice its metaphoric potential, and then I might work the metaphor more deliberately into the story. For example, the writing of my short memoir 'Diamonds in the Red Alley', named after the street in Odessa where I lived as a child, began like this. I simply followed my memory and wrote the following:

> There were not many phones or televisions in the Red Alley, one of the oldest neighbourhoods in Odessa, lined with houses built prior to the revolution. Instead of wires, laundry ropes connected us one to another, and to the wider world. Long and resilient, they stretched between opposing windows like invitations.

This opening paragraph, then, stretched like a laundry rope to the next one to introduce our neighbour, Dusya, with whom we shared a washing line. Laundry ropes, neighbourly proximity, gossip in lieu of technology-based entertainment . . . It dawned on me as I kept writing that my street visually expressed my story's concern with oppressive intimacy and intimate betrayals – Dusya was a KGB informer who spied on my parents' dissident activities.

Of course, my 'organic' way of writing place isn't really that organic. If I hadn't thought a lot about the various ways in which places and people intersect, and if I hadn't paid attention to how other writers use place, surely I'd have failed to notice my own metaphors. It's pretty much the same when we write the body, as we'll see in the next chapter.

FLESHY TRUTHS

One of the common ills affecting writers is our tendency to forget that characters have bodies. Sometimes I finish reading a book without knowing what the protagonist looks like or what they eat. The body, however, is the most basic, and urgent, part of the human story. Without it there is no person. Honest writing reflects this fact as well as that we are embodied in many different ways at once.

Perhaps the most obvious aspect of the body is its appearance, and even this isn't straightforward: appearance can be clothed or nude, transient like the shape of fingernails or permanent like eye colour. Then, the body acts – speaks, smells, runs or shuffles, listens or not, does the dishes, leaks. It has body language – deliberate as well as involuntary – with its variously flavoured smiles, facial tics, that tapping foot we cannot stop. The body feels, deeply: toothache, the taste of the morning's first latte, the mouldy smell of unwashed underwear, the craving or dread of another's touch. And it remembers, even what our conscious mind forgets – tango moves long unpractised, the threat of fire, the scent of a former lover.

It is impossible to write characters vividly and plausibly without showing their physicality. As is the case with any details, effective writing uses the most memorable and idiosyncratic features, like in the following character sketch from Philip Roth's short story, 'Defender of the Faith': 'LaHill was a dark, burly fellow whose hair curled out of his clothes wherever it could. He had a glaze in his eyes that made one think of caves and dinosaurs.'

And here is a more comprehensively embodied description of a character in *A Guide to Berlin*, a novel by the Australian writer Gail Jones:

> Marco talked quietly, with eloquence; he drank in moderation; he seemed the neutral, calm figure in their eccentric crew. He displayed a Roman sophistication they had seen in the movies, a way of tilting his head back after the first listless drag of a cigarette, a habit of leaning towards women as he listened to them, implying automatic intimacy, a tendency to flick open the *Corriere della Sera* when he was bored with conversation. He wore citrus aftershave and expensive clothes. He liked to smooth his springy black curls with a gesture of his palm.

Jones brings Marco to life in all his singularity by employing many physical aspects at once and zooming in on them to achieve fine specificity.

The best physical depictions reveal something about a character's interiority. Roth's brief yet effective sketch introduces a certain attitude towards his 'primitive' character; Jones's description is even more revealing. The American writer and former competitive swimmer Lidia Yuknavitch, known for her embodied writing, explicitly draws attention in her memoir *The Chronology of Water* to how the swimming body can disclose the self:

> You can tell a lot about a person from seeing them in the water. Some people freak out and spaz their way around like giant insects, others slide in like seals, turn over, dive down, effortlessly. Some people kind of tread water with big goofy smiles, others look slightly broken-armed and broken-legged or as if they are in some kind of serious pain.

Corporeal descriptions can also echo the themes of our works, just as places do. D.H. Lawrence's novel, *Lady Chatterley's Lover*, for example, stresses the power of eros and it is sensual not just in its explicit sex scenes, as the following description of people holidaying in Venice (which, coincidentally, happens to reference seals too . . .) shows:

> The Lido, with its acres of sun-pinked or pyjamaed bodies, was like a strand with an endless heap of seals come up for mating. Too many people in the piazza, too many limbs and trunks of humanity . . . all the lying in warmish water and sunbathing on hot sand in hot sun, jazzing with your stomach up against some fellow in the warm nights, cooling off with ices . . .

The passage, infused with physical pleasures, is an apt metaphor for the novel's main concern.

*

Lawrence's celebration of the sensory shouldn't be taken for granted. One of the greatest challenges writers face when describing the body is how to convey such subjective and non-verbal phenomena as physical sensations. It can be tempting to take the easy way out and describe them generically. Poorly written works are rich with sentences such as: 'He kissed her passionately and she shuddered with the pleasure of it.' But what does this sentence tell us about the nature of passion or pleasure? Nothing much, I'm afraid. There is no honesty in such writing.

Yuknavitch acknowledges the difficulty of describing sensations and offers a solution:

> language always falls short of the body when it comes to the intensity of corporeal experience. The best we can do is . . . push on the affect of language. Its sounds and grunts and ecstatic noises. The ritual sense of language. Or the cry. Poetic language – and by that I mean the language of image, sound, rhythm, color, sensation – is probably the closest we bring language to experience.

The Australian author Josephine Taylor uses such poetic, visceral language to capture the suffering of the protagonist of her novel *Eye of a Rook*, a woman afflicted by chronic vulvar pain. The following passage depicts her pain as she urinates:

> Standing, legs apart. Tipped forward, cheeks held open. A quick stream into the toilet bowl. The hissing brand. Skin bubbling and stripping. Oh, no . . . A burst of needles. The fresh knife up and in. Twisting. No. Please, no . . . The consuming ache inside – outside? . . . Slinking to the lounge room, closing doors. Eaten away. Sinews, tendons. 'Who am I?' Raw. Gore. 'Where have I gone?' Throwing her body about. 'Fuck, Fuck.' Beating at the floor. 'God . . . oh, someone.' Pulling at her hair and face. Beseeching the night, 'Please, please.' Howling at the darkness, 'Fucking, fucking, take it away!'

The brevity and incompleteness of Taylor's sentences, and the repeated use of present participles, echo the character's sharp agony and the accompanying shortness of breath. The bold choice of words, including devastating imagery of needles, knives and branding, make the torture of this pain so palpable and specific that I kept squirming and fidgeting as I read this passage.

In her memoir *In My Skin*, Kate Holden uses poetic language to convey sexual attraction: 'Confessions. Poetry. Saturated kisses in dim afternoon rooms . . . His pale body was beautiful, not frightening; it melted under my mouth, under the skimming of my palms.' The description isn't graphic, yet it feels urgent and delicious. The phonetics and the varied rhythm of sentences mimic the slinky, slippery texture of desire.

Another effective way to write sensation is by being hyper-specific, like Hemingway does in this scrumptious description in *A Moveable Feast*:

> natural distilled liqueurs made from purple plums, yellow plums or wild raspberries. These were fragrant, colorless alcohols served from cut-glass carafes in small glasses . . . they all tasted like the fruits they came from, converted into a controlled fire on your tongue that warmed and loosened it.

The list of fruits evokes the taste, whereas the precise image of 'controlled fire' renders the experience at once palpable and relatable.

We can also pinpoint sensations, as well as reveal character, by focusing on people's psychological and behavioural responses to the physical experience. What did that kiss mean to our 'shuddering with pleasure character' in light of her history with the man she'd kissed and of her specific background? What actions did she perform during that kiss?

Emily Gould recounts a kiss in her personal essay, 'Off-Leash', filtering the experience through what went on in her mind at the time as well as describing her behaviour, with fine specificity:

> He starts kissing me, smelling like good coffee and Kiehl's products, and it's what I've been thinking about all day but now it feels off. I'm suddenly aware of the bumps on my arm again . . . But he's so ardent and pushy, more like a wrestler than a boxer, and he pins me eventually. I'm on a cusp of losing myself in it when suddenly up flashes the image of the older cat trembling and straining as he puked. I brush him aside and sit up. And then nothing works out exactly right.

This excerpt skillfully illustrates at once an experience of one specific kiss and the generally volatile nature of desire with its ebbs and flows, shades and shadows. Plus, we see something of Gould's neurotic and cerebral personality.

The Australian memoirist Nicola Redhouse similarly invites us into her mind to describe childbirth pain in *Unlike The Heart*:

> They had tried to coax progress out of me with the drug Syntocinon, with a student midwife who I began to feel responsible for letting down, so that when she stretched my cervix clumsily and caused me searing pain I couldn't bring myself to cry openly.

We wince at the clumsy stretching and searing pain, and we also learn about Redhouse, how even when she is in acute discomfort she is still self-conscious enough to put someone else's feelings before her own, and how much keeping it all together matters to her in this moment.

*

The body, even more than place, not only reflects who we are but also *shapes* us. Everything that happens to us comes from, through or despite it. Even thinking is embodied: fatigue, for example, decreases our cognitive ability whereas a brisk walk can enhance it. The way we look, how we carry ourselves, the volume and tone of our voice, whether we are able or willing to tame certain bodily actions (like burping or farting) – all such factors affect how others perceive and respond to us. These responses, in turn, influence the opportunities available to us as well as our attitudes and the choices we make.

To test my so-far-abstract propositions, consider your own experiences. Think of a time when you went through some significant physical change, like cutting your long hair short, mastering scuba diving, starting to need glasses, getting a tattoo or becoming chronically ill. Has the change affected your sense of self? Has it altered how people treat you? Has it impacted any of your routines, decisions or behaviour? Has it influenced any of your prospects? I suspect you'll answer at least one or two of these questions in the affirmative.

Emotionally honest literature considers such questions, revealing the importance of the body in our lives. Alice Munro describes the enormous impact of a cleft lip on the narrator of her short story, 'Pride'. Having spent his school years 'getting used to . . . what my face was like – and what other people were like in regard to it', he no longer wants to 'break new people in' and so decides to live in self-imposed seclusion. Or here is Joan Didion's searing examination of how her ageing body has affected her writing in her memoir *Blue Nights*:

> My cognitive confidence seems to have vanished altogether. Even the correct stance for telling you this, the way to describe what is happening to me, the attitude, the tone, the very words now elude me . . . Is this another kind of neuropathy, a new frailty, am I no longer able to talk directly?

The bodies of other people also affect our lives. The Australian author Jenny Valentish shows such impact in her creative nonfiction book, *Woman of Substances*, as she recounts the lasting legacy of being sexually abused as a child:

> Post-Adrian [her abuser], I became repelled by George Michael. The two had the same flicky fringe, square face and slant of the eyes. Thirty years on, if I see someone's eyebrow hairs flaring towards the middle, or hear a whiny nasal admonishment, or see a petulant lower lip . . . I recoil. Sometimes I even spot them fleetingly in myself and am revolted.

*

During my first months in Australia, I worked in a video store. One morning, as I was answering the phone, a customer came in. I smiled at her, then habitually pinched together the fingers of my right hand and shook them several times in her direction. The woman looked appalled. It took me some time to realise that the common Israeli gesture meaning 'just one moment' can come across as rude to Australians.

In many significant ways, the body is a cultural phenomenon. The ways we gesture, but also dress and shape, value and discipline our bodies, differ across societies. Just think of the different gender-based restrictions operating on corseted Victorian ladies and on aristocratic women of China with their bound feet. Culture influences even our most private experiences, like desire. Pre-Columbian civilisations, for example, found squinting so attractive they put balls of wax between the eyes of their babies to train them to squint.

Because societies shape bodies to an extent, some bodies become vivid metaphors for the places they inhabit, reflecting local power divisions, aspirations, anxieties. The shocking image from the *Time*'s summer 2010 cover of an Afghan woman whose nose and ears were cut off by the Taliban as punishment for fleeing the house of her abusive in-laws says a lot about that particular society, just as the cosmetically 'young-ified' people we see in western and westernised countries reflect these cultures' dreams of eternal life.

Paying attention to the cultural aspects of the body in writing deepens the analysis and enhances the descriptions of our stories' settings and their inhabitants, our characters. Once I considered how the childhood of my Russian-Israeli-Australian protagonist from 'At the Russian Restaurant' has shaped her taste in food, I was able to describe her outsider status more palpably:

> My palate has always stood out. I love the salty-bitter-fishy flavours despised in the West . . . I take a slice of freshly baked bread, smear it with butter, and pile on crispy beads of red caviar. The red and yellow and black sit blissfully on my tongue.

Writing the body with culture in mind can also promote a richer understanding of characters' motives and behaviours. In her memoir *Lucky*, American writer Alice Sebold recounts the aftermath of her horrific rape and she links her preoccupation with her weight to the trauma she endured and also to the broader pressures placed on women in America during the 1980s.

> That summer I began my makeover. I had been raped but I had also been raised on *Seventeen* and *Glamour* and *Vogue* . . . Mom was losing weight. I decided to join her. We watched Richard Simmons and bought an exercise bike . . . I began to take off pounds . . . [I watched] obese women cry with Simmons . . . Sometimes I cried too.

Writing in this fashion, Sebold avoids reducing her younger self to being solely a rape victim, instead offering a fuller picture of herself as well as an insight into her era.

*

The cultural body strives, or is pressured, to belong. But we also possess what theorists call an 'individual body'. This is the body we shape and exhibit in ways that are meant to differentiate us from others, or at least express us on our terms. To showcase what we see as our essence, we might colour our hair or nails green, practise a swagger or train ourselves to smoke cigars. The individual body is a site of identity, and sometimes of rebellion if it subverts social mores, as in the case of extreme body modification.

The individual body is very useful for writers. Showing how our characters use their bodies to express themselves is another way of deepening their characterisation in a memorable way: a body tattooed with roaring tigers, for example, can tell a story of somebody who lives in a permanent state of war. The individual body can also reveal who the characters *aspire* to be. In another short story by Alice Munro, 'Gravel', a character unhappy with her conventional life, far before leaving it, discards her elegant clothes and buys 'shawls and long skirts and dangling necklaces. She'd left her hair wild and stopped wearing makeup.'

Internal struggles can be manifested through a disparity between what self-body a character displays and how they feel inside. Showing them masking their depression with bright smiles and gaudy clothes, for example, can render their despair particularly poignant as well as say something about this person's sense of propriety and defence mechanisms.

Having made all these distinctions between the physical, cultural and individual bodies, I should now point out that in reality these are rarely discrete. Let's consider our body language, for example, or even more specifically let's consider how my Israeli gesture, on closer inspection, is a tangle of all these aspects. My bunching and shaking of fingers was typical of the society I came from, which is expressive, dramatic and argumentative. But the way I performed it was also impacted by my personality, and by the physical (and cultural and individual!) fact of my long nails that got in the way of the bunching. As a result, my gesturing was relatively subtle if you compare me to some other Israelis, somewhat lacking in zest.

There is much to consider when we write the body and such considerations are often as tangled as my gesturing. That's why it is best during first-draft writing not to ponder too much what bodies *do* in our works and what *more* they can do, and leave such concerns for the redrafting stage. Once the story is told, it is easier to ask, without becoming overwhelmed, such questions as: What aspects of the body are relevant to this scene? Are my characters physical enough? Do my bodily descriptions contribute to developing the story's protagonists and themes? Questions like these probe us to examine deeper what having a body, in all its glorious multidimensionality, *really* means.

CUTTING A SHAPE

During the first three years of working on *The Dangerous Bride* I amassed an obscene amount of words, but the narrative arc still wasn't there. This was my first memoir and, like many novice memoirists, I was under the (mistaken) impression that this would be my only opportunity to describe my life, so I tried to put *everything* into one book. The memoir was about two relationships I had during my early years in Australia, but I also wrote about my preceding love affairs. I wrote about my life in Israel and in Russia, and about my fascination with Australia. I discussed my favourite books and my love of cooking, my relationship with religion, my fear of public speaking. I wrote about my parents, including their lives *before* I was born . . .

Paradoxically, this writing diarrhoea was rooted in my wish to withhold information as much as it was in my drive to tell, because I felt ashamed of my non-monogamous predilection. This may sound ridiculous, but it took me those three years to brave writing the following sentence: 'The dream of love I'd harboured since adolescence entailed commitment but also sexual freedom.' In earlier drafts

I implied that I got into non-monogamous relationships *accidentally*. I kept avoiding my truth, and therefore my subject, by writing around it. The resulting abundance of material obscured the focus of my memoir and without focus I had no clear form.

Writing that sentence was a turning point: I finally got past my shame and committed to the emotional truth of my work. I owned my desire. Now my mind was free to get to real work and formulate something crucial, something which always helps me sift the gold from the sand of my words – a question. The Question. As I mentioned early on, each of my works arises from the desire to answer some question that burns in me. Each work and its own fire . . . *Imperfect*, for instance, I wrote in order to understand how my scars shaped me.

Once I find my question, I use it the way I use a cookie cutter when I bake: I apply it to the ample dough of my material. Whatever words fit within the contours of the question stay in. The rest goes. Unlike in baking, however, the material that remains still needs further shaping – into a coherent narrative.

Usually, the question I need to answer for my own sake also provides the tension necessary to build a narrative. Such tension doesn't need to be extremely high if you aren't writing a thriller, but readers need to be curious about how your work's central problem will be resolved. In investigative creative nonfiction, the question the author personally needs to resolve is often also the problem of the story. In *Imperfect*, for example, I declare from the start that this book is my personal quest, and also a larger quest to understand the relationship between bodily appearance and self. In fiction, however, and often in the more 'straightforward' memoirs, the protagonist's main problem isn't necessarily identical to the author's question, yet the two are always related. The writer's question might inspire a narrative question, the answer to which is already known to the author. For example, will my younger self ever stop hating her scars?

I don't always know from the start why I am drawn to a particular subject. I might write for quite a while until I find what my question is, which isn't a bad thing. Knowing my question affords me some clarity and helps to find structure, but deciding on structure early can inhibit the work's more organic development, tame the magic of exploration. Peter Bishop advises along these lines, suggesting that writers should

> listen carefully to the structure that is being created by the themes you're working with, and the conversations and relationships that are developing among them. Structure is a constellation of things that are alive, each thing reaching out. Don't make decisions too soon: decisions inhibit discoveries and it's discoveries that create structure . . . structure grows from within – it is breath and blood flow rather than straitjacket. The most common problem with a major work is that about halfway through the writer stops listening to the complexities of growth and breathing and allows rigidity to take over.

As I described earlier, I enjoy wandering in the wilderness of the initial writing stages. But too long there and I might lose my way out, might grow fangs and fur . . . With *The Dangerous Bride* I was close to that perilous point. But once I admitted what was sore in me, admitted the paradox of my intimate life, I could formulate my question. It was: If I was naturally non-monogamous then why, when I got the opportunity to love this way, did I fail?

Armed with the question, I was now able to formulate my protagonist's – my younger self's – main problem that would create the narrative tension. And knowing her main problem meant I also knew where to begin the memoir – I wanted the first scene to establish this problem. So, chronologically speaking, my book began in the middle: on the night when for the first time in my second non-monogamous relationship I kissed someone who wasn't my husband. Despite my previous failure at non-monogamy, I was giving it another go with my new partner. But could we pull it off or would this destroy our marriage? As a writer, I already knew the answer – although I wasn't entirely clear why the marriage failed and hoped to find out by writing the book. But for readers, this is where the tension was supposed to be: Will this marriage survive?

The tension informed how I structured my existing material as well as clarified what I still needed to write. My narrative arc was to be the last four months of my second non-monogamous relationship and within this narrative I wove the story of my first non-monogamous relationship wherever it fitted, showing how the problems I had in the first one, unresolved, contributed to the collapse of the second.

Many writers shape their books in this fashion, by following the trail of a question that won't leave them alone. (Sartre's driving question in his childhood memoir, *The Words*, for example, was 'How does a man become someone who writes, who wants to speak of the imaginary?') If you aren't a planner either and struggling with finding structure for your story, you can try out this method. Begin by reflecting on why you are writing this work and what you *must* understand about your subject. Then apply your framing question to your material and keep what's essential. Finally, articulate your main narrative problem as it relates to your question and develop your storyline by trying to resolve this problem.

*

Whenever I ask my friend and formidable reader, Simon, what some book he loves is about, his uniform response is: 'It's about life.' The vagueness of this answer used to irritate me, but, having thought about this more, I get it. The books Simon loves, and the books I love, are usually the kind that don't walk one straight road but venture down labyrinthine pathways. Such books cannot be summed up easily; they fulfil far more than their blurbs promise, because their authors are unafraid of digressing or making connections between seemingly disparate subjects. Amos Oz's *A Tale of Love and Darkness*, for example, ostensibly explores the impact of his mother's suicide on him, but it also explores what it means to be a Jew, the intricacies of Middle Eastern politics, Israel's early history, the forging of a writer's voice. I find such books immensely rewarding in their richness and continuous surprises, and my love for them complicates my cookie cutter metaphor. See, I think that as much as it's important to focus our work, it is no less necessary to nurture complexity.

I know some writers are afraid of coming across as 'too dense'. But thematic cornucopia, as long as it doesn't obscure the work's heart, is a gift to readers. This is what David Grossman felt upon discovering the fiction of the Jewish-Polish writer Bruno Schulz known for its ample allusions, imagery and meanings: 'As soon as I started reading Schulz I was electrified. Every paragraph is an explosion of different realities – of dreams and nightmares, imagination and fantasy. Reading him made me want to live more.'

I know what Grossman means. I felt like this while reading (and re-reading) Geoff Dyer's *Out of Sheer Rage*. Let's consider how Dyer manages at once to stay focused yet also allow complexity and digressions into his memoir, and what such an artistic vision has to do with emotional honesty.

The central question in *Out of Sheer Rage*, the way I understand it, resembles the one I had in *The Dangerous Bride* in that it also explores a failure in realising one's persistent desire. For years Dyer wanted to write a critical study of the works of D. H. Lawrence – the author who possibly had the greatest influence on Dyer's literary (and emotional) life – yet he never managed to complete the book.

Why has he failed? This question provides the book with tension and shape, as the narrative follows Dyer's unsuccessful attempts to compose his study while he moves around the globe, retracing the wanderings of his restless subject – allegedly for research. This narrative, however, is padded with much supposedly redundant dough: anecdotes from Dyer's life, amusing travel sketches and meditations on anything Dyer feels passionate about (Rilke, the Mediterranean character, Dyer's unwillingness to procreate . . .).

As the story unfolds, it becomes apparent that many of these 'redundancies' are actually offshoots of the main theme, which Dyer explores from a delightful and quirky multitude of angles. For example, Lawrence also chose not to have children and this fact had relevance to both writers' art. Still, not all Dyer's departures can be traced back to the book's main problem – the baffling workings of creativity. His penchant for watching television, for one, has no narrative relevance.

None of this is a problem, however. I am with the Anglo-Irish novelist Laurence Stern, who famously said that 'digressions, incontestably, are the sunshine, the life, the soul of reading!' I cannot imagine *Out of Sheer Rage* being as powerful and original as it is without its digressions. As long as we keep digressions in check, as occasional treats that don't obscure the narrative thread, they'll delight by adding surprise to the texture of prose.

Take Graham Greene's memoir about writing, *Ways of Escape*. Fittingly with the subject, the book opens with the description of Greene as a young man, sitting at his parents' house, about to begin writing what would be his first published novel. Nearby, he writes, 'my mother was busy discussing a domestic problem with the parlourmaid. How "period" such a title sounds today, and all those household ranks – kitchenmaid, pantrymaid, nursemaid . . .' Greene spends some more time humorously and vividly evoking that era. Then he moves on to discussing how estranged he feels from his supposedly quaint, younger self, thus engaging with such subjects as memory and continuity of identity. I found this beginning so bewitching in its serpentine unpredictability that I proceeded to read Greene's memoir hyper-attentively. I worried that if I skipped even a line, I'd miss some charming surprises.

Digressions are also oases in which readers take a break from the main preoccupations of the work in order to return to them refreshed. Whereas a story about, say, a bank robber that shows only their criminal activities makes for predictable and therefore tedious reading. There is no shortage of such single-dimension books. Some even sell well, but they appeal to fans of formulaic works. Popular writers, too, if they are any good, digress. Take the bestselling novel, *Three Wishes*, by Liane Moriarty. She enriches her narrative of one family's dramas with a plethora of Australian voices from all walks of life. These brief interjections are supposed to shed light on the protagonists, but actually they hardly advance the story. Mostly, they tell us something about their cameo narrators, together constituting a witty, kaleidoscopic snapshot of our society that deepens the novel while making it entertaining.

Perhaps most significantly, a measure of digression makes a work more real, truer. Life is messy, multidimensional. A novel solely about bank robberies isn't just tedious but also dishonest, because robbers have other things on their minds too, like getting their dog to the vet or finishing the last season of *The Vikings*. Oversimplification can make our work more digestible but can also deaden it. Or as Elena Ferrante puts it: 'A story acquires power . . . when it captures the confusion of existences, the making and unmaking of beliefs, the way fragments from varying sources collide in the world and in our heads.'

The beauty of *Out of Sheer Rage* lies in just such a fragmentary vision, in how it captures the chaos of being alive yet also maintains a clear, tense narrative. I am not saying every book should be as complex as the ones Dyer or Oz have written; the ratios of complexity and digression depend on the writer's temperament. Still, writers must strive to avoid tunnel-vision syndrome.

*

How, in practice, do you find the balance between avoiding said syndrome and remaining true to the heart of your story? I'll try to answer this difficult question through another example, by explaining how I went about finishing *The Dangerous Bride*.

As I was shaping this memoir with my cookie cutter, being as attached to my material as I was, I found it difficult to take out *all* the leftover dough. So I retained certain 'darlings', hoping that in the ensuing drafts my heart would harden enough to murder them. This was indeed the case with many leftovers as I kept redrafting. For example, I removed almost everything about my life in Russia and Israel. I also took out a lot of research, including the love story of the artists Frida Kahlo and Diego Rivera, and several interviews with non-monogamists, as that material didn't contribute anything new to my enquiry.

On the other hand, it occurred to me during redrafting that some of the seemingly unrelated material, like my religious upbringing, was at the root of my unconventional desire. Similarly, the story of my migration to Australia created an emotionally charged backdrop to my misadventures in love and impacted some of my choices. In other words, I realised that my romantic history was inseparable from these aspects of my life. So I not only kept these darlings in but reinstated some more discarded dough and gave my memoir a subtitle to reflect the additional themes: *A Memoir of Love, Gods and Geography*.

My next challenge was to ensure that these newly important themes, my religious past and my migration to Australia, didn't overtake the main subject. I kept applying my cookie cutter to 'gods' and to 'geography', kept discarding more dough, so as to keep these topics as supporting actors rather than lead roles. The material that remained was mostly that which illuminated my love life. One day I might explore these themes in depth, but that will be another book. Or books.

The final version of *The Dangerous Bride* was richer thematically. It also contained some darlings unrelated to love, gods or geography – sprinkled on top like sugary decorations. My terror of public speaking, for example, remained, as did my love of cooking. These brief forays were meant to render me as a multidimensional protagonist, not just a neurotic woman haunted by a messy love life. But also, to be honest, those deviations from the 'grand plan' simply delighted me. I giggled like a schoolgirl as I was writing them, feeling rather naughty about sneaking in something I wasn't supposed to . . .

PART THREE:

ROADBLOCKS TO HONESTY

'Writing requires maximum ambition, maximum audacity, and programmatic disobedience.'

– Elena Ferrante

A writer worries. Always. It is in our job description. We worry about whether we have the talent, or anything to say, or the ability to find the words that do justice to what is burning in us. And even when we manage these creative anxieties, we still have the social world to worry about. What will it make of my story? What will it make of *me*?

Stephen King wrote at the dawn of the new millennium that the writer's job 'boils down to two things: paying attention to how the real people around you behave and then telling the truth about what you see.' But doing this job means you might end up saying stuff you usually don't say aloud, stuff others might not want to hear. To tell the truth is to potentially compromise your image, show yourself in all your imperfect nakedness or 'incorrectness'. It is to potentially upset your nearest and dearest, or anyone else who has some personal stake in your stories. It is to expose yourself to peer critique, and possibly provoke some fierce public critics.

King realised this, of course. He also expressed the view that 'writing . . . as we enter the twenty-first century is no job for intellectual cowards. There are lots of would-be censors out there . . . they all want basically the same thing: for you to see the world they see . . . or to at least shut up about what you do see that's different.' Two decades later, King's words ring even truer – partly thanks to the rise of social media. Then, in this age of climate crisis and social protest, our sensitivities about marginalisation and representation, and our desires for various social changes, are high. In itself, this state of things is positive. However, this has some unintended yet adverse consequences for the world of artistic literature.

Increasingly, creative writers are subject to similar expectations as polemical writers – activists, researchers, social commentators. There are pressures on the former to 'better the world' through their works, or at least to toe a particular ideological line – not dissimilarly to how it was in the Soviet Union of my childhood.

You see this in the flavour of today's many literary events, where the politics of writing are discussed more than the art. You see this in how not infrequently reviews focus on assessing the characters' and/or authors' 'right' or 'wrong' consciousness. Reviewers might even evaluate a literary work based on whether the characters have 'correct feelings'. (This happened to me too, when after the release of *Imperfect* one critic chastised me for feeling shame and grief about my scars rather than the 'correct' pride.) You also see this in the surge of manifesto-style memoirs and novels that declare their agenda loudly.

The contemporary political debates around literature are beyond the scope of this book, but it is underpinned by my conviction that agenda-driven writing and creative writing have their respected places, yet they are different animals with different purposes. The former wants to correct the world. The latter wants to capture it in all its incorrectness and, as the American moral philosopher Susan Neiman writes, 'to give form to contradiction without stifling it, to give voice to tension without dissolving it.' Weaving the two forms together isn't advisable. (Pick up any Soviet novel and you'll see that reading didactic stories isn't much fun.) It's not that writers shouldn't have strong opinions or a social conscience, but we need to try and put these aside as much as possible while writing creatively in order to avoid looking at our subject through the inevitable blinkers of our politics. I'll come back to this last point later in this third part of the book.

Be it for political or personal reasons, nowadays many conversations I partake in with my literary peers are dominated by anxieties about what we feel we can or cannot write. Such anxieties in themselves are not a bad thing. They keep us ethically vigilant. But it should be our conscience we contend with, not the fear of upsetting popular public opinion nor the desire to please at the expense of truth.

A writer, I believe, must at once cultivate sensitivity and

empathy, *and* take risks. I might be naïve, but the optimist in me insists that the risk-taking would ultimately bring rewards, because avid readers have a bloodhound's nose for insincerity. They want from books, as American literary critic Maureen Corrigan writes in her bibliomemoir, *Leave Me Alone, I'm Reading*: 'to get closer to the heart of things . . . In our daily lives, where we're bombarded by the fake and the trivial, reading serves as a way to stop, shut out the noise of the world, and try to grab hold of something real, no matter how small.'

This part of the book explores how we find moral courage to express ourselves with maximum honesty while also considering the impact of our words on others, and how to create our own (as opposed to externally imposed) ethical frameworks. In short, it is about how to keep the torch of emotional honesty switched on to guide us towards our artistic truths and at the same time to keep our personal biases in check. And I hope to convince you that certain obstacles to emotional honesty can actually fertilise and enhance writing rather than kill it. As for other types of obstacles, I offer some practical strategies for turning them into mere detours.

WRITING WITH DISCOMFORT

Whenever I am working on a new book, I am prone to occasional smugness. I get this feeling as if I am carrying inside me a secret – that I am a better person than what I seem and that this superior self lives inside my writing. Wait, I tell myself, till 'they' read my book. ('They' is whoever it is at the time that I decide underestimates me for some reason – neighbours, my mother, the barista in my local café . . .) Then they'll know who I am and think highly of me. But why, on what basis? This essence of me, hopefully captured on my pages, isn't necessarily a pretty one. So it dawns on me, eventually, amid my delusions of grandeur, that once the book is going to be out for all to see, I'll have more cause for embarrassment than for smugness.

The kind of discomfort I just described is supposed to be a good thing for a writer – an indication that their work has high stakes. Then, it is okay for a literary character to come across as unlikeable, but it is never okay to come across as dull. Stripping bare publicly, showing those hidden thoughts and eccentricities that set us apart and reveal our most fundamental confusions and mistakes – all these things, usually invisible in social interactions, are the ones making our work interesting and our words come alive with truth.

I know this, but I am also desperate for people to like me. When writing creative nonfiction or semi-autobiographical fiction, I often fight the urge to portray myself or my stand-in protagonist as a nicer, more moral and politically correct character than I am in real life. Similarly, when I describe my bad behaviour, my initial impulse is to use the examples where I have 'grown out of it', even though this selectiveness also smacks of dishonesty – that of the perpetual happy ending. Then, as much as I fear being disliked, I am also afraid of attracting censure or pity, even though being open about my vulnerabilities – rejections, failures, inadequacies – gives my work greater depth and fosters readers' emotional engagement with my story. But I don't want to be liked for my vulnerabilities. I want people to think highly of me, to like me for my strengths. So, here, too, my first inclination is to write about the frailties I've already overcome – to write from a position of victory. But in reality, not every sin is redeemed nor does every failure turn into eventual success.

I must hold myself in check also when I write fictional protagonists very different from me, because readers of fiction often hold authors accountable for the morals they read in their tales as well as suspect autobiographical inspiration where none exists. Nabokov, for instance is frequently equated with his paedophile character Humbert Humbert or deemed immoral for rendering his protagonist sympathetic in some ways.

Feelings of discomfort can also impede honesty because they reduce our objectivity. To avoid embarrassment or shame, writers might be reluctant to interrogate the truth of the experience. Instead, they could end up writing their (real or fictional) story in order to justify their views or behaviour, vent anger, even take revenge. All this can feel therapeutic, but there is no art in such writing.

To engage more objectively and reflectively with difficult material, you can ask direct questions about it. Even if you write fiction, to practise this I suggest you first use some uncomfortable experience from your own life and ask yourself the following: *Why did this happen? What was my role in what happened? How has this affected me in the short, and possibly long, term?* Later you can apply similar questions to your fictional events and characters.

Mandy Sayer's memoir, *Dreamtime Alice*, engages with just such questions. While its events are poignant and gripping, what makes the book truly captivating is the emotional truth Sayer unearths in her life, as in the following reflection on her time with her father in America:

> What sustained me during those days was not the prospect of 'breaking into show business', nor the hope of meeting a man whom I could love, but the quiet knowledge that I was now lingering on the edges of my father's stories. I wasn't exactly a protagonist, but listening to him yarn to Leonard about our months in New York, I found myself occupying some minor sub-plot of his life. This alone created a little sense out of the chaos of my twentieth year.

I imagine such an insight couldn't have been gained if Sayer was emotionally too close to her material at the time of writing. I've noticed that in her fiction she probes her characters' motivations with similar depth.

But even if you have enough distance to reflect on the confronting truths of your stories, you still need the courage to make them public. And how do you get *that*?

*

When Elena Ferrante writes her novels, she pays 'little attention to the unpleasantness of the operation . . . pull[ing] up from the depths of my experience everything that is alive and writhing, including what I myself have driven away as far as possible because it seemed unbearable.' I share Ferrante's aspirations but, not being as stoic, I'm always trying actively to fight the 'unpleasantness'.

To begin with, I work on reframing my distress – fear, shame, even pain – from being an occupational hazard into an asset. I remind myself that what *all* my works share is that writing them was uncomfortable. I remind myself that, as I suggested earlier, discomfort can lead me to my subject. I also tell myself that while some readers might negatively judge writing that shows vulnerability, many more appreciate it.

Writing about potentially shameful stuff creates an intimate reading experience. Helen Garner's admission of vengefulness as one of her primary reasons for investigating the Canberra murder of a young man by his girlfriend and her friend in *Joe Cinque's Consolation* does that:

> I understand now that I went to Canberra because the breakup of my marriage left me humiliated and angry. I wanted to look at women who were accused of murder. I wanted to gaze at them and hear their voices, to see the shape of their bodies and how they moved and gestured, to watch the expressions on their faces. I needed to find out if anything made them different from me: whether I could trust myself to keep the lid on the vengeful, punitive force that was in me.

Garner's clarity about herself also provides a stark contrast to the opaqueness of the murderers' motives and the disturbing complicity of their milieu. It encourages us to trust that she'll explore other people's inner landscapes with similar insight. More so, her disclosure prompts us to question our own motives and biases as we contemplate various ethical questions this murder raises, and more generally, the complexity of the human psyche.

As I suggested earlier, many readers are grateful for writing that adds yet another ray of light to illuminate the vastness of human nature – warts and all. Good literature reveals something to the reader about themselves, not just about the author. I've been through two divorces and I identify with Garner's 'vengeful, punitive force'. Reading her makes me feel some relief, less alone, more 'normal'.

All this isn't to say exposure is risk-free. I am also aware how easy it is to attract criticism. These criticisms might come from the 'wrong' readers – say, the blinkered ones who seek books to affirm their worldviews or the ones afraid of darkness and complexity – but they still hurt, can feel awfully personal. To fortify myself against that, I read gutsy writers, the ones who say what they think even if this goes against their best interests, even if they attract their share of outrage. I have already mentioned some such authors – Dyer, Knausgaard, Bulgakov, Garner, Camus, Kureishi. And there is also Rachel Cusk, Katie Roiphe and Salman Rushdie, among yet others whose words I soak in to find courage and inspiration.

When reading for these reasons, I don't dip in and out of the books nor do I pick one book to focus on. Rather, I immerse myself systematically, for as many hours as I can afford, in one courageous work after another. The intense reading affects me not dissimilarly to how painkillers would, not curing me of my anxieties but dulling them enough so that I can keep on writing. Take this passage from the Israeli author Etgar Keret's memoir, *The Seven Good Years*:

> The writer is neither saint nor tzaddik nor prophet standing at the gate; he's just another sinner who has a somewhat sharper awareness and uses slightly more precise language to describe the inconceivable reality of our world . . . He's not the least bit better than his readers – sometimes he's a lot worse – and so it should be. If the writer were an angel, the

> abyss that separates him from us would be so great that his writing couldn't get close enough to touch us.

Do you see what I mean? Still, sometimes no words of wisdom are enough to spur me on. It is then that I resort to more hands-on methods.

*

If I can get away with it, I describe only the minimum necessary to convey the emotional truth of an uncomfortable experience. For example, in *The Dangerous Bride*, I only give a few examples of my quite adventurous sex life with my lover J, enough to demonstrate the overall pattern.

Another way to minimise the writing of tough parts is by using the poetic approach, which I discussed in some earlier chapters. You can use stylistic devices, such as word repetition, brief or incomplete sentences, musical rhythm and bold words to convey experiences you find difficult to describe. Such writing spares you from describing some of the more graphic details, while still capturing emotional intensity. In *Imperfect*, once again I felt embarrassed to describe my sex life, but it was intrinsic to telling the story of my scars. So sometimes I used poetic rather than explicit language:

> I took off my stockings and lay naked on his mattress surrounded by stale bongs and guitar strings, in a dark broken only by the glow of a heater, as the rain strummed its ballads outside. We didn't make love; I didn't feel ready for that. But we did other things that were so good I forgot I was a freak.

I left it at that.

However, sometimes writing requires greater elaboration and directness. Or, the little that I have written remains confronting.

Then I might journal about my discomfort. Pinned down on the page, my anxieties often appear smaller, more manageable, than when they chaotically spin in my head. A journal is, generally, a safe place to practise the art of vulnerability. On the other hand, as I previously suggested, journaling can encroach on creative writing. A writer should be mindful of this possibility, aware of the extent of their writing stamina. One writer I know, for whom (like for me) writing doesn't generate *more* writing, solves this issue by journaling about her fears for just ten minutes before she works on her novel – enough to quieten her mind but not enough to exhaust her creative energy.

Another method I use involves writing the difficult parts even faster and wilder than I do when I write my usual first drafts, so as not to leave any space for discomfort to take over. I give myself licence to write associatively, without trying to make sense to anyone but myself, and to say anything, even the most compromising stuff, if it is relevant to the emotional truth of my story. To spur myself on, I remind myself that fist drafts must sear with honesty. That if I don't begin with the raw emotion, the unsavoury content of my intestines, then I have nothing to work with, no living thing. Later, though, I'll wash and perfume my words. I tell myself all that, but leave the editing of these parts until the very end, because by then, when the rest of the manuscript is mostly there, I can hopefully see the value of the uncomfortable material and be so invested in the work that I'll be more game to take risks.

My last strategy for tackling discomfort works on the dual principle of pleasure and distraction. Specifically, it means focusing on humorous and/or vivid details. Even the darkest experiences usually contain some of these aspects, though they might not come to mind at first. So, I deliberately compose a list of such details – recalled or invented, depending on the genre. These can be anything that evokes a feeling: a sway of purple geraniums in the breeze or a piece of toilet paper stuck to a bottom. Each detail can be an entry point into the writing of difficult matter by delighting enough to distract away from anxiety.

To ease myself into writing that disturbing scene in 'Bruised', where my lover holds me captive, threatening murder, I first described the specifics of the place where this happened. I also used the poetic approach: 'The park was dark. The park was dark. The rhyme was as perfect as the night fragrant with a smoky chill, blue with streetlights.' The sensual details and the cadence distracted me from the trauma of what happened, even making the writing enjoyable to an extent.

Humour was instrumental when I struggled with writing in *Imperfect* about my years in Tel Aviv, the time when my anxiety about my body was at its peak. That period also had many hilarious aspects, such as the fridge I had in my rented share-apartment, which was moody: either filling up with ice or giving mild electric shocks. I described such details and then wrote *around* them until the full narrative emerged, complete with the difficult memories.

Not only do such colourful 'distractions' help writers lose inhibition, but as we saw in the previous chapters, they also work miracles on readers. The Dalai Lama once said that you can tell the most terrible truths if you first open the heart with humour, and I think the same applies to vivid details. All such particulars make difficult material more readable – more entertaining and more palatable. And this is precisely when art begins: as the writer's focus shifts from concern for their wellbeing to that of their readers. But what about the wellbeing of the people implicated in our works?

OTHER PEOPLE

After *The Dangerous Bride* was published, I received an email from a woman who had read my memoir. Her name was Anna and she was a Russian migrant living in Melbourne. There was also a Russian 'Anna' (a pseudonym) from Melbourne in my book. The woman felt disturbed by this coincidence and emailed to assert that she and I had never met. I don't want people to think it was me, she wrote.

I was puzzled by her concern. Anna is as common a name among Russians as Anne is among people from Anglo-Saxon backgrounds. Even more perplexingly, the 'Anna' in my book is not a minor but a *fleeting* character – a friend of my aunt whose beautiful home with a rose-filled garden and a whacky cat I briefly housesit. I never imagined someone might get upset on her account. I had, though, many other concerns with this book, particularly that a memoir is never just an author's exposé. A person's story is always bound with other people, and in *The Dangerous Bride* relationships were *the* subject.

During the years of writing this book, I did have inspired, blissful times, when all I cared about was the language and everything else which turns life into art. But mostly I wrote it feeling anxious and guilty. Most obvious was my guilt towards my former partners, especially my ex-husband 'Noah', who made it clear he wasn't happy about me writing the book. I also worried about the people I interviewed – that I didn't adequately represent them or that I might offend them by depicting them as they struck me. Then there was my mother, my most longstanding muse, a wondrous and difficult woman who – to paraphrase Sartre – is lodged like a knife in the writing part of my brain. She features in my works so frequently that whenever I tell her I've begun a new work, she says: 'Oy vey, Lubochka, what will you write about me now? That I drink vodka and beat up your papa?' (For the record, she does neither of these things.) A wig-wearing orthodox Jew, she snuck into *The Dangerous Bride* too, right from the start, after the opening scene set in a fetish club. I was certainly worried about how she would feel reading this memoir. Worst of all, there were times when writing this book almost cost me my present marriage. Daryl didn't care much about his brief appearance on the page, but he did about all the time I spent writing about my past lovers. (Still, he never explicitly demanded I stopped writing the book.)

I wrote this memoir, feeling continuously torn between competing ethical considerations, which pretty much boiled down to one impossible question: Can I portray real people honestly without hurting them? In other words, I was caught between what I owed to my readers (art and truth) and to the people in my works (courtesy and respect). At some stage, my anxiety escalated to the point where every time I sat down to write, my study was crowded, haunted by the ghosts of my characters, who were all telling me that I didn't get them, that I used them, that I was full of shit. Still, I pressed on. I couldn't afford to become blocked again. That possibility terrified me even more than the potential consequences of my book. I knew I couldn't write anything else before finishing this story. It was burning inside me, burning *me*. So I clenched my teeth, literally, and kept going.

*

'There is a splinter of ice in the heart of a writer,' Graham Greene famously proclaimed. Joan Didion echoed him in the preface to her essay collection, *Slouching Towards Bethlehem*, noting that 'writers are always selling someone out'. This is true of writers of nonfiction and of fiction that draws from real life – which is *a lot* of us. (And let's not forget Jonathan Franzen, whose novels are panoramic in their scope and multi-voiced, and who nevertheless, as I mentioned earlier, considers his works to be autobiographical.)

Writers can be placed along a continuum in terms of the ethical decisions they make about how they 'sell out', excuse me – represent others. At one end of this continuum sit the authors of toothless books that cause no harm and tell no truth. Usually these are decent, considerate people who might ask their subjects or people who inspire their fictional characters for permission even before they start writing, then run their drafts by them, modifying them to gain approval. However, while gaining permission may minimise individual hurt and relationship-risk, it maximises writing-risk, most often resulting in a work that reflects how other people *wish to be seen*. And here's the thing about safe material that you are not afraid of anyone reading: 'quite often,' the American essayist Meghan Daum writes, 'no one wants to read it'.

At the other end there are writers like Edmund White, who believes that good writing requires telling everything there is to say about everyone involved. Which is what Karl Ove Knausgaard does, sprawling royally along White with his Proust-like opus, *My Struggle*. There he appears to tell it all – his resentments towards his wife, his mother-in-law's secretive alcoholism . . . And while I wouldn't want to be related to Knausgaard, when I want to get closer to the truth of human experience, I turn to his work. Or to White's.

The uncomfortable truth is that the marriage between literature and decency is an uneasy one. It is public knowledge that some of the people close to Knausgaard have paid a price for the profound and bold art he produces. However, the ethical terrain that lies between Knausgaard and those non-offensive, artless books is vast. It is possible to write with a considerable degree of honesty without completely selling out the people appearing in our books. It is every writer's (difficult) job to locate their place along the continuum. This, of course, depends on their priorities and values, but I hope that by sharing how I composed my ethical framework, something will resonate.

*

I wrote my first three books when I was young and naïve in a way I'll never be again, when I believed that the word 'fiction' stamped on those books was the solution to all my ethical conundrums, no matter that my fiction was inspired by real life. And to some extent, it was a solution. (Although now I know that even completely imagined fiction can get writers in trouble if someone decides they are implicated, as happened, for example, to Graham Greene when another novelist, J. B. Priestley, threatened him with libel action because Greene's character Savory in *Stamboul Train* reminded him of himself.)

When in my early thirties I began writing creative nonfiction, I could no longer ignore the potential impact of my words on others. I believed, however, as I still do, in my right to tell my story and in my obligation to tell it as truthfully as possible, which of course includes the truth about how I've been affected by others, also when they (at least in my opinion) behaved badly. My thinking here is along the lines of Louise DeSalvo's response to an acquaintance who challenged her about publishing a memoir about growing up with a violent father while he was still alive: 'He did what he did . . . and that gave me the right to describe it.' Whatever rights we, writers, might think we have, however, I am also well aware that our pens possess a certain power that is all too easy to misuse. It is to rein in this power that I set some ground rules about how I describe others.

In any genre, my most obvious rule is not to use real names (unless the person wants to be named). I also often alter some other identifying details, like eye colour or occupation. In fiction this is common practice and any liberties can be taken, but in creative nonfiction I don't change anything that meddles with a person's essence. I won't turn a musician into a doctor, for example. I might give them some other artistic occupation, but only if they are a minor character. If they have a significant role in the story, then I cannot depict them authentically without the part music occupies in their psyche.

To blur identification further, some writers create composite characters by combining two or more real people into one. In fiction this, too, is a standard operation. In creative nonfiction, some writers would never do this, while others might employ it liberally. Personally, I am weary of this strategy, because of how it blurs the boundary between fiction and nonfiction. I only use it as a last resort and only if the people-in-question exhibit similar traits and/or convey similar emotional truth, and are minor characters. Kate Holden used this method in this careful way in *In My Skin*, a memoir about her heroin addiction and sex work, when describing some of her clients.

Another principle I follow can be summed up as 'tell your story, not their secrets'. If I consider imparting something potentially compromising about someone, I ask myself: Is this information necessary to tell *my* story? Will omitting it distort the story's emotional truth? If both answers are 'no', I won't write it just because this material is vivid or amusing. (I will sometimes, though, write such compromising stuff about *myself* just to entertain the readers.)

When writing about others, I consider not only which information to withhold and which to impart, but also how to interpret what I do reveal and from what position to write. I find Helen Garner's stance on this latter issue, as described in her essay 'I', useful:

> The deal is this: if I'm rough on myself, it frees me to be rough on others as well. I stress the unappealing, mean, aggressive, unglamorous aspects of myself as a way of lessening my anxiety about portraying other people as they strike me.

Indeed, I find that placing my motives and behaviour under a microscope, before turning my critical eye on others, eases my guilt. This also prevents me from writing with self-righteousness or as a victim. Once I've acknowledged my own imperfections, I am more prone to seeing others through a compassionate and empathic lens (which Garner certainly possesses). This doesn't mean I excuse bad behaviour in others, but I am more vigilant about my biases and judgemental tendencies, I'm less eager to demonise, keener to consider others' point of view. In this way, worrying about the people in my works keeps me on my toes, preventing my writing from sliding into the tedious, artless territory of complaint and revenge. Along these same lines, DeSalvo, who believes she has the right to write about how her father's abuse affected her, also believes in striving to understand how he came to behave the way he did as an integral part of her writing process.

My ethical framework is no magical formula. Following it doesn't mean I do no harm. But, as Garner says in that same essay: 'writing . . . like the bringing up of children, can't be done without causing damage'. Potential damage notwithstanding, the majority of us still have children. A minority of us still writes.

*

Things become even more complicated when I interview people for my works. On one hand, these are informed and consenting adults, and I agree with Robin Hemley, who writes in *A Field Guide for Immersion Writing*: 'you don't want to be someone else's mouthpiece. Your . . . narrative will be compelling to read only if you have full ownership of the story'. On the other hand, I feel that my responsibility to my interviewees is even greater than to the people from my personal life, as the former are in my works only because I've asked them for help and they've agreed, often making themselves vulnerable in the process. So how honestly do I portray them?

The ethics of writing interviews is a vast and complex terrain; I cannot do it justice within this space. But at the most basic level, the crucial question is again: From what position am I writing about these people? Am I doing this with empathy and generosity of spirit? If yes, then I am seemingly in the clear. But can these qualities also blind me, just as their absence can?

To see how such questions can inform writing decisions, let's look at one instance where I struggled to reconcile my commitment to my interviewees with the commitment to writing with integrity. For *Imperfect*, I interviewed more than a hundred people, many of whom had appearances that deviated from the so-called norm, such as dwarfism or burns, and often the stories they shared with me were sensitive. I was grateful for their willingness to talk and for the most part found it easy to stay close to their individual perspective. On several occasions, however, my impressions of the people I spoke to and of what they said left me uneasy, and I felt that flagging my unease was intrinsic to honestly explore the impact of appearance on people. This was particularly the case with Damien. He partook in online communities, which clustered around preferences for people whose bodies didn't conform to our narrow beauty standards. Damien was attracted to larger women and I was uneasy about some generalisations he made about women's character based on their weight, such as that 'skinny' women are more selfish than 'big' ones. Yet I also felt respect for him, the only man from those communities who consented to speak to me face to face. After much deliberation, I resolved to be upfront about my perspective, but at the same time to interrogate my biases and declare my mixed feelings on the page:

> His views reminded me of . . . men who assumed that imperfect [I use this adjective ironically in the book] women would be nicer, kinder. Yet it was Damien who had dared meeting me in the open . . . Was I doing to him the same thing I was judging him for? I kept going around in circles, my ambivalence emblematic of how I'd felt since I'd begun researching [these online communities].

I made my ethical dilemma part of the narrative. I've done so quite a few times, and not only when I write interviews. Admitting and unpacking such struggles can ease their pressure. Sometimes doing so even becomes the solution, because such writing shows that we respect, and care for, the people we write about, even if we don't fully endorse their views or behaviour. As such, writing the ethical issues into the story also potentially enhances our work, deepening its reflective quality. In fact, sometimes accounts of struggles with our material are the most interesting part of the work.

*

I began this chapter with the anecdote about 'Anna' to illustrate how unpredictable the consequences of writing about real people can be. (Which makes me wonder – would she be upset with me again now that I really wrote about her?) Somehow, I managed to offend a stranger, whereas the people I worried sick about showed no serious grievance after the book was published (although 'Noah' as well as Daryl refused to read my memoir).

From what I've seen, often the worst consequences play out inside a writer's mind, particularly because many people actually *like* being written about. I recall the aftermath of the publication of my personal essay 'Me, My Mother and Sexpo', when I was mortified by the possibility that my mother would read it. The work describes my childish attempt at embarrassing her by taking her to Sexpo, and how it was my mother who ended up embarrassing me as she took an unexpected, and sizeable, delight in various shows and exhibits. I kept evading my mother's requests to hand her the anthology featuring this work until one day, during her visit to Melbourne, I came home to find her sitting with the book which she finally unearthed (I deliberately stored it on the most discrete bookshelf), laughing her head off. 'This is hilarious, Lubachka!' was her only comment. (In fact, some people like being written about so much they might convince themselves they are in a book when they aren't. The seventh Earl of Longford, for example, insisted he was a character in his friend Anthony Powell's novel *A Dance to the Music of Time* and even wanted to go brag about this on television.)

This isn't to say there aren't any risks in writing about others. I was lucky, but sometimes people do get hurt. And sometimes they strike back. Truman Capote, for instance, having revealed in his fiction some secrets about his New York socialite friends, found himself ostracised in the last years of his life. Knausgaard faced a severe backlash in Norway, led by his paternal uncle portrayed unflatteringly in *My Struggle*. The English actress Claire Bloom, who described her ex-husband Philip Roth unfavorably in her memoir, *Leaving a Doll's House*, soon after found herself in his novel, *I Married a Communist*, as a mean wife who destroys her husband. Closer to home, several writers I know lost relationships with family members or friends because they wrote about them.

It is my impression, however, that if the published work is of a thoughtful, non-vengeful and non-opportunistic kind (which wasn't Capote's case), then most relationships that are destroyed this way have had levels of toxicity to begin with (the Knausgaard scenario). Healthy relationships will survive. They may even grow stronger, argues Jonathan Franzen, who based a character in *The Corrections* on his brother:

> all loyalties . . . are meaningful only when they are tested . . . what I've learned is that there's potential value, not only for your writing but also for your relationships, in taking autobiographical risks: that you may, in fact, be doing your brother or your mother or your best friend a favor by giving them the opportunity to rise to the occasion of being written about – by trusting them to love the whole you, including the writer part.

Whatever you make of Franzen's argument, the fact is his brother rose to the occasion. My marriage, too, hasn't just survived two memoirs, but grown stronger – at least from my perspective. I feel gratitude towards Daryl. When I offered him to review the parts in *Imperfect* where he appears, before publication (with considerable trepidation, as the book even opens with him, unclothed!), Daryl refused and said, 'Write whatever you want.' Which was what I did.

Things with Daryl or Franzen's brother could have turned out differently, of course. As the Sierra Leonean writer Ishmael Beah points out, even when you write with love or empathy, you write 'your version of the truth about them. You write about how you see them, not how they view themselves.' Every writer has to make their own tough decisions as to potentially jeopardising their relationships. All I can do is point out again that writing about others is not for the faint-hearted or immaculate ones. On the other hand, as Capote said, speaking for many of us: 'all a writer has to work with is the material he's gathered as the result of his own endeavour and observations,' adding, 'he cannot be denied the right to use it. Condemn, but not deny.'

If your anxiety about possible condemnation is crippling, you might like to try an 'accounting exercise'. List all the reasons you are scared of writing about the person-in-question, then all the reasons you desire to/must write about them. Consider which list outweighs the other. Consider also if you tell this story, will it do enough good (to you and your readers) to make it worth potentially (remember, it's always *potentially*) upsetting someone? And do you assume they would be merely upset or profoundly hurt? And would their life be adversely affected?

Once you work out your answers, write the story or don't. But please don't commit to it riddled with reservations. If you do, then I am afraid I'm not optimistic for you. Beah wisely writes: 'Never try to please those you write about. You will not succeed and will certainly ruin your story.' If there are lots of things you feel you cannot say because you are not prepared to face the potential consequences, then this story isn't going to work. Better to write something else than to end up with a false-sounding piece.

In later years, Garner renounced her ethical stance as stated in I. I've heard her say at literary events that now when she suspects her honesty will hurt somebody, she's unlikely to write the story. I have heard some other writers say similar things. I wonder, however, to what extent they are invested in those stories they give up. In my experience, some stories exert such great pressure that left unwritten they end up blocking the author. And some just never go away. Before and during those years of writing *The Dangerous Bride*,

I often begged my tale to just leave me alone, but it persevered, hanging around in dark corners, shadowing me, visiting me at night like an apparition until I succumbed.

So before you make your final decision, the possibly most crucial question to ask is: If I don't write this story, can I go on as a writer? If the answer is 'no', your best option is to learn to live with a splinter of ice in your heart. But I also hope that you don't forget, in the manner of the younger Garner, to cast an even icier eye on yourself.

WRITING IN THE AGE OF SOCIAL MEDIA

Social media has done some marvellous things for the often-introverted writer. Since its inception, I have seen, and partaken in some, thriving online literary communities. Some great things happen there, like practical peer support or the #AuthorsForFireys fundraising campaign in the wake of the 2020 Australian bushfires. Not a few emerging writers, especially from marginalised backgrounds, have found their confidence and occasionally had a career breakthrough by connecting online with literary peers or even agents and publishers.

For most writers, unless they are bestselling authors, using social media professionally is almost unavoidable if they want to get their work noticed. This medium is excellent for networking with event organisers, literary bloggers and podcasters, and possible new readers. It can help prolong a book's life in the landscape where books disappear from bookshop shelves fast. That's why I am there too. A relatively late newcomer, but in the last seven years I've been all over it – tweeting, facebooking, instagramming.

Social media has done some marvellous things for me too.

I have forged literary friendships, which began online and continued unfolding in real life. Speaking engagements, interviews and reviews of my books have come my way. But a couple of years ago, as I was promoting two new books at once and so spent record time online, I found myself afflicted by mild creative depression.

If you are a writer working within the fortress of your (paradoxically, hyperconnected) computer, logging into your social media accounts daily or many times a day, in my experience, sooner or later the boundaries between the virtual and the physical worlds blur. Your life becomes *cyber-flavoured*, populated by disembodied crowds of people you've never met, or you know but barely. (I'm not talking about specialised online support groups but the general usage of social media.) Have you ever dreamed about tweets or FB pages, or caught yourself continuing your online conversations in your head once you are away from screens, going about your usual business? I certainly have.

As I kept regularly merging my brain with that of countless strangers, the part in me that writes progressively became depressed by the ongoing soundtrack of online chatter in my mind. Above all, I've noticed how the social media space amplifies certain factors inherent in the human condition, factors which have always jeopardised writers' emotional honesty. Namely, it promotes the less-noble impulses, such as self-righteousness and conformism.

I haven't felt that opting out of using social media is a realistic option. But I realised I had to take more care with how to be in the electronic, flickering, seductive universe without considerably compromising my integrity as a writer. A crucial step has been to acknowledge the price that I've paid artistically for the social and promotional benefits I've gained online – the harmful ways in which this ah-so-enticing slice of virtual reality has encroached onto my pages. So before I make any specific suggestions about minimising the cumulative impact of time spent in the social media universe on our inner world, let's unpack this impact. It is my hope that the next time we log in into Facebook or Twitter such awareness might act as a useful filter, make us less susceptible to the more harmful aspects of this space.

*

During Melbourne's first lockdown, I posted on Instagram a photo of my son, Luca, queuing in a supermarket for toilet paper amid half-empty shelves. I accompanied the image with a remark about using our waiting time as an opportunity to bore Luca with stories from my Soviet childhood, when food shortages and lining up for essentials were a part of daily life. The post drew various witty comments, but one commenter wasn't amused. She wrote some moderately angry words about the negative impact photos like mine can have on people living with anxiety. I admit, I never considered such a thing. On the other hand, during the pandemic, print and social media was littered with similar images, and if you went shopping you saw what my image showed in the flesh. My reason for sharing this anecdote, however, isn't to discuss whether that commenter had a point or not, but to give an example of the extraordinary multitude of views and sensibilities that social media users expose themselves to.

I probably don't need to convince you that writers are a self-conscious, worried lot to begin with, eager for, yet also mortified by, potential public exposure. As I suggested in previous chapters, such anxieties keep us on our toes artistically, primarily by prompting us to check our biases and/or research our material more thoroughly. But my online contact with masses of people has made me *hyper*-aware of how diverse and perhaps unending the lists of things are that can upset somebody. My self-consciousness has risen to a whole new, often paralysing, level, far greater than any healthy dose of sensitivity – more akin to paranoia. Sadly, I am becoming more reluctant to say things as they strike me for fear of offending somebody. Anybody. Everybody. (I now read the old interviews in *The Paris Review* longingly. How non-cautious writers then sounded . . . Yes, they said lots of rubbish, especially Kerouac, but at least he sounded like Kerouac, not a politician.)

The even sadder truth is my paranoia has as much to do with self-preservation as with considering others. As effective as social media can be for grassroots positive social action, it is just as effective at organising fast and furious collective backlash, otherwise known as online shaming. Considering the real-life implications of such virtual actions, where some publishing houses cancel book tours or even books themselves, expressing nuanced opinions or joking about a potentially touchy subject in a literary work might be the death of a writer's career.

This isn't to say that cancelling an outright ignorant and offensive book is a bad idea. But increasingly, works that intelligently venture into whatever the day deems 'controversial territory', or attempt to dwell in ambivalence, are also attracting online outrage (more on ambivalence and nuance in social media soon). Misinformation spreads online fast (possibly even faster than information) and this includes online 'book critics' who may not have read the book in question but would have a strong view based on a catchy post from somebody else (who possibly also didn't read it).

For all these reasons, writers are now at an increased risk of self-censorship. Once again, not fruitful soul-searching which interrogates our assumptions but plain self-censorship. My friend, the Scottish-Australian writer Paul Dalgarno, put this well in an email conversation we had on the topic:

> It's good that abuse is called out on social media so that people know things like bigotry, racism and sexism are unacceptable, but it also means that writers, myself included, can

> find themselves shitting their pants and second-guessing everything they think for fear of immediate and long-lasting retribution, making it harder to write honestly about a whole host of human experiences. And yet going against the grain, when it's genuine, is precisely what I want to get from reading anyone. Ideally the author wouldn't write things that I find offensive, but I'd rather be thinking 'that writer is a total dickhead' than 'hang on, are they just writing this because it's fashionable?'. For me, authenticity is the gold standard in writing, and the contract a writer is essentially signing with readers is to offer them that, not waste their time with inauthentic (however pretty) writing.

Since joining the social media ranks, I've been haunted by the feeling that I am back in my Soviet childhood where Big Brother is always watching. It's just that now he manifests as the admonishing cacophony coming at once from my laptop screen and from inside my head. It is against these voices that I often, and often on automatic pilot, measure what I write. Is this offensive? Triggering? Or even just merely irritating for someone? And since being 'reprimanded' for that lockdown post I've grown insecure in what I prize most about my voice – my humour – worrying it might not come across as intended. I long to follow Rilke's advice to an aspiring poet: 'only pay attention to what arises within you . . . that is what you must somehow work at, and not lose too much time and too much courage explaining your attitude to people'. But do I have it in me? This chapter, for instance, I've been writing uneasily, imagining various nasty comments it might inspire online.

*

Some experts have argued that social media is one of the chief culprits in the rapid social polarisation that has left little room for nuanced debating. The Welsh author Jon Ronson, for instance, writes in his book *So You've Been Publicly Shamed*: 'with social media, we've created a stage for constant artificial high drama. Every day a new person emerges as a magnificent hero or a sickening villain.' (If you are interested in the subject, I recommend watching Netflix's important, and disturbing, documentary *The Social Dilemma*.)

Browsing various social media feeds, it is indeed easy to see that no matter which side of a debate posters are on, self-reflection is out and self-righteousness in. Doubt is out. Complaint and anger are in. Not that I don't come across fury in the physical world, but anger seems to be magnified, more concentrated, in cyberspace. And it feels so *palpable* when I stare at my computer screen. I can feel it reverberating on my skin. Humour is also out, unless it comes in the shape of catchy witticisms and far-fetched aphorisms directed at the poster's 'opponents'. Earnestness is in. (Some posts remind me of accounting exercises: How many privileges and oppressions do I have? And you?) On Twitter in particular, profile descriptions are often worded either in opposition to something or so as to increase a user's moral virtue.

If you spend considerable time scrolling through feeds and feeding others with your posts, there is the chance of getting infected with a certain smugness this medium enables at the same time as it promotes crippling self-doubt. As much as the social media universe can silence writers, it can also inspire us to be loud, and unequivocal, in expressing those of our opinions that happen to be *popular*. Opinions for which even if we are criticised, there will be many others to defend us; or the kind with which very few would argue (e.g. poverty is bad). Needless to say, the more we express ourselves like this online, the more likely this voice is to trickle onto our pages.

But as Gertrude Stein famously announced, 'I do not write to be right'. She doesn't mean that creative writers shouldn't have convictions (she had plenty of them!), but that these shouldn't be the engines for our writing. And I think we would do far better to use Socrates's suggestion – that wisdom resides in *not-knowing* – as a guideline for our art. Good literature – once again, I am talking about creative, not explicitly polemic, books – is less likely to come from writers perched on barricades, grenade in hand, even when their barricades are built from excellent intentions. David Malouf writes along these lines in his essay 'When the Writer Speaks', saying that the best writing occurs when a writer writes not as 'a good citizen or as a holder of this or that set of views . . . but . . . if he is prepared to go lax and empty.' It is in this emptiness, in the baffling gaps between our convictions, desires and actions, that the truth of human experiences resides.

The best writers acknowledge and interrogate their ambivalence and confusion instead of grinding it down into the smooth paste of moral certainty. It is in this spirit that David Grossman seeks in writing 'to be betrayed, to be taken to a dangerous place that jars the basic presumptions I have about myself, my family, my country'. This isn't a task for the faint-hearted, but it is because of Grossman's willingness to be betrayed that his prose sings.

And don't you worry, your most cherished beliefs will surely still show on the page, only more subtly, and possibly with more nuance, because you've re-examined them during the writing. The big picture inevitably appears in the pages of a seemingly apolitical author. Take the works of Elena Ferrante. Ferrante is adamant that her creative intent has never been to illustrate a certain feminist ideology, even though feminism is important to her: 'The passage through feminist culture is an indispensable part of my experience . . . but telling a story doesn't, for me, mean making it part of a political-cultural battle, even a just one'. Yet her novels imply important things about women's lives in a patriarchal world. Imply, not shout.

But when I spend too much time online – a space where such qualities as tolerance for ambivalence, the ability to work in shadowy territories and critical introspection come under heavy assault – it begins to seem that unless I have a firm agenda, unless I am a moralist, I cannot be a writer. At moments of weakness, my voice on the page grows louder and my laptop screen acquires the rhetorical glare. Until I recall what I believe – that creative writing rooted in uncertainty is far more moral than writing that takes pains to express the author's moral outrage, and not only on account of honesty. I know that when I am uncertain, I am more likely to take interest in a variety of viewpoints, more willing to cast a curious and empathetic look at both the 'hero' and the 'villain' of my story.

But really, the greatest moral act of an artwork, I believe (that is, if there even has to be one), isn't to offer a certain lesson or a call to arms, but to afford readers time out from the waving accusatory fingers on their screens (as well as in real life). Artistic literature at its best offers a still space, away from the rhetoric of big causes, to contemplate the swathes of grey out of which reality is made. My most cherished books have provided me with just such oases to nourish my inner life, to entertain and even elevate my weary mind, to gather courage to greet the next day. They did so by giving me emotional pleasure, layering, deepening and expanding my life. So, I wholeheartedly agree with John Banville's proposition that 'if art has any "duty" to perform, it's to make the reader, the viewer, the listener feel more intensely, more vividly, what it is to be alive.'

*

Today I was online again. I posted a photo of a lentil and vegetable stew I made. The stew was delicious, cooked in homemade chicken stock, flavoured with bay leaves, crushed coriander and fennel seeds. I enjoyed photographing it and sharing my recipe online, reliving the sensual pleasure of making and consuming this dish.

Then I felt mild self-loathing – for spending my time and headspace on the post.

Perhaps even more than complaints and fury, trivia fills social media. The unbearable trivia of being . . . I love writing about food, but my online boasting about a dish I've made is nothing like making poetry out of everyday life. Besides, my delight at sharing my culinary adventures publicly soon morphed into preoccupation with the number of likes and other emoticons my post attracted, and with responding to comments with my own emoticons – something I once resigned to never do and now do daily. These smiley faces and hearty hearts I so abundantly disperse in my social media interactions have crept into my email correspondences too, as they probably have into my soul.

I wonder whether the most damaging impact of social media on writers is how the very furnishings of our brain might rearrange themselves after prolonged use. This process can be so gradual, so subtly incremental, we might not even notice how our thought has assumed the shape of a catchy hashtag, a petty complaint, a slogan, a cutesy little post . . . I don't know about you, but after years of social media usage, I worry I'm losing touch with that famed 'built-in shock-proof, shit detector' that Hemingway thinks every writer needs. And I've noticed my natural urge to please and disperse friendly smiles has intensified to an unprecedented extent. Sometimes I feel all glossy and shiny like a sunray. But, Proust tells us, 'real books should be the offspring not of daylight and casual talk but of darkness and silence'.

The prosaic, and when not petty or nasty then *nice*, saccharine-friendly and chitchatty daylight of our online interactions encroaches on the silent, dark spaces within us. Encroaches on that 'certain strangeness' that the American novelist John Gardner thinks writers must cultivate ('one has to be just a little crazy to write a great novel,' he writes in *On Becoming a Novelist*). I can feel this in my gut, how my online activity, with all its pleasures and rewards, takes over my poetic life. So I cannot see how it is possible to spend hours immersed in the noise of instant opinions and reactions, selfies, rants, photos of kittens and, yes, vegetable casseroles, and still sufficiently water and nourish our 'little craziness'.

*

The longer I spend in the social media world, the easier it is to believe that this space mirrors reality, a reality where all these qualities on which I've always tried to base my creative practice are under attack. The more I am online, the more I believe readers are now keener on unequivocal, humourless voices; that there is little audience, and cultural space, for anything else. And so the more I am there, the more futile my literary pursuit appears – quaint, not combative enough but perhaps still offensive to some, too quiet to be heard amid the cacophony on my screen . . . Still, just as I cannot foresee leaving the online world completely, because I have little faith my books will go on living vital lives if I do, I also cannot stop writing. So I have no choice but to hold onto the hope that in real life authenticity and vulnerability are more compelling and persuasive than righteous fury.

To prevent myself from getting as discouraged as I was a couple of years ago, and to protect my moral courage and the darkest, a-little-crazy corners in my mind, I've settled on a compromise. I haven't stopped using social media, but I changed my approach to how I use it. I'll share what I do and perhaps something will resonate, although you might like to modify this according to your own situation of how much online contact with others you feel you need. (And let's not forget, I'm talking about general social media, not specialised online support groups, which can be life-saving. I, for instance, get a lot out of being a part of a Facebook group for people with albinism and their carers, because my youngest son has this condition.)

Having finally come to terms with the fact that I cannot have it both ways – equally write my best and do my best at promoting my books – I have decided to take regular breaks from social media. You might recall that once, to gain mastery of English, I temporarily gave up on using Russian and Hebrew. Later, to put more time into reading and writing, I gave up television (until COVID lockdowns happened and I lost my Netflix virginity). Nowadays, when I am in the midst of intense writing periods, I might check my social media accounts weekly rather than daily, sometimes even more seldom. It's a bit like doing periodical fasts – mind-purifying. I emerge from these online breaks feeling emotionally cleansed and reinvigorated and, to my surprise, I find my absences don't affect my online connections much.

Perhaps most significantly, I've chosen to disengage emotionally. I gave up the 'leisure aspects' of my social media use to protect my mind from being crowded by trivia and from growing more willing to take offence than to take a good look at itself. I no longer see my tweeting, instagramming and facebooking as harmless distractions, but define them as strictly 'work activities'. Even during the times when I log in into social media regularly, I spend what I see as the necessary minimum time online, checking my accounts on my workdays only to interact with people who contact me there, share some posts. My boundaries between the online and physical worlds are firmer. I am done with developing online conversations, done with the sharing of my feelings and views, and with spending hours reading everyone's posts. I don't use social media to check news updates either. If I want to know what my friends are up to, I speak to them in real life.

This doesn't mean I no longer post photos of my dinners. But I now do this strategically – so that my online output doesn't look like relentless self-promotion but has a personal touch. So I combine casserole photos with more poetic or literary-informative content (for example, links to writerly articles I love), as well as with occasional posts either to promote my own work or that of other writers.

Finally, I've been paying more attention to my voice online. I try to finetune it to sound more like myself, so that my mind doesn't refill with emoticons and exclamation marks again. So that I don't lose myself on the page too.

I know all this isn't an ideal state of affairs, but it's the best compromise between the need to be present in the electronic sphere and the need to be present inside my mind that I've managed so far. I do my little 'social media bit' when I am at my writing desk and the rest of the time I am now my outdated, quaint self. Unplugged.

EXPOSURE

The writers' group I gathered in Israel often met in cafés and collaborated on something we called a 'multimedia art project'. In the writers' group I joined during my first years in Australia, we feasted in each other's houses and went away for weekends. There were pumpkin curries and French cheeses. There were our warm living rooms, the glass-walled house in the greenness of Launceston and the creaking old property in Point Lonsdale. In those groups there was the tension, the magic of artmaking buzzing about, making the air brittle, electric. There was also some workshopping. The writers' group I attended later, when doing my postgraduate degree in writing, was more austere, more focused. We would meet in the University of Melbourne classrooms to critique each other's works, our comments conscientiously punctuated with references to Foucault and Kristeva.

Soon after I finished my MA, it occurred to me that I'd gotten more friends and lovers from my writers' groups than useful writing advice. I did learn quite a bit about copyediting, but not about the heartbeat of art. The groups I attended were mostly composed of intelligent people, some of them successful writers. Yet none of us was immune to the phenomenon of *groupthink*.

In the years since, especially after facilitating workshopping in some of my writing classes, I've come to believe that the feedback people give in groups isn't the same as they'd provide individually, and the latter is far more useful. Group situations can encourage a certain vanity, an (often unconscious) desire to find weaknesses in a work even if there are none, just to show off our critical skills. Then, if our views differ from those of the majority, we might modify our initial assessment of a work – whether out of self-doubt or unwillingness to come across as the 'bad guy' who criticises something others praise, or as 'the fool' who praises what nobody else does.

For these and possibly other reasons, in my experience, group feedback veers towards the conventional, even moralistic, and away from the raw and the experimental. Imagine Milan Kundera submitting a chapter from his novel, *Immortality*, for workshopping. 'Too confusing,' someone might have said, 'too many characters'. Somebody else would have queried: 'How could Goethe meet Hemingway if they lived in different centuries? This is contrived'. 'Show more, tell less,' another critic would have surely chipped in, and everyone would have nodded their heads in solemn agreement. I'd have probably nodded too . . .

My imaginary workshopping session is actually modelled after my own experiences. I am no Kundera, of course, but I do like experimenting with writing conventions, such as bypassing linear narrative or veering in several directions at once. And I don't shy away from provocation. In groups, frequently I'd receive responses along the lines of 'there is too much in this story; it needs to be developed into a novel' or 'I was shocked by that sex scene. Do people really do such stuff?' Eventually, I had to face it that my creative vision didn't sit comfortably within such settings, and leave the groups.

However, I still didn't know how to be alone with my writing. Soon, instead of writers' group there was a mentor. A highly respected novelist. 'Never write from a man's perspective,' he told me while sipping on imported chardonnay. We were sitting in an intimate bar in Melbourne's inner city – his choice of a venue for our sessions. I hadn't shown him anything written from a male perspective, but I was so intimidated by this man whose books I admired that I didn't dare to ask why he imparted this particular advice. (If my mentor had taken some interest in me, he'd have known I'd already published three books featuring narrators of both genders.) So I remained silent, fidgeting with my beer and almost spilling it on my mentor's shorts. Possibly to divert me from such harmful activities, he offered more advice: 'I like what you sent me, but see . . . You're too young to be writing a memoir.' I considered enquiring what the eligible age for memoirists was and whether he even knew my age, but being as nervous as I was, once again I held my tongue.

My main learning from that mentoring relationship, which lasted three meetings before I awkwardly withdrew, wasn't about gender or genre choices, but that it was time for me to take Stephen King's famous advice to write with the door closed.

*

Rilke writes: 'I must be alone with my work, and have as little need of hearing others talk of it as a man might wish to see in print and to collect others' opinions about the woman he loves'. His is a noble sentiment, but few writers complete a decent artwork utterly alone. Published works bear traces of other people, be they the author's peers, mentors, teachers or editors, or some combination of these. King's complete advice is to write with the door closed, but rewrite with the door open. His emphasis is not on solitude but on the timing of exposure – an approach that resonates with me.

Thinking of which, it was also my fault that the feedback I received in writers' groups wasn't of great use to me. Often I sought help too early, when the work and I were at our most fragile. Once, after workshopping a first draft of a short story, I noted enthusiastically in my diary: 'The workshop was fantastic. I got criticised a lot, but this is okay, because people picked on all the faults the story suffers from: I haven't gone deep enough into what it's about, I do too much telling, I jump from topic to topic.' Not long after, however, my enthusiasm petered out. With everyone else's voices in my head, I lost my vision for this work, writing my subsequent drafts to please my critics rather than myself. Eventually, the story simply perished.

The writing of early drafts, the time when we are still fumbling after a story's heartbeat, demands secrecy. Until we find what we are after, people's opinions can hold enormous sway over us and, no matter how well-meaning they might be, can do more damage than good. Even when the heartbeat grows steadier, we might need time alone to roam in the wilderness of our subject, so that no voice of reason inhibits our unreasonably outlandish expedition, our courage, our craziness.

For me, even just talking about my budding work endangers that energy, that strange alchemy that drives literary conception. More than once I have talked a new piece of writing to death. Instead of letting its mystery to build up in me until the pressure is so great it spills onto the page, I released it in conversation. I particularly remember how during one writers' residency, where I was meant to work on my eventually 'murdered' novel, I spent a lovely evening giving a talk in the local library, discussing my plans for the book's plot and characters with a surprisingly engaged audience. Then I spent my three weeks in the residency not writing any of that.

It took me far too long to notice that a story exposed to the world early burns easily, just as photographic film does when taken out of a darkroom – the sacred place where artists have complete control over their medium – before its full development. Once I ended that mentorship, I entered a darkroom and shut the door to work on *The Dangerous Bride* – the memoir I was too young to write.

*

The darkroom doesn't have to be hermetically closed. Occasionally you can invite assistants in – whether to get feedback for a certain section or even just to be held accountable. This can work just fine if this fits your creative process, and you are clear on when exactly you are ready to show an early draft, for what purpose and most importantly – who your (hopefully willing) assistants should be.

It is easy to assume that if we find wisdom in someone's work, they'll also be wise enough to help *our* writing. But writing well and helping others to write their best are different skills (my short-lived mentor is living proof). Good writers are foremost good because they are true to themselves, their vision. This gift doesn't automatically imply an ability to understand what other artists are attempting to achieve. It can even impede this ability. The immense energy required to access your artistic truth might leave little room for imagining someone else's. But this is where the art of constructive criticism resides – in the capacity to transcend your own taste and worldview, and inhabit another's vision. I've seen countless writers assess another's work through the prism of their own passions, encouraging them to write the kind of books *they* want to write and read. ('Cats are fascinating animals with behavioural quirks. *My* cat certainly is. So, why does the cat in your story only appear in one paragraph? Can you elaborate more on the cat character?')

To know whom to ask for help – paid, reciprocal or plain altruistic – is yet another skill a writer needs to develop (and try to become a good critic yourself to offer help in return). Firstly, consider whether this person is genuinely interested in your project and understands it. If they are interested, and willing to help, show them a few pages. Once they respond, consider the following. Does the feedback seem honest? Is it delivered with respect and appreciation for what you're doing? Is it specific enough or made out of opaque observations, such as 'the ending can be stronger' or 'your story doesn't flow', delivered without supporting evidence? Are they judgemental of your characters or your worldview where it doesn't fit with theirs, or capable of judging your work on its literary merit? Finally, having gotten the critique, do you feel inspired, or at least clearer on what to do? (Of course, only after first spending a week anaesthetising your pain with drugs or whisky . . .)

To complete the first draft of *The Dangerous Bride*, I spent several years in a darkroom. But, not being a native English speaker, even then I depended on the help of my friend, Bradley Dawson. He copyedited my book chapter by chapter, so that I could keep fine-tuning the voice. He also provided some gentle, helpful structural suggestions.

Occasionally another friend and my informal mentor, Peter Bishop, to whom countless Australian writers are indebted for inspiration, joined me in the darkroom. Exceptionally knowing about the writing process and writers' neuroses, and accustomed to the mess of first drafts, he was the perfect companion. Peter knew what (not) to expect of my writing at that stage as well as how to lovingly yet firmly cajole its unimpressive cocoon to unfurl into a prettier butterfly. I vividly recall that first time when, full of trepidation, I showed him several sketchy chapters, because at that point I was desperate for a reality check. Having failed with the preceding two projects, I needed to know if this time I was on the right track. Peter read my work, looked at me kindly and said just three words: 'It is strange.' I stared back in horror. *Strange* . . . 'This is what I want from a book,' he added, 'to be strange, to show me something I haven't seen before.'

Peter's response encouraged me so that for a while I needed no other help. Later, as the work progressed, I'd occasionally show him more. He always had something illuminating to say – big picture stuff, which helped me deepen my memoir. And, unlike my short-lived mentor, Peter never imparted his advice from a throne. Rather, he conversed with me, asking questions to help clarify what I was doing, *and* to complicate and layer it.

Two thirds into completing the first draft – the time when many writers experience a sudden energy drop and would rather scrub floors on their hands and knees than write another paragraph – I felt I needed to be accountable to someone to push through this exasperating phase. Luckily, I was awarded a mentorship grant. More aware of my needs now than I'd been during that aborted mentorship, this time I asked the renowned editor Judith Lukin-Amundsen who'd worked with writers I admire – Robert Dessaix and Helen Garner – to mentor me. Judith identified two flaws in the work: my narrator-self could sound preachy and the research overtook the narrative. These were major issues and I could have easily become overwhelmed. Which I was. For the mandatory drug-and-whisky-fuelled painful week. After that, having full confidence in Judith's judgement, and armed with her belief that I had a story worth telling and the voice to tell it, I pulled myself together, fixed the problems and finished the draft.

*

Once I'd written the entire narrative, I spent a long time washing off chemicals – the superfluities, repetitions, lame metaphors. I cleaned my work so thoroughly that its now-brilliant shine blinded me to any of its further faults. Only then did I dry the manuscript and, with trepidation, open the door of my darkroom.

I stood on the threshold blinking vigorously, having grown used to darkness. I was eager to find out if my memoir was still worth anything when illuminated by sunlight. By that time, I was lucky to have established reciprocal working relationships with several writers whose opinions I trusted. So here they were, kindly waiting, ready to assess the freshly glistening images in my shaking hands.

Now, if your chosen readers are as generous as mine, then you're probably in for ample feedback. So ample that you might grow dizzy, no longer able to tell praise from criticism; so ample that you'll have yet another week of drug-and-whisky-fuelled-despair. But once that week is over, as much as you might still feel overwhelmed by how much work remains (there is always more!), I hope you'll also be able to appreciate – despite the hangover – how marvellous, even exhilarating, it is to have others care deeply about something that has obsessed you and you alone for some years now.

So there you are, feeling all these conflicted feelings – despair, gratitude, irritation, fatigue, inspiration. My hope is that, as drunk on this emotional cocktail as you are, you'll still manage to make your way back to the darkroom. Alone again, you'll face the following quandary: What to do about the mass of notes you've received? How to know what advice to take without letting the (thoughtful) thoughts of others overpower your own intuition, the beat of your artistic pulse?

The first thing I do is compare the different lots of feedback. If everyone points out the same flaw, I almost always fix it unless the advice goes completely against my grain. Where opinions differ, I follow my gut feeling. After that I begin a more methodical revision, doing this in reverse to my layering approach. I first address the minor stuff – line-by-line suggestions. Such intellectually not-that-taxing labour makes me feel like I've achieved something and reduces my feelings of overwhelm. Once I finished, I tell myself I need to fix only several more issues, even though these 'several issues' might be major. On their own, they appear more manageable (just as the emails in my inbox that require time-consuming responses appear less demanding if I responded to all the easy emails first). More so, having worked at the line-by-line level for a while, I'm immersed in my work again, can hear its heartbeat and am able to judge better which criticisms resonate and which solutions they require.

*

You won't believe it now, but the time comes when all is done. Or rather, when the writer is so done they would once again prefer to scrub the floor than cast even one more critical look at a possibly redundant comma. Something, however, they aren't done with is exposure. This time it is the exposure to the (Critical? Indifferent? Contemptuous???) eye of the publishing world.

Somebody once estimated that on average a writer gets one acceptance for every twelve rejections. Questionable mathematics aside, there is some truth to this sweeping assertion. Unfortunately, the possibly most common occurrence in a writer's life is facing the ordinary catastrophes of rejections, no matter how gifted you may be. Before Robert Pirsig's *Zen and the Art of Motorcycle Maintenance* became a bestseller, it was rejected 121 times. Eimear McBride kept submitting *A Girl is a Half-formed Thing* for seven years until it found a publisher. And Proust – yes, Proust! – dabbled in self-publishing.

Pirsig, McBride and Proust were still unknown in the days of their struggles. But even success doesn't guarantee smooth exposure to the publishing industry. Your work is less likely to be rejected, but it doesn't mean unreserved reception. By the time Fitzgerald wrote *The Great Gatsby*, he was already something of a literary celebrity. Still, his editor's initial, now-famous, response to his manuscript was: 'You'd have a decent book if you'd get rid of that Gatsby character.' Luckily, Fitzgerald kept that Gatsby in.

Fitzgerald was confident enough in his artistic vision to stick it out, but it's not unheard of for writers to lose all self-belief after an unloving response from publishers. It took one rejected submission for Emily Dickinson to cease sending her work out; almost all of her poems saw light posthumously.

I hope you won't follow Dickinson's path. I hope you'll remember that without receiving rejections you're unlikely to get acceptances either. There is no way around it. Writers must put themselves out there. It is also good to keep in mind that rejection pain does pass eventually (unless you're a very sensitive American poet who locks herself away in a room). It's probably best not to fight the ache (the agony!) but submit to it, with the knowledge that eventually it will go away. Still, if, like me, you belong to the fragile lot, you might need more strategies to protect yourself in order to go on.

Where my short works are concerned, I manage by no longer keeping track of my submissions, even though this means I might forget and resubmit a rejected piece to the same place. For me, the positives outweigh the negatives. Many literary journals notify authors only if their submissions are accepted. Without a submission register, I often forget what I sent where and many rejections pass me by.

However, it is neither possible nor advisable to 'forget' a submitted book. In Israel I was fortunate to have never had one rejected. But in Australia, once I finished my first English-language book, that ratio of 1:12 finally caught up with me. In fact, I almost gave up on sending out *The Dangerous Bride* after receiving one particular rejection, which unlike the others (that were painful all right!) hit me right in the underbelly. It came from a well-known editor to whom I was recommended by Judith Lukin-Amundsen. Judging by that editor's list, it seemed my work might speak to her. Instead, she emailed to say my memoir was well written, but she didn't *love* it enough to publish it.

I was as badly wounded as I'd once been in my mid-twenties, when a new lover ended our relationship, saying he liked me but wasn't in love with me. I had no strong feelings for him either, but his words undid me. Being flawed is redeemable, but unlovable? There was nothing I could do about the fact that I and my art which is also me, didn't arouse strong passions . . .

In the aftermath of the lover's rejection, I spent the day in bed, smoking and thinking unlovable thoughts about my unlovable future, even considering a purchase of blue stockings. I went through a whole pack of Marlboro Lights, and I was only a social smoker. Then I opened a new pack. By nighttime, I felt so nauseous and shaky that my physical suffering overpowered my emotional pain and that, pretty much, was the end of that sorry story.

Unfortunately, by the editor's rejection I no longer smoked. I also had an infant at home and couldn't afford taking to bed. Which didn't prevent me, of course, from thinking unlovable thoughts and resigning myself to a non-writing future. I gave my memoir all I had and now it was clear that all I had wasn't enough.

But, Reader, this time around, instead of my writing marring my life as per usual, it was my life that took a stand and salvaged my writing. My misery was giant but so was the joy I felt at the sight of my firstborn. Besides, my PhD revisions deadline was looming. Despite the dark cloud of an unlovable book hanging over me, I was too preoccupied to devote myself properly to my suffering. Then, it was hard to feel entirely unlovable while lying at night snugly between my handsome husband and my ugly baby, listening to their sleepy breathing. After some weeks equally embroidered with pain, joy and busyness, I clenched my teeth and resumed submitting my book. Rejections kept coming (albeit none was as painful as that one) and I kept crying, and snuggling with my son and husband, and putting finishing touches on my thesis, until eventually a publishing contract came in.

It was as simple and as difficult as that – I finally conceded that writing wasn't *everything*. That I existed beyond it. That gave me the strength to persevere.

Perseverance, however, isn't all a writer needs in the face of rejection. What we also need is honest self-insight. Humility too. To know when it's not forces of darkness that conspire against us but forces of tough love; when a publisher's rejection is an indication that there is more work to do. The Australian poet Alicia Sometimes wrote on my blog along these lines:

> A friend once said to me, 'Far better to have a wonderful poem rejected than a crap one accepted.' This aphorism has been clinking around my head, particularly during this acute pain of rejection when I see the words 'We had a great deal of submissions. Unfortunately . . .' That word. Unfortunately. You don't want to read on. But you should. Lessons can be learnt. Every rejection means you fine-tune: shortening sentences, adding complexities, finding the heart of the story. I am glad I was rejected for so many poems that went on to have stronger lives.

And so you finetune your book. And then it goes on to live a stronger life, as your trembling hand signs a contract. Your unsteady feet cross the darkroom's threshold into the street. What you're likely to notice now that you're finally outside is – life. Life. Shimmering, swarming with pigeons and roses, friends and poodles, simmering casseroles, broken dishwashers . . . Dear just-finished-my-book writer, this is our discovery today – that there is life out there, waiting just around the corner to interfere with your art.

PART FOUR:

HONESTY IN (THE WRITER'S) LIFE

'The hardest thing about being a writer is convincing your wife that lying on the sofa is work.'

– John Hughes

At least until mid-last century, many Russian poets died young, and by unnatural means. American fiction writers abused drink and drugs. English writers of any persuasion were often sickly in pale, doomed, romantic ways. Nationality notwithstanding, most of the notable writers specialised in messy love lives, and I suspect many still do today.

Scholars have long tried to unpick the correlation between private turbulence and writing. What causes what? And why? Nobody is sure, but Arthur Rimbaud took a good guess. His belief was that the living writers do is integral to their art and the wilder it is the better the work. His famous advice to writers was to make themselves 'a seer by a long, prodigious and rational disordering of all the senses. Every form of love, suffering, madness . . .'.

Until my mid-thirties, at least as far as love and suffering are concerned, I followed Rimbaud's advice, and it worked. Most of my writing has been inspired by my earlier, stormy life. I believe I have enough past left to fuel several more books, which is fortunate, as nowadays I spend my non-writing time planting roses, making meatballs, tearing Ipads away from my children's sticky hands and reading other people's books for a living.

This tamer life affects my art too, sometimes counterproductively, as I struggle to keep those sticky little hands also away from my laptop and, more importantly, struggle to keep away my mother-and-wife-self when I write. But while my current life is hectic in non-inspiring ways (once I write those 'several more books', I may have to find new methods to disorder my senses), in other ways it is actually suited to writing. Its relative stability makes it easier for me to establish a working routine and rather than being distracted from writing by living, writing is now my distraction away from my relatively wholesome existence – my wild, dirty secret.

Possibly, the relationship between literature and life is so unclear because of how enmeshed the two are. A writer cannot separate work and the rest of their day (and sometimes night) as neatly as, say, an engineer might. If you're anything like me, you would hang your washing out to dry (that is, if you are also like me environmentally opposed to dryers), or try to get sexually aroused with your partner, or breastfeed your child, but what would really occupy your mind is how to kill that irritatingly resilient character or that reviewer who just tore your new book apart, or why your friend was selected for some literary award but you weren't . . .

If you are a writer, your fresh washing is likely to fall on the ground and get dirty. Your spouse is likely to develop chronic sexual hunger. Your breastfeeding child might soon enter therapy. In the last part of this book, I cannot guarantee to help you prevent any such calamities. But I am inviting you to contemplate the impact our personal lives have on our art and, in turn, the price that a writing life exacts from us and our loved ones. Cultivating a deliberate, candid reflection about these issues I believe (hope) can help make our lives more conducive to literary labour without the latter completely overtaking the former.

LITERARY FRIENDS

I won't name names, but a writer friend calls to discuss a mutual friend – also a writer. 'I really, really, really wish her well. Really do . . .' she says with barely contained angst, and I know she means it. 'But if only X stopped licking all those literary arses! Every time I check my social media, she's there – either promoting her new book or raving profusely about somebody else's book, somebody who is more famous.'

Thank goodness! Lately I've had precisely the same shameful, conflicted thoughts, but I wasn't brave enough to admit them. What a relief to hear it's not just me.

'And Y,' my friend continues, 'he just got that prize . . .'

'That's mainly because his topic is fashionable,' I chip in gladly, revelling in my awfulness. 'I mean, the book is good, but . . .'

Right now my friend and I are in a similar place, battling our budding works without having nailed them yet, so our pettiness towards anyone with a new book out, even someone we like, flares up as easily as our insecurities. Jealousy is a common and possibly the most humiliating occupational hazard for writers. Liking someone doesn't eradicate it, but can actually enhance it as well as bring on much guilt.

After your book is out, it is just as difficult not to compare yourself to others, because opportunities for disappointment are rife. Perhaps your book was released into silence. Or was slashed by critics. Or received well critically but not listed for awards. Or you didn't sell as many books as that other writer you know and dislike. Then there was that writers' festival, where they put you up in Quest and not in the posh hotel with the more important speakers . . . Even such renowned writers as Helen Garner are not immune. Upon discovering she wasn't included in the *Oxford Anthology of Australian Literature*, Garner noted in her diary that she felt 'wretched . . . People must laugh at me behind my back. I posture as a writer and at forty-two I can't even get into the Oxford book.' Later, at the good news of being shortlisted for a prestigious award but convinced she wouldn't win, Garner recorded the following response: 'I determine not to go to the presentation. Never again, that shameful public torment.'

All these petty feelings aren't something I can share, not even with my husband, without feeling judged. Only another writer understands. As my friend and I keep airing our grievances, I feel increasingly better in a way that reminds me of the instances when I absent-mindedly clench my teeth for a while, then become aware of the persisting discomfort and unclench. We end our conversation by laughing off our pettiness and I resume writing, feeling purged and re-energised.

*

Orhan Pamuk says that a good writer:

> is a person who does not belong to a community, who does not share the basic instincts of community, and who is thinking

> and judging with a different culture than the one he is experiencing . . . He is an outsider, a loner. And the richness of his text comes from the outsider's voyeuristic vision.

This quote resonates with me. The way I interpret it is writers should stay away from any communal orthodoxies and truisms, be these conservative or progressive. But writers also create communities – idiosyncratic communities of their own. The age-old Rapunzel story of a writer shut in an impossibly high, doorless and stairless tower is both fact and fiction. It is true that solitude is our necessity, that it nourishes us, and that a book isn't a collaborative affair. But writers need other writers. Even recluses like Flaubert and Rilke maintained some literary friendships (though predominantly by epistolary means).

We need our writer friends to share resentments (and successes) with and to be our security blankets to ease the blows of rejection. We need them to steel our creative selves against the ongoing assaults of the so-called book market and its representatives (publishers, publicists, agents, event organisers, media squads). And if Kerouac hadn't typed up the handwritten pages he'd found strewn across William Burroughs's filthy floor in Tangier while Burroughs slept off the heroin (at Burroughs's request) and, along with Allen Ginsberg, put them in a coherent order, *The Naked Lunch* would never have materialised.

I see my friendships with other writers – particularly those that have provided oxygen for my art and kept me honest about it – as an inseparable part of my writing process. I see them as the ultimate intersection of life and art. In this spirit, you might like to consider to what extent your social environment nurtures your writing and whether you can nourish it even more through the connections you make – in ways I'll examine now or in some other fashion.

*

There was a period in my life when I was desperate not just for literary friendships but a milieu. I was new to Australia and married to a man who didn't read. Our mutual friends talked mostly about sex, food and drugs. I knew several writers, but we, too, mostly talked sex and food (less so drugs) and about how difficult it was to write and get published. I was into all those topics, but I felt as if a certain, intellectual, part of me was atrophying. Plus, I was at the peak of my writer's block. Desperate to quench the dryness in me, I enrolled in the University of Melbourne's masters in writing.

The School of Creative Arts was a revelation. The air under its arched wooden ceilings was dense, electric, buzzing with ideas – you could stretch out a hand and catch some. I wandered around in a dream, imbibing the teachings of Marion May Campbell who spoke in her film-noir-smoky voice about the hard self-work that it takes to become a writer: *We should encourage our students to hone their critical skills and read as widely as possibly across disciplines and cultures before and while they write* . . . I worshipped Marion and I tried to copy my classmates, who read Freud and argued over the comparative merits of French versus German feminism on their lunch breaks. The school appeared to me as a magical space, caught between past and present. It was easy to believe that soon Hemingway might bang the door open, pour himself a dry scotch and launch into a conversation with Gertrude Stein, who would advise him to invest his earnings in modern painting.

It was no coincidence that Hemingway and Stein were the subjects of my daydreaming. I was an avid reader of literary biographies, particularly versed in the lives of writers who spent their evenings together in the cafés of Saint-Germain-des-Près and Montparnasse. I was acutely jealous of those soupy milieus, wondering how much of their genius the members owed to all that joint drinking, flirting and theorising – their words clinking against each other like amorous swords.

But soupy milieus aren't exclusive to modernists. Writers have a long history of banding together intentionally and intensely, a tendency perhaps best expressed in the tradition of literary salons which began around the sixteenth century and blossomed in the mid-1700s when the novel as a genre grew more complex and ambitious, and the status of novelists increased. Some wealthy readers, predominantly women, eager to bathe in 'genius', opened their comfortable houses to literati, offering them a reprieve from the solitude of writing, good quality cognac and even help with their love lives. (It was in such a gathering that George Sand first laid eyes on Chopin.) Most importantly, salons stimulated writers' intellects with their thoughtfully orchestrated mix of thinkers and personalities. The conversations were typically rich and challenging, dissecting literary, scientific and political matters. In fact, by the end of the eighteenth century, many such gatherings became almost as structured as university seminars: typically, there would be a reading of some guest's work followed by a sustained debate on its subject.

By the time of Hemingway and Stein, literary salons were fading out. Writers migrated to cafés and to their own, usually modest, abodes. In the Paris of the forties, Marguerite Duras cooked stews at her home for her literary comrades as they argued about communism and danced. In the fifties, the Beats came together in Greenwich Village bars and cramped San Francisco apartments to trip high into the sky. In the seventies, Yona Wallach drank Turkish coffee with her fellow poets in Tel Aviv cafés. These gatherings weren't as structured as the salons but they still provided a fertile ground for art. The Beats, for instance, developed a distinctive vision of writing as a spiritual quest and exploration of the human condition, drawing on Eastern religions and their experiences with psychedelic drugs.

In the twenty-first century, it seems writers have less and less time or inclination to while away hours together. When we do, too often we end up bemoaning our advances and book sales, day jobs and children. I wonder if we have lost some inner wilderness, some mental space to ponder why we write and what art is, what sacrifices it requires, what compromises it can tolerate, and more broadly, the miracles we call 'life' and 'the universe'. It was in pursuit of some such comradeship – where deep conversation is preserved like an endangered species, writing is treated as sacred and I'd be pushed to write my best — that I joined writers' groups, travelled far and wide to share artistic residencies, and gathered with other writers under the guise of higher education.

Sometimes I found what I was seeking, often I didn't. And when I did, as during my postgraduate writing study, it didn't last very long. By nature, groups are vulnerable to power struggles and other such maladies (or are temporary by design, as my degree was). But mostly I didn't find what I was after because something as pure as that might be the fruit of my imagination. Surely Virginia Woolf banged on about publishing deals too, surely Hemingway discussed where to find a good sausage . . .

In any case, perhaps longevity isn't the right measure of a literary milieu. After my masters was done, my writer's block persisted for another year. However, my brain synapses were no longer the same – they were flooded with new ideas and perspectives (no matter that many of them pissed me off!). I stored those learnings behind my mind's dam and later, when the writer's block lifted, the dam opened and its waters revived my pages. I thought broader, placing my stories within history and other larger narratives, and I was a better critic of my writing.

*

Perhaps individual friendships have a better chance at longevity than milieus. It is true that relationships among writers can be complicated, rife with ambivalence and barely concealed rivalries or even full-blown feuds – Hemingway and Fitzgerald, Sartre and

Camus, Truman Capote and Harper Lee, to name a few. However, literary history also brims with tales of joyful, artistically fruitful, soul-filling friendships.

Charles Dickens helped his younger friend, Wilkie Collins, advance his writing career by giving him a platform in *Household Words*, a weekly literary periodical he ran. Later, as Collins matured as a man and artist, their relationship became more equal. The two collaborated on theatre works and, in an interesting twist of fate, after Dickens published Collins's suspense novel, *The Woman in White*, in his other periodical, *All the Year Round*, the work was so popular that the periodical's circulation increased by almost ten times.

The college friends Sylvia Plath and Anne Sexton didn't pen poems together, but their works contained thematic overlap. This is unsurprising given the women used to discuss, among all else, their shared fascination with the allure of death and that of bright, difficult men. Their conversations were instrumental in the realisation of the poets' artistic potential and in the expression of their singular visions (but sadly, not in them leading happier lives).

Hannah Arendt and Mary McCarthy met as fully fledged adults and writers, and yet their friendship, which lasted a quarter of a century until Arendt's death, has left irrevocable traces on their works. The biographer Claudia Roth Pierpont describes in *Passionate Minds* how the two were driven to investigate the nature of morality and each exerted influence on the writing of the other as they debated various isms (communism, Cartesianism, existentialism) and the power of evil. And of sex, of course. They also supported each other through the storms in their creative (and personal) lives. When Arendt's controversial work, *Eichmann in Jerusalem*, was released, instantly making her infamous, McCarthy went as far as to write a passionate essay in defence of the book. The essay only got Arendt (and McCarthy) into more trouble, but their friendship persisted and Arendt even appointed McCarthy as her posthumous literary executor.

McCarthy and Arendt's relationship was so intense that some of their friends referred to it as a 'love affair'. It is actually not uncommon for writers to marry other writers – something that can get us into trouble or benefit our art, or, as in the case of Sylvia Plath and Ted Hughes's marriage, do both . . . For Virginia Woolf, who, like Plath, died by suicide, her marriage to the novelist and critic Leonard Woolf arguably delayed rather than hastened her death. Their relationship was a hotbed of creation, at least for Virginia. Leonard, recognising her gifts, put her art before his. He became her editor and publisher as well as carer and household manager, freeing her to write.

The Victorian poets Elizabeth Barrett Browning and Robert Browning were devoted to each other's art more equally. Elizabeth admired Robert's talent long before the world began to love his works. Eleven years before her masterpiece *Aurora Leigh* was published to roaring applause, Elizabeth shared her vision for the work with her husband. Robert was astute enough to know greatness even in its incubatory stage. His encouragement verged on exaltation. He wrote to her: 'the fearless fresh living work you describe, is the only Poem to be undertaken now by you or anyone that is a Poet . . . it is what I have been all my life intending to do, and now shall be much, much nearer doing, since you will be along with me.'

A more contemporary literary couple, American writers Michael Chabon and Ayelet Waldman, have often publicly discussed the pivotal roles they play in each other's writing. In one such instance, midway through writing his novel, *Telegraph Avenue*, Chabon grew so discouraged he almost gave it up. Fortunately, Waldman, who had read what he'd already written, talked him out of it. She urged him to write the book if not for his then for her sake, because 'she cared too much about these characters and wanted to find out what became of them'. So Chabon kept going until the book was complete. This wasn't the only time, he said, when Ayelet had had 'to lash me to the tiller and keep me there long enough to get through the bad patches'.

For better or worse, I've avoided marrying writers, but in my twenties I had a relationship with one. To keep peace at home, we rarely critiqued each other's works. But we talked incessantly, deep into the night, sometimes until dawn about bookish and other matters. We talked about antiquity, Tolstoy, Thailand, which he knew intimately, Russia, which I had in my blood, and what we desired to write. We were together while I wrote my second book, a collection of short stories, and when I peruse it, I find traces of our conversations everywhere.

The Dangerous Bride – the book on account of which I've suffered the most and the book that has possibly meant the most to me out of everything I've written – is imprinted with someone else. Not a paramour but a friend – Peter Bishop. As much as this book is me, it would not have fully been what it is if Peter and I hadn't met.

I wrote in the previous chapter about Peter's help in the darkroom, but there is far more to say about his contribution to my writing. Like that very first time when we met, which was also when I first came to Varuna where he was the director. The softly spoken, blond-bearded stranger welcomed me with a big smile, losing no time to small talk. 'So you're the writer who writes about Russia,' he said enthusiastically as I wheeled in my overstuffed suitcase. 'Have you heard that story, when Anna Akhmatova unintentionally irked Stalin . . .?' Without a pause, we launched into a lengthy conversation about matters of high importance to us – poetry, free speech, irony . . . All of which later ended up creeping into my memoir.

Over the course of our friendship, Peter pulled me more than once out of the lowest lows, where I wallowed during my writer's block, with his unwavering belief in me. He also expanded my vision of what is possible in literature by giving me new perspectives on my subjects and introducing me to a bunch of authors who have also affected the shape of my art – Bruno Schulz, Louis Simpson, Beverley Farmer, Sasha Soldatow. In return, I gave Peter books by Amos Oz and Aharon Appelfeld, and read his writing drafts.

Peter and I live in different states and since I've had children it is impossible for us to meet as regularly as we once did. But this friendship has a permanent room in my heart, where I can retreat when I feel flat, uninspired. There, a fire is always blazing in a fireplace. A meaty stew is slow-cooking. Fierce Siberian wolves are howling outside. On an antique coffee table, Akhmatova's tome lays open and some, probably German, opera singer is crooning, probably something about love and life and death and love.

*

'The only people for me,' Kerouac famously wrote in *On the Road*, 'are the mad ones, the ones who are mad to live, mad to talk, mad to be saved, desirous of everything at the same time, the ones who never yawn or say a commonplace thing, but burn, burn, burn like fabulous yellow roman candles . . .'

Kerouac depended on the fire of others to write, but these 'others' weren't all literati. The friend who left the greatest footprint on his pages wasn't a writer but a flesh-and-blood muse. Neal Cassady – an adventurer, petty thief, speed-driver, lover of Ginsberg, bigamist and father of at least four children, a man always on the run from something and towards something else, a perpetually burning man. He lived so dangerously, so intensely, that he made everyone in his vicinity feel acutely alive. Essentially, *On the Road* is Kerouac's love poem to Cassady, who is the model for its unforgettable character Dean Moriarty and whom Kerouac's stand-in narrator trails around America. Around him, Kerouac wrote, 'I knew there'd be girls, visions, everything; somewhere along the line the pearl would be handed to me'.

Cassady had enough fire in him to inflame some more Kerouac books, as well as the works of several other writers. John Clellon Holmes wrote him into his novel *Go*. Tom Wolfe described Cassady's later reincarnation, when the criminal-turned-beatnik became a psychedelic drug enthusiast and bus driver for the Merry Pranksters, in his creative nonfiction book *The Electric Kool-Aid Acid Test*. Ken Kesey wrote a fictional account of Cassady in his short story 'The Day After Superman Died'.

It makes sense to expand my definition of literary friendships to include such natural born muses, such naturally burning people, as Cassady. It is common for writers to depend on real people to inspire their works, particularly on the complex, even dubious characters, seekers of sorts who live close to the edge. Henry Miller and Anaïs Nin had June, who was Miller's wife as well as a failed actress and a glamorous swindler fond of opium and gangsters. Mayakovsky wrote about, and for, Lilya Brik, who lived with him and her husband Osip Brik as she sculpted, danced all night and played tennis naked. Such living muses have provided plots for writers as well as expanded their outlook on life.

My art, too, feeds on people who are on fire. The first of them was my friend Miriam, whom I described in one story as 'the queen of hashish and orgies, the professional teenage runaway and con artist'. Miriam was the toughest girl in our tough neighbourhood in Ashdod, an industrial Israeli port city. We met when we were seventeen and, not unlike Kerouac with Cassady, I grew convinced that life was most worth living wherever Miriam was and began shadowing her. We would hitchhike around Israel, share drinks with petty criminals and sleep in strange places, but I always felt safe. I trusted in Miriam to protect me and she always did, carrying a pocketknife everywhere. She was fearless and she fucked the kind of men whose sex appeal has been made unfashionable by feminism – men with unshaven faces, crooked teeth, calloused hands. Sometimes she and her lovers shared the details of their sex with me, still a virgin, in a way that felt more comradely than sordid. 'She's a writer,' Miriam would tell her men. 'She needs to know this stuff.'

My years with Miriam, before her metamorphosis into a pious wife and mother, have given me some tantalising plots and nurtured my appetite for adventure. It is also thanks to her that in anything I've ever written someone is always burning. Finding living muses involves luck but also a skill, an openness, an alertness of sorts. Since Miriam, at my own peril I have always been on the lookout for seductive, destructive or self-destructive friends – so-called bad girls and boys, drama queens, perpetual vagabonds. Like comets they sweep through my life, leaving scorched trails behind. And when the fire and smoke get too much, I throw down my Rapunzel tresses and gratefully watch my writer friends climb up to cool me and my laptop down.

THE PRAM IN THE HALLWAY

I delayed motherhood until I was almost forty for several reasons, the main one being my suspicion that having a child would be incompatible with being a writer. While I could imagine myself not having children, albeit with some pain, I couldn't imagine not being a writer. So, I chose the risk of trying for children when my fertility was already on the decline over the risk of not expressing myself creatively.

It would be convenient to blame English critic Cyril Connolly for my supposition that children and writing cancelled each other out. Connolly famously scared generations of artists, particularly of the female kind, by declaring that 'there is no more sombre enemy of good art than the pram in the hallway'. He frightened me too, but to be fair – I was terrified long before I knew Connolly existed. I grew up to the tune of my mother's refrain that a woman's main mission is to have children. I had other missions in mind. Plus, watching some women (and a few men) I knew shed their selfhoods once children came along made me even warier of these overbearing creatures that would surely devour everything I'd ever cared about: my independence, intellectual curiosity, libido and writing, of course.

My eventual decision to 'get myself a kid', as I came to refer to it – faking lightness where there was none – took years. The thing that tilted the scales in child's favour was finishing a draft of *The Dangerous Bride*. This was the first time in nine years that I'd completed a book-long narrative, so I felt more inclined to sacrifice myself at the altar of The Baby. At that point, my main sacrificial motivations were the fear of growing old alone and the desire to make Daryl happy. Some vague craving for baby-cuteness aside, my biological clock wasn't working. Perhaps it was paralysed with terror.

When, one fine autumnal evening, our baby arrived, I discovered there was far more pleasure to motherhood than I'd expected. In fact, pleasure wasn't an adequate word for the euphoria I felt once Luca emerged out of me and deftly attached himself to my breast. Having my son made me happier in a lasting way too and within weeks this happiness trickled into my feelings about my writing, not dissimilarly to what had happened five years before the birth, when I met his father. As with falling in love, my baby took the edge off my urgency to look for the ultimate fulfilment in writing. Paradoxically, once the urgency diminished, I wanted to write more, because now writing was less bound with anxiety. But how to realise this desire in the face of the sleepless nights and mountains of dirty bibs I hadn't a clue.

*

Now that I've had eight years of testing Connolly's proposition, I no longer believe children stop their parents from making literature. What the pram in the hallway is more likely to do is provide a solid excuse to follow the pathway of self-doubt or some other fear and avoid writing. If a writer is determined to persevere, then I believe they will find a way back to writing, albeit for some it might be a long road. But is this necessarily a bad thing?

Some writers, particularly those who start a family early, only begin writing after their children are grown. Others pause their work during early childhood years, preferring to live this precious experience to the full. Neither of these choices is problematic from the artistic perspective, as long as this choice is made not out of guilt and the writer is genuinely fine with postponing their work. Hiatuses for whatever reason are an essential part of the writing process (more on this in the next chapter). Besides, our so-called non-writing time often ends up being creative. My friend, the Australian writer Leah Kaminsky, for example, waited until her children became teenagers before writing her first novel, *The Waiting Room*. However, in the meantime she kept contemplating her book and taking notes. That long gestation resulted in an exquisitely thought-through work that has garnered success.

The thing to do, I now believe, is to consider honestly what creative pathway you want to wheel your pram along. Do you really wish to integrate writing with parenting of young children (and often with paid work too)? For some, life isn't all about writing, and writing isn't as fragile as we might think. It can wait until we are ready.

But *I* didn't want to wait. Not even during the babyhood of my firstborn, when he had a magical hold on me and I was consumed by his physicality – his milky scent, silky tummy, various noises, the folds of his inner thighs, the dimples on his cheeks. Not even when my experience of cyclical time changed and day was no longer a clearly delineated entity with fixed rituals, as I couldn't predict when my baby would be awake or asleep, or for how long he would breastfeed.

I wanted to keep writing, but I didn't know how to disentangle myself from this amorphous existence of the baby–mother dyad to resume the strict routines that writing requires. In fact, I didn't even want to give up my new, floating, moment-by-moment life composed of breastfeeds during which I'd read guilt-free, playtime, naps, housework and rest. This was a reprieve from my usual structured self. Did this mean Connolly was right after all? I don't think so. It meant it was time for me to consider the practicalities of weaving parenting and writing together, and what I was willing to compromise on in each of these mighty endeavours.

At some point, an obvious but not obvious to me, epiphany struck me: I should forget my writing 'rules', or rather, I should adjust them to my new circumstances. There was no harm in scaling my ambitions down during Luca's first year. I could fit my writing *around* our dyad, just often enough for the work to stay alive.

I resumed writing six weeks after Luca's birth, mostly working during his daytime naps instead of catching up on sleep or housework. In this new 'routine', leisure and work became enmeshed and I grew used to writing for unpredictable, often short, periods several times a day. Later, when my child slept less, I enlisted support from my husband and part-time childcare. By the end of Luca's second year, I'd completed the final edits of *The Dangerous Bride*, finished my PhD and written several short works while doing some teaching too. That I accomplished all this while still spending considerable time with my baby might imply that I'd resolved the hostile pram issue, which was exactly what I believed – to the extent of braving another pregnancy.

Some writers choose to have one child, so that they have more time to parent and to write (and to sleep). This is as sound a choice as any. But for me, to have one child when I wanted two was a sacrifice I wasn't prepared to make. Plus, by now I felt quite smug, confident I could manage it all. Little did I know that I'd find the transition from having one child to two far more earth-shattering than from zero to one. Nor did I guess that my early, blissful days of parenthood were no indication of the shape this experience would assume later, particularly when my adorable firstborn would begin showing emotional and behavioural difficulties. In short, I naïvely assumed parenthood could be forecast like tomorrow's weather.

*

Two days after Ollie, my second son, was born, I sat at a desk in a hotel room (it was a part of my hospital stay) with bandages over my freshly cut abdomen and a hospital tag around my wrist, high on Endone and scrolling furiously through my emails. Near me, a tiny blond creature dozed in a cot. Behind me, on a king-sized bed Daryl was reading *Hairy Maclary* to our toddler. I kept scrolling through various congratulatory emails, without opening them, trying to locate an email which required an urgent response. It was from a contributor to an anthology I was co-editing and due to deliver to my publisher in just four months. And there was also that literary event to prepare for . . .

Once we left the bubble of the hotel, things went from difficult to nearly impossible. Not only did I have looming deadlines but also a chaos-filled house and a furious toddler, unprepared to share his royal place in our family with the baby. And just as it became apparent that the expression 'sibling rivalry' could never account for the civil war happening in our house, Ollie was diagnosed with albinism – a condition that causes low vision and high sensitivity to the sun.

Now those initial secluded six weeks I'd had with Luca and the subsequent amorphous months of work and leisure came to seem like some utopian fairytale. I entered permanent emergency mode, continually pacifying my toddler while adjusting practically and emotionally to Ollie's diagnosis and breastfeeding two children in tandem. At the same time, I kept taking on any work that came my way, including signing a contract for my next book to be delivered within eighteen months. I could have refused some things, but I rarely did. Was it cowardice? Fear of missing out? Denial of my changed circumstances? I tick all these boxes. But it was also the nature of the writing industry, where you hardly ever get a second chance if you decline something.

Now the entirety of my waking hours was composed of responsibilities (breastfeed, give mentoring feedback, draw with Luca, take Ollie to a medical appointment, write, take Luca to a therapy appointment, cook dinner, give a library talk, breastfeed . . .). I discovered I could work in the following conditions: on the floor near Ollie's playmat; hiding in the bedroom while my husband minded Luca, Ollie dozing near me; at midnight, fortified with obscene quantities of coffee; in cafés with Ollie strapped to me in a baby carrier. I recall one afternoon when I was editing an essay by the Australian memoirist Rochelle Siemienowicz, 'Resisting the Nipple', for my anthology while breastfeeding Ollie. I was supporting him with one hand and writing my comments with the other. When I reached Rochelle's (far more peaceful) description of breastfeeding her son, tears welled for no apparent reason. I suppose it was some hormonal response to something only my hormones knew about. There was no time to pause and investigate what was happening inside me. I kept editing and leaking – tears, milk and ink.

I now think that moment was emblematic of what I'd become during Ollie's first years – an automaton who was all brain yet also all body, a self-unaware paradox. I finished editing that essay on time, just as I did everything else back then. Fulfilling my writing commitments became crucial to proving to myself, as well as to the world (and to Connolly, and to my mother, most of all my mother), that I was still a writer, my leakages notwithstanding. As Ollie edged towards his third birthday, I submitted *Imperfect*, missing the contract deadline only by a fraction.

*

Ironically, the book I wrote while nursing two boys with special needs ended up being the book I wrote the fastest, with the least amount of procrastination. Parenthood turned me into a more adaptable, resilient writer (I can now write even during the ten minutes of waiting in a car during school pickup). But there is more to my writing-while-parenting story.

My pram turned out to be an ambiguous object. The efficiency came at a price. Writers need to write, but they also need time to think, and especially to daydream. Unfortunately, since the birth of my children, my headspace lacks some romance, a measure of languidness required to put me in touch with my subconscious, to allow formless, strange beings to rise from its depths. Among myriad mundane concerns filling my days – packing school lunches, supervising playdates, sourcing the next Moomintroll book – the strangeness that creative work requires is more elusive. Without time to laze with music and books, and no longer able to retreat to a writers' residency – that liminal space that cancels the ticking clock and my intense domestic reality – for more than a few days, it is more difficult for me to call on the muses, easier to produce mediocre words.

Nowadays, I must hunt for liminality in snatches, deliberately, in the manner of the young Nabokov's expeditions in search of rare butterflies. I take walks to encourage daydreaming and sometimes I write at night – not out of necessity but to capitalise on that time when spooky creatures leave their dark corners to cast shadows on my laptop screen. I am also more attentive when I read at night, when odd thoughts are more likely to arise in response to others' words, and I record these in a notebook. On my next working day, I revisit those notes, hoping their glimmer hasn't faded at daylight and I can use them.

*

Where I've been most tested by the pram is in the personal domain. Yes, I can have it all, but at what price? Before I had children, whenever I contemplated, Hamlet-style, to be or not to be that mythical vomit-covered-mother (my children indeed turned out to be gifted vomiters), I used to recall, with admiration and horror, all those biographical liner notes on books. *X, the author of 394 books, lives with her husband, three dogs, two cats and 4.5 children . . .* I thought those writer-parents were heroes, made of material I wasn't. My assumption gained confirmation when Leah Kaminsky gifted me Irish writer Anne Enright's memoir of motherhood, *Making Babies*. Enright describes writing mostly in the evenings, when her husband was home from work to take over the children, and late into the night. I never wanted to follow in Enright's stoic footsteps. I'd grown excessively attached to spending evenings revelling in the satisfaction of 'having-written' and indulging guilt-free in reading, film watching and other leisurely pursuits. With one child, I could still do some of this. But after Ollie was born, I followed Enright's example.

Then, a minor matter, there is the impact on my family to consider. During my second pregnancy, I asked the Australian novelist Ellie Marney how she manages raising four (four!) children while writing. Ellie said she does this by compartmentalising the writing and the parenting parts of her. Because when she is with her children she is fully present, she doesn't feel guilty about the time she spends writing.

I want but rarely manage to follow Ellie's fine example. I play Uno with my boys or watch them perform The Beatles songs for the hundredth time, but my mind often drifts to my anxieties about some deadline or event, or tries to solve some writing problem. The truth is I am perpetually compromised as a parent. I am crap at compartmentalising and I am nowhere near being that archetypal mother who packs homemade muffins into homemade lunchboxes (which Greek myth is she from?). I've often left my boys (in my husband's care) to attend writers' festivals, teach, or just lock myself somewhere for a night to meet a deadline. When I do this, I grow hyper-emotional. I feel at once heartbroken and exhilarated (oh, the ravishing pleasure of eating room service in bed with a book on my lap!). But sometimes it's just heartbreak, like the day when I was teaching an all-day memoir class and somebody read a moving passage about their baby. Immediately my breasts began leaking and I ended up spending the day with my arms crossed over my chest.

Intellectually, I know that to be a working writer I have to drop my parenting standards. I have to continuously make decisions about which sacrifices for my art are acceptable and which would cause too much damage (like, going away for two nights is possible, but three nights means I might not find all my household members alive upon my return). But emotionally, I struggle to accept the fact of any sacrifices at all. So, a lot of the time I feel like a shit mother. I think: Did I have children to be with them or to work around them? And: Is a book-writing mother in the corridor an enemy of her offspring? (Memoirs of writers' unhappy children are a subgenre of their own.) But just as I start fantasising about full time devotion to my boys, I remember what happens on those occasions when I try acting these fantasies out, switching off my laptop to dedicate myself to every question coming from little mouths, every little hand needing to be washed or kissed. By the end of such a time (it never lasts longer than a week), I am usually an emotional and physical wreck, irritable and alienated from myself, not great company for my family.

My dirty secret is that as much as writing interferes with my parenting, it also makes it more bearable. Parenting is rarely easy for anyone, but in our family it is even harder than average as Daryl and I have been learning how to optimise the lives of a child with low vision and another afflicted with tantrums that can turn into violent rages. During the first years of my boys' coexistence, when our house was a war zone, sometimes my writing time felt like salvation, an escape from reality. I'd leave my study and return to my family with more energy and goodwill to manage our frequent crises. I'll try to remember this the next time dreams of full-time parenting descend upon me.

*

My process of writing this chapter reminds me of how I parent. Forever divided and seeing a con for every pro, I never feel as if I 'nailed' it. I'm struggling to say something of substance, distil from my singular experience something useful for other writers who are, or want to be, parents. But what can I offer besides my confusions?

I suppose primarily this: ongoing self-reflection is an absolute must for any writer, but particularly a parenting one. Both endeavours are creative, tough, capricious, deeply rewarding and maddeningly demanding. They give rise to visceral passions, and require stamina and guts. Writing parents make important choices every day, many times a day, and we need to be candid about our needs and priorities and those of our loved ones. Not usually one for regrets, I now wish I had more insight into what was happening inside me following Ollie's birth. Perhaps if I knew then how much I *needed* writing, I'd have spared myself much of the guilt I felt. And possibly I'd have been braver at not taking on *any* work but just enough to save myself, so that the rest of the time I could be more present for my family. And do my nails more often.

Nowadays I am trying harder, more consciously, to strike a balance between parenting and writing, as well as my more 'frivolous' needs. Then, there is also that. I am writing this chapter eight years, one month and fifteen days since that autumnal night that turned me into someone's mother. Things are different once again. My boys require a little less physical care and supervision;

my youngest already reads independently and my eldest, on his good days, can play with him for several hours without exploding. In fact, we have more good days now that Daryl and I have finally accepted Luca needs medication to manage his moods. Unsurprisingly, I am somewhat less highly strung too.

Now that the parenting feels a little easier, the eros of creativity has weakened for me. I want to spend more time with my boys and I am more easily drawn away from my laptop and into the adventures of Moomintroll, which we like reading huddled together on our porridge-stained couch, or into joint muffin-baking (yes, those homemade muffins are finally happening). On days when the boys are content and floors aren't too sticky, I think: What if it's time to press pause now that I've proven to myself that parenthood and art can coexist?

I don't regret too much how I've lived these last eight years, but the costs have been high and we all need a break. I am seriously considering doing what I did in my younger years, when my appetite for living through my senses (as opposed to in my head) was ferocious, when I wouldn't write *all the time* but at intervals, because I desired so much else. So, Connolly, it looks like you weren't totally off the mark after all. I swear, yesterday I saw our (long-unused) pram acquire that ominous glow you see in horror films . . .

THE WRITING TIMES AND THE LIVING TIMES

The Booker Prize-winner John Banville published his first book when he was twenty-five. Now, fifty years since that publication, as well as producing a plethora of journalistic works he's written so many books (some under a pseudonym) that midway through counting them I lost my stamina. Another 'hyper-writer', the five-time Pulitzer finalist Joyce Carol Oates, uncannily also published her first book at twenty-five. Over the next fifty-seven years, she wrote about 150 books in a staggering variety of genres (fantasy, literary fiction, biography, criticism, plays, memoir), some of which – in yet another curious parallel to Banville – were published under a pen-name. Oates's name is 'synonymous with productivity,' *The New York Times* once opined.

To be so extraordinarily fertile you must be quite single-minded. Another prolific writer, Stephen King, writes every day while working on a book (and he is almost always working on a book) – weekends, Christmases, family birthdays. Balzac, who in 1842 alone published eight books, kept an even stricter writing schedule. This is how he described his daily routine:

> I go to bed at six or seven in the evening, like the hens. I am awakened at one o'clock in the morning and work till eight. At eight I sleep for an hour and a half. Then I have something light to eat, and a cup of black coffee, and harness my wagon until four. I receive callers, I take a bath or I go out, and after dinner I go back to bed.

Some biographers blame Balzac's fragile health and premature death at fifty-one on his taxing routine. (His habit of fuelling himself with obscene quantities of Turkish-style coffee, which he prepared with little water as a mud-thick brew, didn't help either.) Still, I suspect many writers would be envious of his workaholism, considering how commonly we bemoan our inability to write faster and faster, more and more.

The question is, should we be?

Much has been said about the virtue of slow writing, but not so much about the virtue of slowing down between books, and not only in order to wait for the right subject. Even if you already know what to write next, it doesn't mean the best thing is to begin it immediately after finishing the previous work. First, I suggest pondering the reasons for the urgency you might feel. Is it artistic urgency? Do you really need to express so much that it requires constant writing, or is it more about ambition and peer pressure, so prevalent in literary milieus?

It is not uncommon to feel inadequate, a fraud, not only in the face of Balzac but writers you might know personally, the ones who churn out a novel every year, and perhaps expect you to do the same. The American poet Kate Angus, in her essay 'Maybe the Secret to Writing is Not Writing?' describes such pressures:

> Whenever I see people at parties, frequently one of the first questions posed is 'What's your latest project?' And if I dare

to log on to any social media site, my newsfeed unscrolls a series of status updates from friends and acquaintances posting about their recent publications. It's so easy to feel like I'm falling behind, like I should always be producing.

But writing a book can be deeply depleting. The work rarely stops after writers leave their proverbial writing desk. They watch television or chat with friends and all the while their mind consciously and unconsciously mulls over their projects. Sometimes this intense cognitive and emotional labour goes on even in dreams. One day, however, the work is finished. The overdriven brain stops in its tracks, baffled, exhausted yet unused to a pause, and now unsure what to do next. The feeling of emptiness that can follow a lengthy period of creation can be profoundly discomforting. Not a few books are begun in the hurry to resolve such discomfort, to fill the void, to avoid the not-writing.

However, the rush from one book to another (which is, by the way, pretty much how I used to conduct my love life) isn't particularly conducive to doing your artistic best. The quality of ultra-productive writers' oeuvres varies. Not every book by Balzac or Oates does justice to the extent of their talent. Some would have clearly benefited from slow-cooking, from more thought and distance, and some just lack that certain magic that the author's other works possess.

On the other end of productivity continuum, things are also not clear-cut. Take J. D. Salinger who, having never been particularly prolific, closed shop in his mid-forties, then lived for several more decades occasionally writing just for his private pleasure. (The rest of the time he spent falling in and out of love, fathering children and, my favourite, indulging his passion for movies.) Or Rimbaud, who surpassed even Salinger in cutting brilliance short. Having said, poetically, what he had to say by the age of twenty, he left his native France to traverse three continents and do the kind of living overachieving writers never do, including a sojourn in a jungle, and trading in coffee and firearms. Yet (this 'yet' is particularly aimed at the ambitious among us), the small literary oeuvre Rimbaud and Salinger left behind counts for so much. The two are a part of literary canon just as Balzac is and, arguably, more so than Banville, King and Oates are.

So, the next time you decide to beat yourself up for not being up to Balzacian standards, for slipping in your devotions, please consider that prolific output isn't necessarily a virtue. It is not synonymous with better art. On the other hand, pausing between books for some months, or even years, whatever feels right, can be actually conducive to creativity.

*

Kate Angus likens creative hiatuses to the regeneration of farming soil. Her metaphor makes sense to me. It is easy to see how by letting a depleted mind rest, while nourishing it with fertilisers, you allow ideas – about what to write next or about the particulars of a planned work – to germinate and grow. In this spirit, for some years now I've viewed taking a break between books as a part of my writing process.

What fertilisers writers use, or in less metaphorical terms, what we do during the break, varies between writers. You may like to spend some time to reflect on what works best for you. Sometimes a writer might just rest – get some sleep (while paying attention to their dreams!), read, take their family to the beach. Louise DeSalvo writes that with time Virginia Woolf 'learned to be less obsessive about her art and to take more time for relaxation . . . to enrich her work. She subsequently spent time bowling, doing needlepoint, knitting, bread baking, and listening to music.'

Other writers prefer to fill their breaks with new impressions and experiences, so that all that living composted in the conscious and the unconscious will make their writing, once it's resumed, more fecund and vital. Or as Ann Patchett poetically puts this, on such pages 'life itself stokes the flames of the writing, makes the words whistle and crack, and draws the reader closer to this warm, bright place'. It must be not accidental that so many writers have an appetite for travel. Such a pursuit is likely to layer their works with new sights, tastes, legends, mindsets. Perhaps in line with Rimbaud who suggested writers enrich their art by living risky lives, Graham Greene travelled extensively and deliberately to dangerous places, like Kenya during the Mau Mau Rebellion or Israel just after the Six Day War. Anaïs Nin took risks in other ways, for example, by conducting challenging love affairs, some in tandem, in between (as well as during) writing her books. And Hemingway, oh Hemingway, when he didn't write he was indiscriminately chasing any perils, be it wrangling a shark or hunting for German submarines during the Second World War.

I think about all this whenever I catch myself yet again bemoaning the fact that rather than dedicating myself to writing and working in writing-friendly jobs from a young age, until my mid-thirties I greedily sampled other demanding occupations, which put temporary breaks on my creative practice. Among other things, I worked in a singles' agency and in mental health, organised dance parties and taught social sciences across several universities. A part of me still mourns those unfocused years, but another part recognises how my adventures and misadventures have given me some of my writing subjects. More so, they've given me a perspective through which to sift my creative impulses. It is this latter part of me that is puzzled by the fact that some writers *can* write well without doing intense living, without immersing themselves in the ocean of reality swarming with sharks and knitting needles. But maybe if they did they'd have been even better writers?

*

What if, by some magic, I was endowed with the ability to write dozens of good books without pausing, if only I cared to? *Should* I care? Should I spend the lion's share of the time allocated to me on earth writing?

The Scottish poet Iain Crichton Smith wrote a poem after attending an exhibition of manuscripts by that other ultra-prolific writer, Walter Scott: 'Walking the room together in this merciless galaxy of manuscripts and notes, I am exhausted by such energy . . . What love he must have lost to write so much.' To lead a life chained to a quill, pen, typewriter or keyboard, one is sure to miss out on some love. And sunsets, birds, conversations among the velvet of night, roses, storms external and internal . . . But what if, the devil's advocate in me asks, incessant writing can afford comparable aliveness? Here I am, back full circle to this perennial question of why we write.

Scott (and Balzac) worked relentlessly primarily for prosaic reasons – financial need (and greed?). Today, however, when literature is rarely a lucrative profession, such reasons are less common. Instead, Banville identifies as a graphomaniac, saying that for him stopping writing would be dangerous. Oates echoes him as she describes, in an interview, feeling 'rather melancholy, or derailed, or simply lost, because I completed a novel some weeks ago and haven't begun another.' Stephen King says writing is his favourite place to be. Perhaps this is the thing about the intense need of these authors to write – that it originates in the escapist impulse, to be somewhere else.

This motivation isn't exclusive to ultra-prolific writers. I, for instance, work most productively when I am at my most settled, when nothing electrifying is unfolding in my life, so I seek to experience intensity in the space of writing. At such times, writing is my playground, a liminal place where adulthood is suspended. I play there often feeling lost. Sometimes even bored. Or bullied. But I would rather not go home yet.

Still, for me writing is a fallible escape. Like a sandcastle, my creative space cannot withstand for long the pressures of reality – wind, ocean waves, my emotional baggage. My earthly sorrows, joys and desires eventually follow me there. Perhaps some writers are more immune to reality than others. Or for some living is more a passion, for others more a chore. Some need to escape from whatever it is that haunts them – loss, boredom, private terrors, the unbearable lightness (and brevity) of being – more than others do. In this line of thinking, ultra-productivity can be framed as a matter of temperament and personal history, and a preference for a different kind of happiness. Or compulsion? Listen to Kafka confessing in his diary:

> When it became clear to my organism that writing was the most productive direction for my being to take, everything rushed in that direction and left empty all those activities which were directed towards joys of sex, eating, drinking, philosophical reflections, and above all music.

So perhaps another question to ask yourself before you worry what to say about your 'new book' at the next literary soiree is: What life do I want to live?

I wish I'd asked myself this earlier. There were times when I tried to do everything at once – those demanding jobs, intense love affairs and friendships, elaborate housekeeping *and* regular writing; I lived at an Olympian pace, not doing anything particularly well. At other times, I'd follow Kafka's example and prioritise writing over all else. But in my case, I did this out of vanity rather than an artistic need. I'd sacrifice relationships and other essentials at the altar of publication dreams. Or I wouldn't write at all, instead living adventurously and passionately, but suffering excessive guilt about not writing.

Now that I've approached middle age and my horizon is shrinking, I no longer have the stamina to live so hectically, or give up what I love, or live in a state of permanent frustration. I have no choice but to face the truth: I don't want to live *in order* to create. I prefer it the other way around. As absorbing as writing is, I also love getting my hands dirty in the garden soil or cake dough, or to use them to caress my husband. I love the drama of life and also to live slowly, horizontally, dreamily, with someone else's words in my hands or on the screen in front of me. Often, more than writing I love to *have written*, so that I can then indulge without guilt in all that other stuff . . . And once I have done my indulging, I return to writing with renewed desire.

There is also this. When my writing goes well, time disappears. More than once I have emerged at the end of a workday dazed, dishevelled, exhilarated but also anxious that I am shortening my life by swallowing chunks of it too quickly, greedily. I don't want to die so soon.

Fortunately, between Rimbaud's retirement at an age when many writers haven't even begun their creative lives and Oates's handwringing over not-writing for several weeks there are plenty of other modes of being a writer. Even though I rarely lack a writing subject, I have decided to return to my earlier fluctuations between writing and not writing, just without feeling so much guilt about either mode, particularly considering that even during 'non-writing times' I still write, but irregularly and without deadlines. I might do some short works or experiment with longer ones that either don't take off or remain simmering in my neural circuits until I feel ready for the writing stage of my cycle, when once again completing a book takes priority. And how do I know when it is time to do the latter? It's hard to explain; it is this feeling I get akin to what Virginia Woolf describes:

> as for my next book I am going to hold myself from writing it till I have it impending in me: grown heavy in my mind like a ripe pear; pendant, gravid, asking to be cut or it will fall.

Cyclical writing will not suit every writer, but it is useful periodically to take stock of your artistic and personal needs, to be aware of what makes you happy and fulfilled as opposed to what you think *should* fulfil you. If you take joy in living as monastic a life as Philip Roth did, reduced in his last years to five essentials – food, writing, exercise, sleep and solitude (he called this 'a wonderful experience'), then do it. But if you don't, following your non-writing happiness shouldn't stop your work, as long as when you do write you dedicate yourself to it. And I'll tell you one more thing: it took me a while to accept that I can take my time to live and still be a writer, but once I did, the air turned clearer, the sky brighter and the flapping sound of muses' splendid wings grew louder in my ear.

EPILOGUE: STOKING THE FLAMES

1.
'The freedom to create is somehow linked with facility of access to those obscure regions below the conscious mind,' writes the philosopher of nature Loren Eiseley. If he's right, which I think he is, then it is not on Mount Helicon but in the underground geography of us that muses huddle, their dark heavy wings folded as they stoke their terrifying fires.
2.
The poet Andrew Motion took Beechams Powders to fool his body into simulating cold symptoms. The fever created a tunnel in his mind, which spiralled downdowndown, away from the ego and into the flames.
3.
The prose writer Erica Jong took lovers.
4.
Kurt Vonnegut didn't know how to write about love. Hemingway would rather discuss bullfights than writing. Kerouac could only play 'Afro-Germanic music' on the piano. The greats can talk about anything, gossip, travel or in the case of Knausgaard changing

nappies, and their words make me burn. It is the *dimensions* of their speech – the expanse of their flair and the depth – that light my fire. I feel elevated when I dip into their minds as captured in *The Paris Review* interviews, letters, diaries, memoirs, biographies. Such reading makes me want to be sharper, bolder, invest more in my inner world and in my art.

5.

Rachel Carson listened to Beethoven. His sixth, seventh and ninth symphonies, she wrote to her lover, made 'some little bit of his marvelous creativeness . . . seep through into my brain cells.'

6.

I listen to my students. In our writing classes small talk doesn't exist. The embers of the spoken words crackle in the air. I return to my study smelling of smoke.

7.

Art begets art. Chagall's crooked villages and violinists, Magritte's faceless lovers and the whippets of Lucian Freud stir the lava of my yearnings and terrors. So do Pina's dancers, their hair flowing along with their gowns and emotions. As I edge towards another's fires, the heat melts the outer world. My throat grows parched, my eyes glow red, my heart pumps blood into my typing fingertips faster, faster . . .

8.

And David Lynch. I love the wit of his dialogue, the suspense, the colours and the beauty of his actors. But his main allure for me resists logical explanation. It has something to do with the closeups of lit matches, the Red Room, Club Silencio wrapped in blue shadows, the eerie vocals of Julee Cruise. It is as if Lynch's imagery and soundscapes are coded expressions of my foundational longings for which I have no exact language – some yearning for mystery but also for penetrating unseen layers of life, and the impulse to weave reality into a myth. His art illuminates and gives form to my miasma, reassuring me not so much of my sanity but that I can be understood in my madness.

I want to write the way Lynch makes cinema.

I begin my writing day by playing a scene from *Fire Walk With Me.*

9.

Maya Angelou brought a Bible with her when she wrote in hotels, to read it aloud: 'And I'll remember how beautiful, how pliable the language is, how it will lend itself.' She also brought bottles of sherry.

10.

In my twenties, I briefly dated a man whom I so displeased (for reasons unclear to me) that after our breakup he referred to me as 'that woman who *fancies* herself a writer'. His words spurred me into action. I promptly finished writing my second book and had it published. Now, *this* would show him! Or more importantly, show my mother . . . My mother considered my ambition to live a literary life to be *yerunda*, bullshit, advising me to dedicate myself to *real* occupations – social work, marriage, childrearing. For the natural-born rebel that I am, her opposition was a potent spark. And now that she has grown proud of my books and I no longer date disgruntled lovers, it is harder to come across opposing forces. Most recently, I hit the jackpot when my publisher suggested I write this book. I agreed immediately, because I wanted to, but also because I was terrified of my then-plan to revive my 'dead novel'. Yet once I began working to a deadline and the plan was cancelled, the novel's fire rekindled. Defiantly, I now sneak off for an occasional illicit rendezvous with my old flame.

11.

Upon visiting Paris, Albert Camus remarked: 'I now have the kind of attachment to this city that one has for women who cheat on you, which is to say I'd be extremely unhappy if I lived here, but at the same time so enriched that I'd be obliged to write.' Soon after, he moved to Paris.

12.

Inspiration isn't a myth, scientists say, but the time when our inhibition drops its guard and falls asleep. It is then that ideas, which normally don't associate, get together for a close dance to the tune of alpha waves. To induce this state, I first empty my mind of mundane concerns, pinning them down onto to-do lists (harvest tomatoes, pick up children . . .). Then I recline on the couch and re-read some passages from my work-in-progress. Afterwards I wait. I stare at the bright-red bougainvillea visible through the glass backdoor until my mind warms up and loosens. If I am lucky, random images and phrases appear. *An orange frock . . . She could easily imagine him as a snake . . . The eucalyptus bush . . . A dying animal . . .* The fragments pair, pirouetting past me. *The terror of the woman in the orange frock watching the animal dying among eucalyptuses. And her snake-like lover, who wouldn't even get out of the car to help . . .* By now I am no longer still, my fingers drumming on the keyboard in an effort to capture the fire burning on the dance floor.

13.

Rilke insisted that 'what is needed is, in the end, simply this: solitude, great inner solitude'.

14.

Some stories can be only told at night, under the cover of darkness and silence, when the mind is exhausted, inclined to play havoc with us. These stories have the sound of a whisper, a stifled gasp. They bear a nocturnal signature, a particular menace impossible to create at daytime. I listen to the sleeping breath of my husband. The stars are burning just beyond the partly open blinds in our bedroom, their gleaming fingers pointing towards my study. I am drowsy and can barely keep my eyes open. I am coming.

15.

'Always be drunk,' said Baudelaire.

16.

'Write what makes you blush,' I say again and again in my classes. And always somebody is defiant: Why should they? Why shouldn't writing be a distraction, a fun thing rather than all that . . . *burning ache?* Who knows, perhaps this might be true for some, but here is the truth embedded in my body – I blush and the heat of my skin regenerates the fire in me.

MY FOUR WRITING TENETS

1. To write is to read.
2. All writing is rewriting.
3. Write what is urgent.
4. Write what makes you blush.

MY 100 BOOKS (MENTIONED AND UNMENTIONED IN *THE WRITER LAID BARE*)

The following is a mixture of fiction and creative nonfiction books for children and adults (not including poetry and plays, which require their own separate lists). The only thing these books share is that their stories have impressed themselves on my mind permanently, possibly affecting the shape of my thought and writing, and certainly giving me much pleasure.

1. Ali, Monica, *Brick Lane*
2. Andersen, Hans Christian, *Fairy Tales*
3. Åbrink, Elisabeth, *1947: When now begins*
4. Athill, Diana, *Somewhere Towards The End: A Memoir*
5. Auster, Paul, *Leviathan*
6. Auster, Paul, *The New York Trilogy*
7. Babel, Isaac, *The Complete Works of Isaac Babel*
8. de Balzac, Honoré, *Father Goriot*
9. Barnes, Julian, *Flaubert's Parrot*
10. Batuman, Elif, *The Possessed: Adventures With Russian Books And The People Who Read Them*

11. Byatt, A. S., *Angels and Insects*
12. Bulgakov, Mikhail, *The Master and Margarita*
13. Burke, John Muk Muk, *Bridge of Triangles*
14. Capote, Truman, *In Cold Blood*
15. Carroll, Lewis, *Alice in Wonderland*
16. Carter, Angela, *The Bloody Chamber*
17. Chandler, Raymond, *The Big Sleep*
18. Chekhov, Anton, *Collected Stories*
19. Conan Doyle, Arthur, *Sherlock Holmes: The Complete Novels and Stories*
20. Cusk, Rachel, *A Life's Work: On Becoming a Mother*
21. Dalton, Trent, *Boy Swallows Universe*
22. Daum, Meghan, *My Misspent Youth*
23. Dessaix, Robert, *Night Letters*
24. Didion, Joan, *The White Album*
25. Didion, Joan, *Slouching Towards Bethlehem*
26. Dovlatov, Sergei, *The Suitcase*
27. Dumas, Alexandre, *The Count of Monte Cristo*
28. Dumas, Alexandre, *The Three Musketeers*
29. Duras, Marguerite, *The Lover*
30. Dyer, Geoff, *Out of Sheer Rage: Wrestling with D. H. Lawrence*
31. Dyer, Geoff, *Zona: A Book About a Film About a Journey to a Room*
32. Ferrante, Elena, The Neapolitan Novels
33. Fitzgerald, Scott, *The Crack-Up*
34. Fitzgerald, Scott, *The Great Gatsby*
35. Flanner, Janet, *Paris Was Yesterday, 1925–1939*
36. Flaubert, Gustave, *Madame Bovary*
37. Forster, E. M., *A Passage to India*
38. Franzen, Jonathan, *Freedom*
39. Funder, Anna, *Stasiland*
40. Gaiman, Neil, *American Gods*

41. Garner, Helen, *Monkey Grip*
42. Garner, Helen, *Joe Cinque's Consolation: A true story of death, grief and the law*
43. Garner, Helen, *Yellow Notebook: Diaries Volume 1 1978–1987*
44. Giggs, Rebecca, *Fathoms: The World in the Whale*
45. Gogol, Nikolai, *The Collected Tales*
46. Goldman, Francisco, *Say Her Name*
47. Grealy, Lucy, *Autobiography of a Face*
48. Greene, Graham, *Travels With My Aunt*
49. Grimm, Jacob & Grimm, Wilhelm, *Grimms' Fairy Tales*
50. Halligan, Marion, *The Taste of Memory*
51. Hammond, Victoria, *Letters from St Petersburg*
52. Hemingway, Ernest, *A Moveable Feast*
53. Hemley, Robin, *Oblivion*
54. Hugo, Victor, *The Hunchback of Notre Dame*
55. Hustvedt, Siri, *A Plea for Eros*
56. Irving, John, *The Hotel New Hampshire*
57. Irving, John, *A Widow for One Year*
58. Jansson, Tove, The Moomins books (particularly *Moominsummer Madness*)
59. Jong, Erica, *Fear of Flying*
60. Jung, Carl, *Memories, Dreams, Reflections*
61. Keret, Etgar, *The Seven Good Years: A Memoir*
62. Knausgaard, Karl Ove, *My Struggle* series (particularly, *A Man in Love* and *The End*)
63. Kundera, Milan, *The Unbearable Lightness of Being*
64. Kundera, Milan, *The Book of Laughter and Forgetting*
65. Kureishi, Hanif, *Something to Tell You*
66. Lessing, Doris, *The Sweetest Dream*
67. Limonov, Eduard, *It's Me, Eddie*
68. Malcolm Janet, *The Silent Woman: Sylvia Plath and Ted Hughes*
69. de Maupassant Guy, *Complete Original Short Stories*

70. McEwan, Ian, *Black Dogs*
71. Miller, Henry, *Nexus*
72. Millet, Catherine, *The Sexual Life of Catherine M.*
73. Molina, Antonio Muñoz, *Winter in Lisbon*
74. Morris, Jan, *Conundrum*
75. Munro, Alice, *The Beggar Maid*
76. Murakami, Haruki, *The Wind-Up Bird Chronicle*
77. Nabokov, Vladimir, *Lolita*
78. Nafisi, Azar, *Reading Lolita in Teheran: A Memoir in Books*
79. Nelson, Maggie, *The Argonauts*
80. Oz, Amos, *A Tale of Love and Darkness*
81. Patchett, Ann, *Truth and Beauty: A Friendship*
82. Prose, Francine, *Blue Angel*
83. Pung, Alice, *Her Father's Daughter*
84. Rabinyan, Dorit, *Persian Brides*
85. Remarque, Erich Maria, *Arch of Triumph*
86. Remarque, Erich Maria, *Shadows in Paradise*
87. Roiphe, Katie, *In Praise of Messy Lives*
88. Roth, Philip, *Zuckerman Unbound*
89. de Saint-Exupéry, Antoine, *The Little Prince*
90. Sayer, Mandy, *Dreamtime Alice: A Memoir*
91. Shriver, Lionel, *The Post-Birthday World*
92. Shteyngart, Gary, *The Russian Debutante's Handbook*
93. Smith, Zadie, *Changing My Mind: Occasional Essays*
94. Soldatow, Sasha, *Mayakovsky in Bondi*
95. Thomas, D. M., *The White Hotel*
96. Travers, P. L., The *Mary Poppins* Books
97. Tsiolkas, Christos, *The Slap*
98. Tumarkin, Maria, *Traumascapes: The Power and Fate of Places Transformed by Tragedy*
99. Turgenev, Ivan, *First Love*
100. Ugrešić, Dubravka, *Baba Yaga Laid an Egg*

FURTHER READING ON THE ART OF WRITING (AND READING)

I love books on writing and have a separate bookshelf dedicated to them in my study. None of these, however, are what you'd call 'how-to' books, the kind that offer step-by-step guidelines for building a story followed by writing exercises. To my mind, such books are likely to encourage rather formulaic work; on top of that, they can create (possibly inadvertently) the impression that creative writing is nothing but a skill.

The books that live on my shelf are of a different ilk. They acknowledge the mystery of literary creation. They approach their subject with some degree of reverence – not to master and conquer it but to tentatively brush up against its glory and in the process tell us something useful about our own art.

These books reliably spark my inspiration, but not in the fluffy, zany way of 'connecting you to your inner muse'. Rather, they push me out of my comfort zone, introduce me to new worlds of literature and ideas, provoke me to think in more complex ways about the ethics of writing and about life in general, and sometimes sweep me off my feet by the sheer beauty of their prose. Some of them are for creative writers of all genres, others are more specialised. And not all of them are what we traditionally define as 'writing books'. Some are collections of interviews with renowned authors executed by impressive interviewers (often themselves writers), others are written in the form of letters, or contain fictional elements or literary criticism, or are autobiographical. Whatever their shape may be, all of them, I find, guide me to places where writers should go – to the precipice.

Appelfeld, Aharon, *A Table for One: Under the Light of Jerusalem*

Bashevis, Singer Isaac & Burgin, Richard, *Conversations with Isaac Bashevis Singer*

Benedict, Elizabeth (ed.), *Mentors, Muses and Monsters: 30 Writers on the People Who Changed Their Lives*

Bird, Carmel, *Dear Writer . . . Revisited: The Classic Guide to Writing Fiction*

Brophy, Kevin, *Explorations in Creative Writing*

Carman, Luke, *Intimate Antipathies*

Ferrante, Elena, *Frantumaglia: A Writer's Journey*

Gardner, John, *On Becoming a Novelist*

Gornick, Vivian, *The Situation and the Story: The Art of Personal Narrative*

Grenville, Kate and Woolfe, Sue, *Making Stories: How Ten Australian novels were written*

Hemley, Robin, *A Field Guide for Immersion Writing: Memoir, Journalism and Travel*

Koval, Ramona, *Tasting Life Twice: Conversations With Remarkable Writers*

Lazar, David (ed.), *Truth in Nonfiction: Essays*

Marfording, Annette, *Celebrating Australian Writing: Conversations with Australian authors*

Miller, Henry, *The Books in My Life*

Miller, Patti, *Writing True Stories: The complete guide to writing autobiography, memoir, personal essay, biography, travel and creative nonfiction*

Nabokov, Vladimir, *Strong Opinions*

Prose, Francine, *Reading like a Writer: A Guide for People Who Love Books and for Those Who Want to Write Them*

Rilke, Rainer Maria, *Letters to a Young Poet*

Walker, Brenda (ed.), *The Writer's Reader: A Guide to Writing Fiction and Poetry*

Wood, James, *How Fiction Works*

The Paris Review Interviews volumes (more interviews are available on the magazine's website for free: http://www.theparisreview.org/interviews)

ACKNOWLEDGEMENTS

For some years I'd entertained a timid little dream to make a book out of my ongoing blog on writing called *The Writing Life* (an offspring of a monthly blog I used to write for Writers Victoria). At the same time, the oh-so-familiar refrain of 'who even *are you* to advise others?' kept playing in my head, so, apart from a few non-committal remarks to my husband and a couple of friends, I never discussed this idea with anyone. If I was more superstitious, however, I'd have said I must have manifested my desire to a rather attentive universe, because this is what happened in 2019. My dear publisher, Jane Curry of Ventura Press, called a meeting – to discuss some book idea she had in mind for me, she said. I thought it would be another anthology to follow the two I'd already edited for Ventura. But then Jane said, 'You know this blog you've got. We would like to see a book from you on this topic.' Oh man . . .

Certainly, the biggest thank you for this book's existence goes not to the universe but to Jane. It is not often, at least in my experience, that an author meets the publisher of their dreams (or a publisher who is also a mind-reader). Working with Jane feels like home – literary home that is. Thank you also to Ventura's current and former team – Edward Schiller, Zoe Hale, Holly Jeffery and Sophie Hodge – for their warm and unwavering support, and expertise. And, Katia Ariel, your wise editing has made a great difference; thank you!

A recurrent theme of this book is the importance of relationships in writers' lives. In this department I feel blessed. Bradley Dawson, who has seen almost everything I've ever written in English, cast his usual magic on the earlier drafts of *The Writer Laid Bare*. Dmetri Kakmi, my generous friend, spent many hours on a later draft, armed with his proverbial professional editor's red pen, knocking my book into shape. Cassie Lane and Rochelle Siemienowicz were my close writing companions throughout the gloom of lockdowns, helping me to persevere and offering insightful feedback. Kate Murdoch promptly read a draft, making excellent suggestions. And I am grateful to the following friends for reading parts of the book and for their overall (ongoing!) support: Paul Dalgarno (thank you also for your and Jon Ronson's quotes), Kate Goldsworthy, Myfanwy Jones, Ashley Kalagian-Blunt, Leah Kaminsky, Nicola Redhouse and Jenny Valentish.

It took me two years to write *The Writer Laid Bare*, but really this work is a culmination of my lifelong passion for books and for the art of creating them, and my literary worldview has not been formed in isolation. Dorit Zilberman and Lior Ofek were instrumental in my youth, when I still lived in Israel. In Australia, I was fortunate to come across Peter Bishop whose wisdom, erudition and unmatched passion for (any) arts were essential to who I became as a writer in English. Gratitude also to the following literary friends who for years have been expanding my mind with conversation and book recommendations (and with their own writing!) as well as offering practical help: Caroline Baum, Josiane Behmoiras, Perle Besserman, Nadine Davidoff, Karla Dondio, Robin Hemley, Kate

Holden, Belinda Johnson, Ross Karavis, Hayley Katzen, Simon Klimowitsky, Ramona Koval, Jane Messer, Alice Nelson, Virginia Peters, Alice Pung, Angela Savage, Graeme Simsion, Jane Sullivan, Maria Tumarkin and Linda Weste.

I thank the following literary organisations, which have been important to my writing life: Varuna the Writers' House, Writers Victoria and Writing NSW. And deep gratitude to my current and former writing students and mentees, starting with my very first students at Prahran Mission whose words and dear faces are forever imprinted on my psyche – I thank you for your contagious passion for storytelling and your willingness to share it with me.

One of the greatest misfortunes that can happen to a family is to have a writer born into it. My parents Geula and Avraham Kofman, my brothers Moshe, Gershom and Israel Kofman, and my sisters-in-law Svetlana Bregman and Vivi Kofman have dealt with this problem with grace and fortitude, and I cannot tell you how lucky I feel to have you in my life. My gorgeous husband, Daryl Efron, willingly walked into the said misfortune and remained there throughout the many trials and tribulations of my book creations, putting up with my moods and insane deadlines, my writing-related travels and anxieties. All my love to you!

Finally, I thank all those dead and living writers who have been my literary beacons, whose artistic courage and wisdoms help me daily to navigate the perils of laying myself bare on the page.

REFERENCES

PROLOGUE

p.viii: 'As Philip Roth said . . .' Philip Roth, The Art of Fiction. In Gourevitch, Philip (ed.) (2009). *The Paris Review Interviews, Vol.4.* Canongate Books: Edinburgh, p.206

'Or as the bestselling American novelist James M. Cain puts it . . .' James M. Cain: The Art of Fiction. In Gourevitch, Philip (ed.) (2006). *The Paris Review Interviews, Vol.1.* Picador: New York, p.224

p.ix: 'so it was easier to write as Jonathan Franzen thinks writers should . . .' Franzen, Jonathan (2016). Introduction. In Franzen, Jonathan (ed.). *The Best American Essays 2016.* Houghton Mifflin Harcourt: New York, p.xx.

PART ONE

p.4: 'like in this (not atypical) account by Albert Camus . . .' Todd, Olivier (1997). *Albert Camus: A life.* Carroll & Graf Publishers: New York, p.228

Where writing springs from

p.8: 'Oz writes that the one impulse that underpins his otherwise diverse works is . . .' Oz, Amos (2005). *A Tale of Love and Darkness.* Vintage: London, p.305

p.9: 'He offers four, arguing that . . .' Orwell, George (1946). Why I Write. https://www.orwellfoundation.com/the-orwell-foundation/orwell/essays-and-other-works/why-i-write/

p.10: '"Being an egomaniac and a narcissist, I had to make my inner world public," John Banville announced publicly.' Anonymous (18 November 2017). The SRB Interview: John Banville. *Scottish Review of Books.* https://www.scottishreviewofbooks.org/2017/11/the-srb-interview-john-banville/

'the Norwegian writer Karl Ove Knausgaard wrote . . .' Knausgaard, Karl Ove (2018). *The End.* Harvill Secker: London, p.164

p.11: 'The American writer Anna Quindlen thinks that . . .' Quindlen, Anna (2014). In Paul, Pamela (ed.). *By the Book: Writers on literature and the literary life from* The New York Times Book Review. Picador: New York, p.164

p.12: 'Some scientists think creative writing can also promote the wisdom of *self*-understanding.' For example, see Bolton, Gillie (1999). *The Therapeutic Potential of Creative Writing.* Jessica Kingsley Publishers: London; Pennebaker, J.W. & Seagal, J. D. (1999). Forming a story: The health benefits of narrative. *Journal of Clinical Psychology*, Vol.55(10), pp.1243–1254; Sampson, Fiona (ed.) (2004). *Creative Writing in Health and Social Care.* Jessica Kingsley Publishers: London.

'Studies show the reflective writing phase helps reduce pathological cognitive patterns . . .' Damianakis, T. (2001). Postmodernism, Spirituality, and the Creative Writing Process:

Implications for social work practice, *Families in Societies: The journal of contemporary human services*, Vol.82(1), January, pp.23–40; Freely, M. (2004). Writing as Therapeutic Practice. In Sampson, Fiona (ed.). *Creative Writing in Health and Social Care*. Jessica Kingsley Publishers: London, pp.79–91; Klauser, Henriette Anne (2003). *With Pen in Hand*. Perseus Publishing: Seattle.

'Jonathan Franzen argues in his essay 'On Autobiographical Fiction' that . . .' Franzen, Jonathan (2012). *Farther Away*. Fourth Estate: London, p.129

p.13: 'In his masterpiece, *The End*, Knausgaard suggests a certain psychological void . . .' Knausgaard, Karl Ove (2018). *The End*. Harvill Secker: London, p.633

Finding your subject

p.18: 'as V. S. Naipaul put it . . .' V. S. Naipaul, The Art of Fiction. In Gourevitch, Philip (ed.) (2009). *The Paris Review Interviews, Vol.4*. Canongate Books: Edinburgh, p.279

p.19: 'Isaac Bashevis Singer talks along these lines . . .' Bashevis Singer, Isaac & Burgin, Richard (1986). *Conversations with Isaac Bashevis Singer*. Farrar, Straus & Giroux: New York, p.87

'Elena Ferrante describes in *Frantumaglia* how she chooses her subjects in this spirit . . .' Ferrante, Elena (2016). *Frantumaglia: A writer's journey*. Europa Editions: New York, p.73

'The American writer Kate Christensen describes in her memoir, *Blue Plate Special*, how she wrote her wounds . . .' Christensen, Kate (2013). *Blue Plate Special: An autobiography of my appetites*. Doubleday: New York, p.252

p.20: 'Jonathan Franzen, who rarely fictionalises events from his life, nevertheless . . .' Franzen, Jonathan (2012). *Farther Away*. Fourth Estate: London, pp.129–130

'As Bashevis Singer tells us . . .' Bashevis Singer, Isaac & Burgin, Richard (1986). *Conversations with Isaac Bashevis Singer*. Farrar, Straus & Giroux: New York, p.87

'Graham Greene writes in his memoir, *Ways of Escape* . . .' Greene, Graham (1999). *Ways of Escape*. Vintage: London, p.79

'Amos Oz in his younger years, for instance, was ashamed of his desire . . .' Oz, Amos (2005). *A Tale of Love and Darkness*. Vintage: London, pp.470–471

p.21: 'As the renowned American literary critic James Wood puts it . . .' Wood, James (2008). *How Fiction Works*. Picador: New York, p.126

'Highsmith, who argued, with her characteristic aplomb . . .' Highsmith, Patricia (2016). *Plotting and Writing Suspense Fiction*. Sphere: London, p.122

p.22: 'Dessaix writes that the only shared denominator . . .' Dessaix, Robert (2012). Climbing the Helicon. In Dessaix, Robert. *As I Was Saying*. Random House: North Sydney, p.114

'She had good reasons, Garner writes in *Joe Cinque's Consolation* . . .' Garner, Helen (2005). *Joe Cinque's Consolation: A true story of death, grief and the law*. Picador: Sydney, pp.12–13

p.24: 'The Guyanese-British writer Fred D'Aguiar, for example, is concerned with race relations . . .' Weste, Linda (2020). *Inside the Verse Novel: Writers on writing*. Australian Scholarly: North Melbourne, p.2

p.25: 'Karl Ove Knausgaard speaks along these lines in his interview for *The Paris Review* . . .' Wood, James & Knausgaard, Karl Ove (2014). Writing *My Struggle*: An exchange. *The Paris Review*, issue 211, Winter. https://www.theparisreview.org/miscellaneous/6345/writing-my-struggle-an-exchange-james-wood-karl-ove-knausgaard

p.26: 'Franzen's conviction that . . .' Franzen, Jonathan (2012). *Farther Away*. Fourth Estate: London, p.130

Into the wilderness

p.29: 'Helen Garner, for example, describes the initial sketches . . .' Grenville, Kate & Woolfe, Sue (2001). *Making Stories: How ten Australian novels were written*. Allen & Unwin: Crows Nest, p.224

p.30: 'There is even some neuroscientific evidence of this, that creative activity in its initial stages is an intuitive process.' Claxton, Guy (2005). *The Wayward Mind: An intimate history of the unconscious.* Abacus: London, p.224

'Interestingly, the visual artist Max Ernst described his creative process . . .' Zunshine, Lisa (2008). *Strange Concepts and the Stories They Make Possible: Cognition, culture, narrative.* Johns Hopkins University Press: Baltimore, p.142

'To enable such chance meetings, the cognitive scientist Guy Claxton advises . . .' Claxton, Guy (2005). *The Wayward Mind: An intimate history of the unconscious.* Abacus: London, pp.267–268

Builders and renovators

p.37: 'Ian McEwan, who works like this, says he pretends . . .' Begley, Adam (2002). Ian McEwan, The Art of Fiction No. 173. *The Paris Review*, issue 162, Summer. https://www.theparisreview.org/interviews/393/the-art-of-fiction-no-173-ian-mcewan

'William Styron perfects . . .' William Styron, The Art of Fiction. In Gourevitch Philip (ed.) (2009). *The Paris Review Interviews, Vol.4.* Canongate Books: Edinburgh, p.4

'He has even developed a formula that reliably works for him, where he completes a novel in what he calls. . .' King, Stephen (2001). *On Writing: A memoir of the craft.* Hodder & Stoughton: London, p.248

'Carey begins writing each chapter . . .' Carey, Peter (n.d.). *Author Q&A.* Gotham Writers. https://www.writingclasses.com/toolbox/author-q-a/peter-carey?page=2

p.38: 'The American novelist Richard Price works similarly . . .' Richard Price, The Art of Fiction. In Gourevitch, Philip (ed.) (2006). *The Paris Review Interviews, Vol.1.* Picador: New York, p.384

'Not only does she revise them as she creates a story, but she retypes them . . .' Joan Didion, The Art of Fiction. In Gourevitch, Philip (ed.) (2006). *The Paris Review Interviews, Vol.1.* Picador: New York, p.476

'John Steinbeck advises along these lines . . .' Popova, Maria (13 March 2012). 6 Writing Tips From John Steinbeck. *The Atlantic.* https://www.theatlantic.com/entertainment/archive/2012/03/6-writing-tips-from-john-steinbeck/254351/

Writing as layering

p.44: 'The American poet Marianne Moore once remarked . . .' Marianne Moore, The Art of Poetry. In Gourevitch, Philip (ed.) (2009). *The Paris Review Interviews, Vol.4.* Canongate Books: Edinburgh, p.47

p.45: 'Sometimes all the first draft is good for, says the Australian novelist Finola Moorhead . . .' Grenville, Kate & Woolfe, Sue (2001). *Making Stories: How ten Australian novels were written.* Allen & Unwin: Crows Nest, p.217

'Graham Greene's novel *Brighton Rock*, for example . . .' Greene, Graham (1999). *Ways of Escape.* Vintage: London, p.77

p.46: 'Neuroscientists agree that pausing the creative activity reactivates our unconscious and that this part . . .' Claxton, Guy (2005). *The Wayward Mind: An intimate history of the unconscious.* Abacus: London, pp.223–224

'He would find that in the morning . . .' Greene, Graham (1999). *Ways of Escape.* Vintage: London, p.275

'our work-in-progress potentially remains . . .' Krauss, Nicole (25 May 2011). *On Writing 'Great House'.* HuffPost. https://www.huffpost.com/entry/nicole-krauss-on-writing-_b_764806

p.47: 'Vladimir Nabokov rewrote his words so much that . . .' Nabokov, Vladimir (2000). *Speak, Memory: An autobiography revisited.* Penguin: New York, p.157

Taming the lion

p.48: 'The American writer Annie Dillard writes . . .' Dillard, Annie (1990), *The Writing Life.* Harper Perennial: New York, p.52

p.51: 'While we're working on a book, Helen Garner says . . .' Grenville, Kate & Woolfe, Sue (2001). *Making Stories: How ten Australian novels were written.* Allen & Unwin: Crows Nest, p.62

p.53: 'Here is Albert Camus writing to his lover . . .' Todd, Olivier (1997). *Albert Camus: A life.* Carroll & Graf Publishers: New York, p.407

'John McPhee, one of the pioneers of the creative nonfiction genre . . .' Hessler, Peter (2010). John McPhee, The Art of Nonfiction No. 3. *The Paris Review*, issue 192, Spring. https://www.theparisreview.org/interviews/5997/the-art-of-nonfiction-no-3-john-mcphee

p.55: 'The American writer A. J. Jacobs writes along these lines . . .' Kofman, Lee (29 August 2014). That Damn First Draft. *The Writing Life.* http://leekofman.com.au/the-writing-life/damn-first-draft/

'The Australian novelist Charlotte Wood prefers . . .' Kofman, Lee (29 August 2014). That Damn First Draft. *The Writing Life.* http://leekofman.com.au/the-writing-life/damn-first-draft/

'When the Australian memoirist Kate Holden writes . . .' Kofman, Lee (29 August 2014). That Damn First Draft. *The Writing Life.* http://leekofman.com.au/the-writing-life/damn-first-draft/

p.56: 'Trollope used this method strictly . . .' Parini, Jay (30 July 1989). The More They Write, the More They Write. *The New York Times.* https://www.nytimes.com/1989/07/30/books/the-more-they-write-the-more-they-write.html

'Hemingway, for example, was satisfied with writing as little as 450 words a day . . .' see Ernest Hemingway, The Art of Fiction. In Gourevitch, Philip (ed.) (2006). *The Paris Review Interviews, Vol.1.* Picador: New York.

p.57: 'I'll quote Jeanette Winterson's writing advice . . .' Anonymous (20 February 2010). Ten Rules for Writing Fiction (Part Two). *The Guardian.* https://www.theguardian.com/books/2010/feb/20/10-rules-for-writing-fiction-part-two

'Camus – an enthusiastic dancer and womaniser who often had three or four lovers . . .' Todd, Olivier (1997). *Albert Camus: A life.* Carroll & Graf Publishers: New York, p.101

'To do this violence, Camus would leave his wife, children and mistresses . . .' Todd, Olivier (1997). *Albert Camus: A life.* Carroll & Graf Publishers: New York, p.406

The writer's space

p.58: 'he describes in his memoir, *A Table for One* . . .' Appelfeld, Aharon (2007). *A Table for One: Under the light of Jerusalem.* The Toby Press: New Milford, p.63

p.59: 'It was also in cafés that he honed his skills of observation and learned how to translate abstract emotions . . .' Appelfeld, Aharon (2007). *A Table for One: Under the light of Jerusalem.* The Toby Press: New Milford, p.34

'The Turkish novelist Orhan Pamuk writes that . . .' Orhan Pamuk: The Art of Fiction. In Gourevitch, Philip (ed.) (2009). *The Paris Review Interviews, Vol.4.* Canongate Books: Edinburgh, p.376

p.60: 'Maya Angelou used to set up . . .' Maya Angelou, The Art of Fiction. In Gourevitch, Philip (ed.) (2009). *The Paris Review Interviews, Vol.4.* Canongate Books: Edinburgh, p.239

p.61: 'he installed a specially designed gigantic desk with two working surfaces in his study . . .' Parini, Jay (30 July 1989). The More They Write, the More They Write. *The New York Times.* https://www.nytimes.com/1989/07/30/books/the-more-they-write-the-more-they-write.html

'He has said his "productivity breakthrough" came when he disconnected the computer . . .' Child, Lee (2014). In Paul, Pamela (ed.). *By the Book: Writers on literature and the literary life from* The New York Times Book Review. Picador: New York, p.116

p.62: 'Louise DeSalvo, for example – that most plan-oriented of writers – likes working in busy public places . . .' DeSalvo, Louise (2014). *The Art of Slow Writing: Reflections on time, craft and creativity.* St Martin's Griffin: New York, p.64

'Not dissimilarly, the Australian writer Beverley Farmer recounts in her book, *A Body of Water* . . .' Farmer, Beverley (1990). *A Body of Water.* University of Queensland Press: Brisbane, p.78

'The Austrian satirist Karl Kraus had even higher expectations . . .' Scambler, Graham (n.d.). Vienna's Cafe Central. *Graham Scambler.* http://www.grahamscambler.com/viennas-cafe-central/

p.147: 'The wellbeing he experienced in those places fueled his work . . .' Hemingway, Ernest (1996). *A Moveable Feast.* Arrow Books: London, p.5

The writer's body

p.67: 'Woolf then, as her scholar Louise DeSalvo writes . . .' DeSalvo, Louise (2014). *The Art of Slow Writing: Reflections on time, craft and Creativity.* St Martin's Griffin: New York, p.50

'Philip Roth also used to walk . . .' Henley, Jon (13 May 2013). How Dan Brown and Other Authors Defeat Writer's Block. *The Guardian.* https://www.theguardian.com/books/shortcuts/2013/may/13/dan-brown-authors-writers-block

p.68: 'The bestselling novelist Dan Brown is the most acrobatic writer . . .' Henley Jon (13 May 2013). How Dan Brown and Other Authors Defeat Writer's Block. *The Guardian.* https://www.theguardian.com/books/shortcuts/2013/may/13/dan-brown-authors-writers-block

'Joyce Carol Oates, who runs regularly in between blocks of writing . . .' Ripatrazone, Nick (12 November 2015). Why Writers Run. *The Atlantic.* https://www.theatlantic.com/entertainment/archive/2015/11/why-writers-run/415146/

'He makes the point that . . .' Ripatrazone, Nick (12 November 2015). Why Writers Run. *The Atlantic.* https://www.theatlantic.com/entertainment/archive/2015/11/why-writers-run/415146/

p.69: 'In *The Paris Review* interview he discusses his predilection . . .' Paul Auster, The Art of Fiction. In Gourevitch, Philip (ed.) (2009). *The Paris Review Interviews, Vol.4.* Canongate Books: Edinburgh, p.310

'He usually uses a computer, but when he faces problems . . .' Robert Stone, The Art of Fiction. In Gourevitch, Philip (ed.) (2006). *The Paris Review Interviews, Vol.1.* Picador: New York, p.308

'John Banville also thinks the pace of writing matters.' Anonymous (18 November 2017). The SRB Interview: John Banville. *Scottish Review of Books.* https://www.scottishreviewofbooks.org/2017/11/the-srb-interview-john-banville/

p.71: 'Truman Capote did that while also indulging . . .' Truman Capote, The Art of Fiction. In Gourevitch, Philip (ed.) (2006). *The Paris Review Interviews, Vol.1.* Picador: New York, p.28

'In turn, Hemingway, another writer who turned vertical with ageing . . .' Ernst Hemingway, The Art of Fiction. In Gourevitch, Philip (ed.) (2006). *The Paris Review Interviews, Vol.1.* Picador: New York, pp.36–37

The writer's library

p.73: 'As Philip Roth puts it, for a writer reading is . . .' Philip Roth, The Art of Fiction. In Gourevitch, Philip (ed.) (2009). *The Paris Review Interviews, Vol.4.* Canongate Books: Edinburgh, p.207

'Elena Ferrante is sterner on the topic . . .' Ferrante, Elena (2016). *Frantumaglia: A writer's journey.* Europa Editions: New York, p.269

'Reading can, and should, make us . . .' Miller, Henry (1969). *The Books in My Life.* Penguin: New York, p.32

'Paul Auster's account of his reading as a young writer in his memoir *Hand to Mouth* is more typical . . .' Auster, Paul (1997). *Hand to Mouth: A chronicle of early failure.* Faber & Faber: London, p.29

p.74: 'For Ian McEwan, Philip Larkin's poems are . . .' Ash, Alec (n.d.). Ian McEwan on the Books That Shaped His Novels. *Five Books.* https://fivebooks.com/best-books/ian-mcewan-books-that-shape-his-novels/

'Reading the Austrian writer Peter Handke inspired the younger Helen Garner . . .' Garner, Helen (2019). *Yellow Notebook: Diaries Volume 1 1978–1987.* Text: Melbourne, p.124

'Isabel Allende says *One Hundred Years of Solitude* was instrumental . . .' Allende, Isabel (11 July 2017). *Isabel Allende's Book Bag: 5 Books That Influenced Me.* Daily Beast. https://www.thedailybeast.com/isabel-allendes-book-bag-5-books-that-influenced-me

'In all these ways, as American fantasy writer and literary critic Lev Grossman puts it . . .' An interview with Lev Grossman in Price, Leah (ed.) (2011). *Unpacking My Library: Writers and their books.* Yale University Press: Connecticut, p.90

'That's why whenever Joan Didion begins a new novel . . .' Joan Didion, The Art of Fiction. In Gourevitch, Philip (ed.) (2006). *The Paris Review Interviews, Vol.1.* Picador: New York, p.481

p.76: 'David Sedaris is one, hoping . . .' David Sedaris (2014). In Paul, Pamela (ed.). *By the Book: Writers on literature and the literary life from* The New York Times Book Review. Picador: New York, p.3

p.78: 'Virginia Woolf even set herself . . .' DeSalvo, Louise (2014). *The Art of Slow Writing: Reflections on time, craft and creativity.* St Martin's Griffin: New York, p.60

'reading how Nabokov's character in *The Gift* . . .' Nabokov, Vladimir (2001). *The Gift.* Penguin: London, p.7

'I'll never be capable of writing a sentence as good as the one above or the following one . . .' Nabokov, Vladimir (2000). *Speak, Memory: An autobiography revisited.* Penguin: New York, p.73

p.79: 'As Stephen King writes, sometimes reading . . .' King, Stephen (2001). *On Writing: A memoir of the craft.* Hodder & Stoughton: London, p.166

p.81: 'Salman Rushdie reads poetry while composing his stylish prose . . .' Livings, Jack (2005). Salman Rushdie, The Art of Fiction No. 3. *The Paris Review*, issue 186, Summer. https://www.theparisreview.org/interviews/5531/the-art-of-fiction-no-186-salman-rushdie

The writer's dread

p.83: 'The prolific American novelist Ann Patchett, for example, thinks writer's block is a myth . . .' Patchett, Ann (2011). The Writing Life: Examined in a Digital Minibook. *Nieman Reports.* https://niemanreports.org/articles/the-writing-life-examined-in-a-digital-minibook/

'Another fertile writer, Philip Pullman . . .' Masson, Isidora (n.d.). Read Like a Butterfly, Write Like a Bee. *Journal.* https://vocal.media/journal/read-like-a-butterfly-write-like-a-bee

p.85: 'My semi-educated guess has some support with researchers who have studied the phenomenon of writer's block.' See, for example, Claxton, Guy (2005). *The Wayward Mind: An intimate history of the unconscious.* Abacus: London; and Weaver Flaherty, Alice (2005). *Midnight Disease: The drive to write, writer's block, and the creative brain.* Mariner Books: Boston.

p.87: 'Hunter S. Thompson was fond of remarking . . .' Anonymous (20 February 2005). Hunter S Thompson: In His Own Words. *The Guardian.* https://www.theguardian.com/books/2005/feb/21/huntersthompson

'there is the advice of Hilary Mantel, who thinks solitude is crucial during vulnerable times.' Mantel, Hilary (22 February 2010). Hilary Mantel's Rules for Writers. *The Guardian.* https://www.theguardian.com/books/2010/feb/22/hilary-mantel-rules-for-writers

p.88: 'Anne Lamott believes less in a writing routine and more in loose . . .' Lamott, Anne (2008). *Bird By Bird: Some instructions on writing and life.* Scribe: Carlton, p.92

Fail better

p.90: 'Recently I came across a quote by American visual artist William Bailey . . .' Fallon, Michael (9 September 2008). The Day the Music Died. *Mn Artists.* https://mnartists.walkerart.org/essay-the-day-the-music-died

'Midway into composing his masterpiece, *The Stranger*, Camus wrote to his wife-to-be . . .' Todd, Olivier (1997). *Albert Camus: A life.* Carroll & Graf Publishers: New York, p.108

p.91: 'Garner's difficulties with writing her next book led her to conclude that . . .' Garner, Helen (2019). *Yellow Notebook: Diaries Volume 1 1978–1987.* Text: Melbourne, p.10

'Five years and two more successful books later, she expressed . . .' Garner, Helen (2019). *Yellow Notebook: Diaries Volume 1 1978–1987.* Text: Melbourne, p.91

'Think of V. S. Naipaul who for the first nine months of writing his novel, *A House for Mister Biswas* . . .' V. S. Naipaul, The Art of Fiction. In Gourevitch, Philip (ed.) (2009). *The Paris Review Interviews, Vol.4.* Canongate Books: Edinburgh.

p.92: 'Chabon managed to use the dead bones . . .' Gourney, Douglas (30 December 2010). Michael Chabon: How to salvage a wrecked novel. *The Atlantic.* https://www.theatlantic.com/entertainment/archive/2010/12/michael-chabon-how-to-salvage-a-wrecked-novel/68665/

p.93: 'Rilke writes along these lines in *Letters to a Young Poet* . . .' Rilke, Rainer Maria (2008). *Letters to a Young Poet.* BN Publishing: Hawthorne, p.42

p.94: "I hope you suffer prettily in Paris," somebody said to the American writer Djuna Barnes upon her arrival in that city.' Barnes, Djuna (1974). *Vagaries Malicieux: Two stories.* Small Press Distribution: Berkeley, p.19

PART TWO

p.98: 'Karl Ove Knausgaard says that . . .' Rothman, Joshua (11 November 2018). Karl Ove Knausgaard Looks Back on 'My Struggle'. *The New Yorker.* https://www.newyorker.com/culture/the-new-yorker-interview/karl-ove-knausgaard-the-duty-of-literature-is-to-fight-fiction

'David Grossman, for whom writing means . . .' David Grossman, The Art of Fiction. In Gourevitch, Philip (ed.) (2009). *The Paris Review Interviews, Vol.4.* Canongate Books: Edinburgh, p.421

Voice is you

p.101: 'The American writer A. Alvarez argues in *The Writer's Voice* that . . .' Alvarez, A. (2005). *The Writer's Voice.* Norton: New York, p.17

p.102: 'Or as Raymond Carver puts it . . .' Carver, Raymond (1985). On Writing. *Mississippi Review*, Vol.14(1–2), Winter. https://www.jstor.org/stable/20115383

'Isaac Bashevis-Singer says, along these lines, that . . .' Bashevis Singer, Isaac (1967). Knut Hamsun. Artist of Scepticism: Introduction. In Hamsun Knut. *Hunger.* Picador: London, p.6

p.103: 'Or take this brief passage from Geoff Dyer's memoir *Out of Sheer Rage* . . .' Dyer, Geoff (2009). *Out of Sheer Rage.* Abacus: London, p.86

p.104: 'Filtered through Pung's darkly humorous mind . . .' Pung, Alice (2006). *Unpolished Gem.* Black Inc.:Melbourne, pp.1–2

'Elena Ferrante puts it this way . . .' Ferrante, Elena (2016). *Frantumaglia: A writer's journey.* Europa Editions: New York, p.86

p.105: 'Take this sentence from *The Big Sleep* . . .' Chandler, Raymond (2008). *The Big Sleep.* Penguin: Australia, p.46

p.106: 'In this vein, King advises . . .' King, Stephen (2001). *On Writing: A memoir of the craft.* Hodder & Stoughton: London, pp.225, 184–185

'Knausgaard points out in *The End* . . .' Knausgaard, Karl Ove (2018). *The End.* Harvill Secker: London, p.912

p.107: 'Perhaps it was to counter such denial that Saul Bellow, one of the finest American stylists, felt . . .' Saul Bellow, The Art of Fiction. In Gourevitch, Philip (ed.) (2006). *The Paris Review Interviews, Vol.1.* Picador: New York, p.95

'A unique voice, Knausgaard continues, goes . . .' Knausgaard, Karl Ove (2018). *The End.* Harvill Secker: London, p.912

p.112: 'I thought of Rilke who advised an aspiring writer . . .' Rilke, Rainer Maria (2008). *Letters to a Young Poet.* BN Publishing: Hawthorne, p.12

Voice is style

p.114: 'Take this passage from the novel *The Lover* . . .' Duras, Marguerite (1997). *The Lover.* Pantheon: New York, p.7

p.115: 'Elena Ferrante writes . . .' Ferrante, Elena (2016). *Frantumaglia: A writer's journey.* Europa Editions: New York, p.261

'Or as Proust puts it . . .' Proust, Marcel (2003). *Time Regained.* Modern Library: New York, p.931

p.116: 'Flaubert's contemporaries, the French writers Goncourt Brothers, report him as saying. . .' Taylor, Irene & Alan (eds.) (2008). *The Assassin's Cloak: An anthology of the world's greatest diarists.* Canongate Books: Edinburgh, p.148

'Helen Garner's lyrical as well as sharply ironic prose . . .' Garner, Helen (2008). *The Feel of Steel.* Picador: Sydney, p.54

p.117: 'As E. B. White writes . . .' E. B. White, The Art of the Essay. In Gourevitch, Philip (ed.) (2009). *The Paris Review Interviews, Vol.4.* Canongate Books: Edinburgh, p.151

p.119: 'As far as expressing content goes, a satisfactory sentence, the English novelist Anthony Burgess tells us . . .' Farmer, Beverley (1990). *A Body of Water.* University of Queensland Press: Brisbane, p.156

'The prose in the following excerpt from Kerouac's *On the Road* does just that.' Kerouac, Jack (1976). *On the Road.* Penguin: New York, p.113

p.120: 'As Kerouac said in an interview for *The Paris Review,* when he writes he aspires to follow . . .' Jack Kerouac, The Art of Fiction. In Gourevitch, Philip (ed.) (2009). *The Paris Review Interviews, Vol.4.* Canongate Books: Edinburgh, p.103

'That's why, during revision, the American writer Christopher Beha continuously asks . . .' Beha, Christopher (ed.) (2012). *The Writer's Notebook II: Craft Essays.* Tin House: Portland, p.193

p.121: 'Orhan Pamuk, for example, prefers long sentences . . .' Orhan Pamuk, The Art of Fiction. In Gourevitch, Philip (ed.) (2009). *The Paris Review Interviews, Vol.4.* Canongate Books: Edinburgh, p.397

'There they made a living by performing music and tap dancing . . .' Sayer, Mandy (1999). *Dreamtime Alice.* Vintage: Milsons Point, p.3

p.122: 'Paul Auster's books even originate in what he calls . . .' Paul Auster, The Art of Fiction. In Gourevitch, Philip (ed.) (2009). *The Paris Review Interviews, Vol.4.* Canongate Books: Edinburgh, p.329

Invitation issued

p.124: 'My memoir *Imperfect* opens in this spirit . . .' Kofman, Lee (2019). *Imperfect: How our bodies shape the people we become.* Affirm Press: South Melbourne, p.1

'Take the opening of *The Great Gatsby,* hailed by some critics as the perfect novel . . .' Fitzgerald, F. Scott (2008). *The Great Gatsby.* Penguin: Australia, p.7

p.125: 'Other openings bewitch with what the legendary American editor Gordon Lish calls "magical utterances . . ."' in Tuck, Lily (2009). The Seducer. In Benedict, Elizabeth (ed.). *Mentors, Muses & Monsters: 30 writers on the people who changed their lives.* Free Press: New York, pp.169–179

'The siren call of Nabokov's first line in *Lolita* comes to mind . . .' Nabokov, Vladimir (2000). *The Annotated Lolita.* Penguin: London, p.9

p.126: 'Or consider the magical utterances of Arundhati Roy in the opening of, *The God of Small Things* . . .' Roy, Arundhati (2002). *The God of Small Things.* Penguin: New Delhi, p.1

'In his novel *Something to Tell You,* the English writer Hanif Kureishi comes across as a skilful salesman . . .' Kureishi, Hanif (2008). *Something To Tell You.* Faber & Faber: London, p.3

p.127: 'Annie Dillard advises writers to opt . . .' in Chee, Alexander (2009). Annie Dillard and the Writing Life. In Benedict Elizabeth (ed.). *Mentors, Muses & Monsters: 30 writers on the people who changed their lives.* Free Press: New York, pp.59–69

'This is what Paul Auster does in the opening of his novel *Leviathan* . . .' Auster, Paul (1993). *Leviathan.* Penguin: New York, p.1

p.128: 'It can even utterly shape it, as it does the short story "My Brother and the Girl from Surat Thani" . . .' Ofek, Lior (1998). *Bangkok Stories*. Gvanim: Tel Aviv, p.9 [my translation].

'This is how Bruce Chatwin's novel *On the Black Hill* begins . . .' Chatwin, Bruce (1984). *On the Black Hill*. Penguin: New York, p.9

p.129: 'We can win over readers by starting with the familiar, the relatable, like Jeffrey Eugenides does . . .' Eugenides, Jeffrey (2011). *The Marriage Plot*. Fourth Estate: London, p.3

p.130: 'Similarly, there is nothing particularly dramatic about the opening lines of *The Master and Margarita* . . .' Bulgakov, Mikhail (2003). *The Master and Margarita*. Vintage: London, p.13

Authentic characters

p.133: 'Still, Styron says, they . . .' William Styron, The Art of Fiction. In Gourevitch, Philip (ed.) (2009). *The Paris Review Interviews, Vol.4*. Canongate Books: Edinburgh, p.11

p.134: 'Here is one of the instances where Paul Auster sketches in Benjamin Sachs, the man whose death opens *Leviathan* . . .' Auster, Paul (1993). *Leviathan*. Penguin: New York, p.23

p.135: 'According to Hemingway, in his fiction "there is seven-eights of [iceberg] underwater for every part that shows".' Ernest Hemingway, The Art of Fiction. In Gourevitch, Philip (ed.) (2006). *The Paris Review Interviews, Vol.1*. Picador: New York, p.57

'And notice how detailed and probing are Helen Garner's notes on Dexter . . .' Grenville, Kate & Woolfe, Sue (2001). *Making Stories: How ten Australian novels were written*. Allen & Unwin: Crows Nest, p.72–73

p.139: 'Joyce Carol Oates suggests that . . .' Oates, Joyce Carol (2006). *Uncensored: Views & (re) views*. Harper Collins: New York, p.349

'When I read the following statement . . .' Dyer, Geoff (2009). *Out of Sheer Rage*. Abacus: London, p.125

p.140: '*Lolita*, for instance, is one of the most widely read modern novels notwithstanding the fact . . .' Nabokov, Vladimir (2000). *The Annotated Lolita*. Penguin: London, p.10

p.143: 'Look at the singular fashion in which Hannah, the mentally unravelling protagonist of Amos Oz's novel . . .' Oz, Amos (1991). *My Michael*. Vintage: London, p.89

'Albert Camus does this in his novel *The Fall*, where his protagonist's observations . . .' Camus, Albert (1956). *The Fall*. Random House: New York, p.12

p.144: 'David Grossman finds it useful to write letters . . .' David Grossman, The Art of Fiction. In Gourevitch, Philip (ed.) (2009). *The Paris Review Interviews, Vol.4*. Canongate Books: Edinburgh, p.415

'Peter Carey journals in a stream-of-consciousness fashion, as in these excerpted notes . . .' Grenville, Kate & Woolfe, Sue (2001). *Making Stories: How ten Australian novels were written*. Allen & Unwin: Crows Nest, p.45

Writing emotions

p.146: 'the American writer Emily Gould, who articulates her adolescent infatuation in her personal essay . . .' Gould, Emily (2010). *And the Heart Says Whatever*. Free Press: New York, p.20

p.147: 'In her personal essay "Close to the Bone", the Australian writer Georgia Blain . . .' Blain, Georgia (2008). *Births, Deaths, Marriages: True tales*. Random House: North Sydney, p.162

'In my short story "Floating Above The Village", which describes . . .' Kofman, Lee (2007). Floating Above the Village. In Drewe, Robert (ed.). *The Best Australian Stories 2007*. Black Inc.: Melbourne, p.81

'The Australian novelist Mireille Juchau describes the breakup . . .' Juchau, Mireille (2016). *The World Without Us*. Bloomsbury: London, p.79

p.148: 'Or you can combine physical sensations *and* thoughts, which is how Alice Munro conveys her character's bereavement . . .' Munro, Alice (2013). *Dear Life*. Vintage: London, p.90

'Or here is Jane's love for Mr Rochester in *Jane Eyre*, marvellously captured . . .' Brontë, Charlotte (2003). *Jane Eyre*. Penguin: London, p.177

p.149: 'Flaubert excels in capturing such experiences clearly and vividly, like in this passage from *Madame Bovary* . . .' Flaubert, Gustave (1979). *Madame Bovary*. Penguin: Middlesex, p.49

p.150: 'As a rule, we would better wait until we "exhaust the emotion", as Truman Capote suggests . . .' Truman Capote, The Art of Fiction. In Gourevitch, Philip (ed.) (2006). *The Paris Review Interviews, Vol.1*. Picador: New York, p.24

p.151: 'My hope was that these details would convey my terror . . .' Kofman, Lee (2019). Bruised. In Kofman, Lee (ed.). *Split: True stories of leaving, loss and new beginnings*. Ventura Press: Edgecliff, p.247

'Here is another example from my work, this time *The Dangerous Bride*. I use . . .' Kofman, Lee (2014). *The Dangerous Bride: A memoir of love, gods and geography*. Melbourne University Press: Carlton, p.136–137

'Oz expresses his anger at losing his mother to suicide by likening the suicidal urge to a seducer . . .' Oz, Amos (2005). *A Tale of Love and Darkness*. Vintage: London, p.209

To tell you the truth

p.154: 'When the protagonists of "The Feeder", the Australian author Glenys Osborne's short story about doomed love . . .' Osborne, Glenys (12 January 2008). The Feeder. *The Age*. https://www.theage.com.au/entertainment/books/the-feeder-20080112-ge6lht.html

p.155: 'Here is an example from Zadie Smith's novel *On Beauty*. When one of its protagonists . . .' Smith, Zadie (2005). *On Beauty*. Penguin: Australia, p.75

p.156: 'In this other snippet from *On Beauty*, Smith's descriptive and reflective narration . . .' Smith, Zadie (2005). *On Beauty*. Penguin: Australia, p.183

p.157: 'like in this excerpt from Philip Roth's novella . . .' Roth, Philip (1986). *Goodbye, Columbus*. Penguin: Middlesex, p.13

p.158: 'That's why in *The Dangerous Bride* I chose to introduce my ex-partner, J, through . . .' Kofman, Lee (2014). *The Dangerous Bride: A memoir of love, gods and geography*. Melbourne University Press: Carlton, p.71

'The English novelist Monica Ali expertly uses it for such a dual purpose throughout *Brick Lane* . . .' Ali, Monica (2004). *Brick Lane*. Black Swan: London, p.45

p.159: 'as it does in this excerpt from *On Beauty*, where a chairman at a conference . . .' Smith, Zadie (2005). *On Beauty*. Penguin: Australia, p.215

p.161: 'Stephen King writes . . .' King, Stephen (2001). *On Writing: A memoir of the craft*. Hodder & Stoughton: London, p.217

Caress the details

p.164: 'Fans of Raymond Chandler relish the extravagant richness of his descriptions of urban environments . . .' Chandler, Raymond (2008). *The Big Sleep*. Penguin: Australia, p.172

p.165: 'like the following memorable detail from *The Tale of Love and Darkness* . . .' Oz, Amos (2005). *A Tale of Love and Darkness*. Vintage: London, p.238

'"Goodbye to All That", Joan Didion's seminal essay about living in New York, for example, is . . ." Didion, Joan (2006). *We Tell Ourselves Stories in Order to Live: Collected nonfiction*. Knopf: New York, p.173

'Consider the following "mobile" character description from Kate Grenville's novel *Lilian's Story* . . .' Grenville, Kate (2021). *Lilian's Story*. Text Classics: Melbourne, p.13

p.166: 'Those details, as the American writer Francine Prose writes in *Reading Like A Writer*, tell . . .' Prose, Francine (2007). *Reading Like a Writer: A guide for people who love books and for those who want to write them*. Harper Perennial: New York, p.198

'Thomas Hardy writes that the writer's job is to create . . .' In Wood, James (2008). *How Fiction Works*. Picador: New York, p.240

'Marguerite Duras emphasises the clothes of the fifteen-year-old narrator . . .' Duras, Marguerite (1997). *The Lover*. Pantheon: New York, p.11

p.167: 'One day I randomly jotted down some details that had stuck with me . . .' Kofman, Lee (2020). At the Russian Restaurant. *Griffith Review*, issue 69, p.201

p.168: 'I wrote down some of the details I knew or imagined about it . . .' Kofman, Lee (2020). At the Russian Restaurant. *Griffith Review*, issue 69, p.200

'I wrote down that realisation too . . .' Kofman, Lee (2020). At the Russian Restaurant. *Griffith Review*, issue 69, p.201

Landscapes of our minds

p.170: 'But, as he wrote in his recollections, he simply couldn't help himself . . .' Alexander, Sidney (1990). *Marc Chagall: An intimate biography*. Ladori: Tel Aviv, p.270

p.171: 'Raimond Gaita describes, in this vein, the crucial role of place in the writing . . .' Gaita, Raimond (2011). *After Romulus*. Text: Melbourne, p.115

'However, even most vividly detailed descriptions risk being flat, or "ornamental", in the words of Hilary Mantel . . .' Mantel, Hilary (22 February 2010). Hilary Mantel's Rules for Writers. *The Guardian*. https://www.theguardian.com/books/2010/feb/22/hilary-mantel-rules-for-writers

p.172: 'Elena Ferrante, for example, describes Naples as . . .' Ferrante, Elena (2016). *Frantumaglia: A writer's journey*. Europa Editions: New York, p.65

'Here is Paris in Miller's autobiographical novel *Nexus* . . .' Miller, Henry (1965). *Nexus*. Grove Press: New York, p.267

p.173: 'The choices Joan Didion makes when describing a certain Californian region in her essay . . .' Didion, Joan (2006). *We Tell Ourselves Stories in Order to Live: Collected nonfiction*. Knopf: New York, p.13

p.174: 'The Russian-American poet Joseph Brodsky observes in *Watermark*, a memoir about . . .' Brodsky, Joseph (2013). *Watermark: An essay on Venice*. Penguin: London, p.47

'Albert Camus thinks temperature matters . . .' Todd, Olivier (1997). *Albert Camus: A life*. Carroll & Graf Publishers: New York, p.395

'Perhaps this is why in Joan Didion's novels, as American critic John Leonard suggests . . .' Leonard, John (2006). Introduction. In Didion, Joan. *We Tell Ourselves Stories in Order to Live: Collected nonfiction*. Knopf: New York, p.xiii

'And here is Didion herself, pondering the impact of environment on humans . . .' Didion, Joan (2006). *We Tell Ourselves Stories in Order to Live: Collected nonfiction*. Knopf: New York, p.164

'Lorrie Moore observes wryly in her short story . . .' Moore, Lorrie (2009). *The Collected Stories*. Faber & Faber: London, p.371

'In his essay "The Grand Illusion", Robert Dessaix makes the following witty distinctions . . .' Dessaix, Robert (2012). *As I Was Saying*. Random House: North Sydney, p.134

p.175: 'No wonder then that the narrator of *The Great Gatsby* towards the end concludes . . .' Fitzgerald, F. Scott (2008). *The Great Gatsby*. Penguin: Australia, p.167

p.176: 'In the following excerpt from the novel *Late in the Day*, the British writer Tessa Hadley . . .' Hadley, Tessa (2019). *Late in the Day*. Jonathan Cape: London, p.49

p.177: 'The opening of the Jewish-Russian writer Isaac Babel's short story . . .' Babel, Nathalie (ed.) (2002). *The Complete Works of Isaac Babel*. Norton: New York, p.203

'And Raymond Chandler's quirky, dark novel, *The Big Sleep*, unfolds within . . .' Chandler, Raymond (2008). *The Big Sleep*. Penguin: Australia, p.185

p.178: 'For example, the writing of my short memoir . . .' Kofman, Lee (2016). Diamonds in the red alley. *The Lifted Brow*, no. 30, June, pp.76

Fleshy truths

p.180: 'like in the following character sketch from Philip Roth's short story . . .' Roth, Philip (1986). *Goodbye, Columbus*. Penguin: Middlesex, p.127

'And here is a more comprehensively embodied description of a character in *A Guide to Berlin* . . .' Jones, Gail (2015). *A Guide to Berlin.* Random House: Australia, p.11

'The American writer and former competitive swimmer Lidia Yuknavitch, known for her embodied writing . . .' Yuknavitch, Lidia (2010). *The Chronology of Water: A memoir.* Hawthorn Books: Oregon, p.99

p.181: 'D. H. Lawrence's novel, *Lady Chatterley's Lover*, for example, stresses the power of eros . . .' Lawrence, D. H. (2008). *Lady Chatterley's Lover.* Penguin: Australia, p.270

p.182: 'Yuknavitch acknowledges the difficulty of describing sensations and offers a solution . . .' Yuknavitch, Lidia (2010). *The Chronology of Water: A memoir.* Hawthorn Books: Oregon, p.297

'The following passage depicts her pain as she urinates . . .' Taylor, Josephine (2021). *Eye of a Rook.* Fremantle Press: Fremantle, p.83

p.183: 'In her memoir *In My Skin*, Kate Holden uses poetic language to convey sexual attraction . . .' Holden, Kate (2005). *In My Skin: A memoir.* Text: Melbourne, p.9

'Another effective way to write sensation is by being hyper-specific, like Hemingway does in this . . .' Hemingway, Ernest (1996). *A Moveable Feast.* Arrow Books: London, p.13

'Emily Gould recounts a kiss in her personal essay . . .' Gould, Emily (2010). *And the Heart Says Whatever.* Free Press: New York, p.122

p.184: 'The Australian memoirist Nicola Redhouse similarly invites us into her mind . . .' Redhouse, Nicola (2019). *Unlike the Heart: A memoir of brain and mind.* The University of Queensland Press: St Lucia, pp.7–8

p.185: 'Alice Munro describes the enormous impact of a cleft lip on the narrator . . .' Munro, Alice (2013). *Dear Life.* Vintage: London, p.144

'Or here is Joan Didion's searing examination of how her ageing body . . .' Didion, Joan (2011). *Blue Nights.* Fourth Estate: London, p.116

'The Australian author Jenny Valentish shows such impact in her creative nonfiction book, *Woman of Substances* . . .' Valentish, Jenny (2017). *Woman of Substances: A journey into addiction and treatment.* Black Inc.: Carlton, p.23

p.187: 'Once I considered how the childhood of my Russian-Israeli-Australian protagonist . . .' Kofman, Lee (2020). At the Russian Restaurant. *Griffith Review*, issue 69, p.202

'In her memoir *Lucky*, American writer Alice Sebold recounts the aftermath of her horrific rape . . .' Sebold, Alice (2002). *Lucky.* Picador: London, p.210

p.188: 'In another short story by Alice Munro . . .' Munro, Alice (2013). *Dear Life.* Vintage: London, p.93

Cutting a shape

p.192: 'Peter Bishop advises along these lines, suggesting that writers should . . .' Kofman, Lee (29 August 2014). That Damn First Draft. *The Writing Life.* http://leekofman.com.au/the-writing-life/damn-first-draft/

p.193: 'Sartre's driving question in his childhood memoir, *The Words*, for example, was . . .' Bakewell, Sarah (2016). *At the Existential Café: Freedom, being, and apricot cocktails.* Other Press: New York, p.220

p.194: 'This is what David Grossman felt upon discovering the fiction of the Jewish-Polish writer Bruno Schulz . . .' David Grossman, The Art of Fiction. In Gourevitch, Philip (ed.) (2009). *The Paris Review Interviews, Vol.4.* Canongate Books: Edinburgh, p.417

p.195: 'Take Graham Greene's memoir about writing . . .' Greene, Graham (1999). *Ways of Escape.* Vintage: London, p.11

p.196: 'Or as Elena Ferrante puts it . . .' Ferrante, Elena (2016). *Frantumaglia: A writer's journey.* Europa Editions: New York, p.344

PART THREE

p.201: 'Stephen King wrote at the dawn of the new millennium that the writer's job . . .' King, Stephen (2001). *On Writing: A memoir of the craft.* Hodder & Stoughton: London, p.222–223

'He also expressed the view that . . .' King, Stephen (2001). *On Writing: A memoir of the craft.* Hodder & Stoughton: London, p.219

p.202: 'The latter wants to capture it in all its incorrectness and, as the American moral philosopher Susan Neiman writes . . .' Neiman Susan (2003). *Evil in Modern Thought: An alternative history of philosophy.* Scribe: Melbourne, p.203

'They want from books, as American literary critic Maureen Corrigan writes . . .' Corrigan, Maureen (2005). *Leave Me Alone, I'm Reading: Finding and losing myself in books.* Vintage: New York, p.xvi

Writing with discomfort

p.206: 'Mandy Sayer's memoir, *Dreamtime Alice*, engages with just such questions. While its . . .' Sayer, Mandy (1999). *Dreamtime Alice.* Vintage: Milsons Point, p.137

'When Elena Ferrante writes her novels, she pays . . .' Ferrante, Elena (2016). *Frantumaglia: A writer's journey.* Europa Editions: New York, p.226

p.207: 'Helen Garner's admission of vengefulness as one of her primary reasons for investigating . . .' Garner, Helen (2005). *Joe Cinque's Consolation: A true story of death, grief and the law.* Picador: Sydney, pp.25

p.208: 'Take this passage from the Israeli author Etgar Keret's memoir, *The Seven Good Years . . .*' Keret, Etgar (2016). *The Seven Good Years.* Granta Books: London, p.106

p.209: 'In *Imperfect*, once again I felt embarrassed . . .' Kofman, Lee (2019). *Imperfect: How our bodies shape the people we become.* Affirm Press: South Melbourne, p.73

p.211: 'To ease myself into writing that disturbing scene in 'Bruised', where my lover . . .' Kofman, Lee (2019). Bruised. In Kofman, Lee (ed.). *Split: True stories of leaving, loss and new beginnings.* Ventura Press: Edgecliff, p.246

Other people

p.214: 'Joan Didion echoed him in the preface . . .' Didion, Joan (2006). *We Tell Ourselves Stories in Order to Live: Collected nonfiction.* Knopf: New York, p.7

'And here's the thing about safe material that you are not afraid of anyone reading . . .' Maran, Meredith (ed.) 2016. *Why We Write About Ourselves: Twenty memoirists on why they expose themselves (and others) in the name of literature.* Plume: New York, p.85

p.215: 'Although now I know that even completely imagined fiction can get writers in trouble . . .' Greene, Graham (1999). *Ways of Escape.* Vintage: London, p.27

'My thinking here is along the lines of Louise DeSalvo's response to an acquaintance . . .' DeSalvo, Louise (2014). *The Art of Slow Writing: Reflections on time, craft and creativity.* St Martin's Griffin: New York, p.265

p.217: 'I find Helen Garner's stance on this latter issue, as described in her essay . . .' Garner, Helen (n.d.). I. *Meanjin Quarterly.* https://meanjin.com.au/essays/i/

'But, as Garner says in that same essay . . .' Garner, Helen (n.d.). I. *Meanjin Quarterly.* https://meanjin.com.au/essays/i/

p.218: 'On one hand, these are informed and consenting adults, and I agree with Robin Hemley, who writes . . .' Hemley, Robin (2012), *A Field Guide for Immersion Writing: Memoir, journalism, and travel.* The University of Georgia Press: Athens, p.47

p.219: 'After much deliberation, I resolved to be upfront about my perspective . . .' Kofman, Lee (2019). *Imperfect: How our bodies shape the people we become.* Affirm Press: South Melbourne, p.273

p.220: 'I recall the aftermath of the publication of my personal essay . . .' Kofman, Lee (2016). Me, my mother and Sexpo. In Katsonis, Maria & Kofman, Lee (eds.). *Rebellious Daughters: True stories from Australia's finest female writers.* Ventura Press: Edgecliff, pp.77–98

'The seventh Earl of Longford, for example, insisted . . .' Taylor, Irene & Alan (eds.) (2008). *The Assassin's Cloak: An anthology of the world's greatest diarists*. Canongate: Edinburgh, pp.548–549

p.221: 'They may even grow stronger, argues Jonathan Franzen . . .' Franzen, Jonathan (2012). *Farther Away*. Fourth Estate: London, pp.139–140

'As the Sierra Leonean writer Ishmael Beah points out, even when you write . . .' Maran, Meredith (ed.) 2016. *Why We Write About Ourselves: Twenty memoirists on why they expose themselves (and others) in the name of literature*. Plume: New York, p.8

p.222: 'On the other hand, as Capote said, speaking for many of us . . .' Capote, Truman (2012). *Music for Chameleons*. Vintage: New York, p.xiv

'Beah wisely writes . . .' Maran, Meredith (ed.) 2016. *Why We Write About Ourselves: Twenty memoirists on why they expose themselves (and others) in the name of literature*. Plume: New York, p.8

Writing in the age of social media

p.228: 'I long to follow Rilke's advice to an aspiring poet . . .' Rilke, Rainer Maria (2008). *Letters to a Young Poet*. BN Publishing: Hawthorne, p.27

p.229: 'The Welsh author Jon Ronson, for instance, writes in his book . . .' Ronson, Jon (2015). *So You've Been Publicly Shamed*. Riverhead Books: New York, pp.78–79

p.230: 'David Malouf writes along these lines in his essay . . .' Malouf, David (2014). *The Writing Life*. Knopf: North Sydney, pp.34–35

'It is in this spirit that David Grossman seeks in writing . . .' David Grossman, The Art of Fiction. In Gourevitch, Philip (ed.) (2009). *The Paris Review Interviews, Vol.4*. Canongate Books: Edinburgh, p.414

'Ferrante is adamant that her creative intent has never been to illustrate . . .' Ferrante, Elena (2016). *Frantumaglia: A writer's journey*. Europa Editions: New York, p.309

p.231: 'So, I wholeheartedly agree with John Banville's proposition that . . .' Anonymous (18 November 2017). The SRB Interview: John Banville. *Scottish Review of Books*. https://www.scottishreviewofbooks.org/2017/11/the-srb-interview-john-banville/

p.232: 'But, Proust tells us . . .' Proust, Marcel (2003). *Time Regained*. Modern Library: New York, p.257

'Encroaches on that "certain strangeness" that the American novelist John Gardner thinks . . .' Gardner, John (1999). *On Becoming a Novelist*. Norton: New York, p.56

Exposure

p.238: 'Rilke writes . . .' Rilke, Rainer Maria (2008). *Letters to a Young Poet*. BN Publishing: Hawthorne, p.45

'King's complete advice is to write . . .' King, Stephen (2001). *On Writing: A memoir of the craft*. Hodder & Stoughton: London, p.249

p.247: 'The Australian poet Alicia Sometimes wrote on my blog along these lines . . .' Kofman, Lee (11 July 2017). And More on Failure. *The Writing Life*. https://leekofman.com.au/the-writing-life/failure/

PART FOUR

p.251: 'Nobody is sure, but Arthur Rimbaud took a good guess. His belief was that . . .' Rimbaud, Arthur (1966). *Complete Works, Selected Letters*. Chicago University Press: Chicago, p.307

Literary friends

p.254: 'Upon discovering she wasn't included in the *Oxford Anthology of Australian Literature*, Garner noted . . .' Garner, Helen (2019). *Yellow Notebook: Diaries Volume 1 1978–1987*. Text: Melbourne, p.144

'Later, at the good news of being shortlisted for a prestigious award but convinced she wouldn't win, Garner . . .' Garner, Helen (2019). *Yellow Notebook: Diaries Volume 1 1978–1987*. Text: Melbourne, p.228

'Orhan Pamuk says that a good writer . . .' Orhan Pamuk, The Art of Fiction. In Gourevitch, Philip (ed.) (2009). *The Paris Review Interviews, Vol.4.* Canongate Books: Edinburgh, p.391

p.255: 'And if Kerouac hadn't typed up the handwritten pages he'd found strewn across . . .' Weinreich, Regina (2016). Kerouac and Burroughs in Tangier. *CLCWeb: Comparative Literature and Culture,* Vol.18(5). https://docs.lib.purdue.edu/cgi/viewcontent.cgi?article=2974&context=clcweb

p.259: 'The biographer Claudia Roth Pierpont describes in *Passionate Minds* . . .' Roth Pierpont, Claudia (2000). *Passionate Minds: Women rewriting the world.* Scribe: Carlton, pp.251–287

p.260: 'The poets Elizabeth Barrett Browning and Robert Browning were devoted to each other's art more equally. Elizabeth . . .' Popova, Maria (2019). *Figuring.* Pantheon Books: New York, pp.88–89

'A more contemporary literary couple, Michael Chabon and Ayelet Waldman . . .' Fox, Killian (9 September 2012). Meet the author: Michael Chabon. *The Guardian.* https://www.theguardian.com/books/2012/sep/09/michael-chabon-telegraph-avenue-interview

p.262: 'Kerouac famously wrote in *On the Road* . . .' Kerouac, Jack (1976). *On the Road.* Penguin: New York, p.9

'Around him, Kerouac wrote . . .' Kerouac, Jack (1976). *On the Road.* Penguin: New York, p.11

The pram in the hallway

p.265: 'Connolly famously scared generations of artists, particularly of the female kind, by declaring that . . .' Connolly, Cyril (2009). *Enemies of Promise.* Chicago University Press: Chicago, p.116

p.270: 'I recall one afternoon when I was editing an essay by the Australian memoirist Rochelle Siemienowicz . . .' Siemienowicz, Rochelle (2016). Resisting the Nipple. In Katsonis, Maria & Kofman, Lee (eds.). *Rebellious Daughters: True stories from Australia's finest female writers.* Ventura Press: Edgecliff, pp.275–296

The writing times and the living times

p.276: 'Oates's name is "synonymous with productivity," *The New York Times* once opined.' Parini, Jay (30 July 1989). The More They Write, the More They Write. *The New York Times.* https://www.nytimes.com/1989/07/30/books/the-more-they-write-the-more-they-write.html

'Balzac, who in 1842 alone published eight books, kept an even stricter writing schedule . . .' Parini, Jay (30 July 1989). The More They Write, the More They Write. *The New York Times.* https://www.nytimes.com/1989/07/30/books/the-more-they-write-the-more-they-write.html

p.277: 'The American poet Kate Angus, in her essay . . .' Angus, Kate (24 September 2019). Maybe the Secret to Writing is Not Writing? *Lit Hub.* https://lithub.com/maybe-the-secret-to-writing-is-not-writing/

p.279: 'Louise DeSalvo writes that with time Virginia Woolf . . .' DeSalvo, Louise (2014). *The Art of Slow Writing: Reflections on time, craft and creativity.* St Martin's Griffin: New York, pp.108–109

p.280: 'Or as Ann Patchett poetically puts this, on such pages . . .' Patchett, Ann (2013). Introduction. In Wolff, Geoffrey. *A Day at the Beach.* Vintage: New York, p.xvii

p.281: 'The Scottish poet Iain Crichton Smith wrote a poem . . .' Parini, Jay (30 July 1989). The More They Write, the More They Write. *The New York Times.* https://www.nytimes.com/1989/07/30/books/the-more-they-write-the-more-they-write.html

'Instead, Banville identifies as a graphomaniac, saying that for him stopping writing would be dangerous.' McKeon, Belinda (2009). John Banville, The Art of Fiction No.200. *The Paris Review,* issue 188, Spring. https://www.theparisreview.org/interviews/5907/the-art-of-fiction-no-200-john-banville

'Oates echoes him as she describes, in an interview, feeling . . .' Phillips, Robert (1978). Joyce Carol Oates, The Art of Fiction No.72. *The Paris Review,* issue 74, Fall-Winter. https://www.theparisreview.org/interviews/3441/the-art-of-fiction-no-72-joyce-carol-oates p.282: 'Listen to Kafka confessing in his diary . . .' Cited in Malouf, David (2014). *The Writing Life*. Knopf: North Sydney, p.199

p.283: 'It's hard to explain; it is this feeling I get akin to what Virginia Woolf describes . . .' Cited in Burnham, Sophy (1996). *For Writers Only*. Ballantine Books: New York, p.112

p.284: 'If you take joy in living as monastic a life as Philip Roth did, reduced . . .' Tharp, Twyla (2006). *The Creative Habit: Learn it and use it for life*. Simon & Schuster: New York, p.238

EPILOGUE: STOKING THE FLAMES

p.285: '"The freedom to create is somehow linked with facility of access to those obscure regions below the conscious mind," writes the philosopher of nature . . .' Eiseley, Lauren (1 November 2010). The Mind as Nature. *The American Poetry Review*. https://www.thefreelibrary.com/The+Mind+as+Nature-a0242306448

'The poet Andrew Motion took Beecham Powders . . .' Claxton, Guy (2005). *The Wayward Mind: An intimate history of the unconscious*. Abacus: London, p.223

'Kerouac could only play "Afro-Germanic music" on the piano.' Jack, Kerouac, The Art of Fiction. In Gourevitch, Philip (ed.) (2009). *The Paris Review Interviews, Vol.4*. Canongate Books: Edinburgh, p.108

p.286: 'Rachel Carson listened to Beethoven. His sixth, seventh . . .' Popova, Maria (2019). *Figuring*. Pantheon Books: New York, pp.462

p.287: 'Maya Angelou brought a Bible with her when she wrote in hotels . . .' Maya, Angelou, The Art of Fiction. In Gourevitch, Philip (ed.) (2009). *The Paris Review Interviews, Vol.4*. Canongate Books: Edinburgh, p.240

'Upon visiting Paris, Albert Camus remarked . . .' Todd, Olivier (1997). *Albert Camus: A life*. Carroll & Graf Publishers: New York, p.64

'Inspiration isn't a myth, scientists say, but the time . . .' Claxton, Guy (2005). *The Wayward Mind: An intimate history of the unconscious*. Abacus: London, pp.267–268

p.288: 'Rilke insisted that . . .' Rilke, Rainer Maria (2008). *Letters to a Young Poet*. BN Publishing: Hawthorne, p.27

BIBLIOGRAPHY

Alexander, Sidney (1990). *Marc Chagall: An intimate biography*. Ladori: Tel Aviv.

Ali, Monica (2004). *Brick Lane*. Black Swan: London.

Allende, Isabel (11 July 2017). *Isabel Allende's Book Bag: 5 Books That Influenced Me*. Daily Beast. https://www.thedailybeast.com/isabel-allendes-book-bag-5-books-that-influenced-me

Alvarez, A. (2005). *The Writer's Voice*. Norton: New York.

Angus, Kate (24 September 2019). *Maybe the Secret to Writing is Not Writing?* Lit Hub. https://lithub.com/maybe-the-secret-to-writing-is-not-writing/

Anonymous (18 November 2017). *The SRB Interview: John Banville*. Scottish Review of Books. https://www.scottishreviewofbooks.org/2017/11/the-srb-interview-john-banville/

Anonymous (20 February 2010). Ten Rules for Writing Fiction (Part Two). *The Guardian*. https://www.theguardian.com/books/2010/feb/20/10-rules-for-writing-fiction-part-two

Anonymous (20 February 2005). Hunter S Thompson: In His Own Words. *The Guardian*. https://www.theguardian.com/books/2005/feb/21/huntersthompson

Appelfeld, Aharon (2007). *A Table for One: Under the light of Jerusalem*. The Toby Press: New Milford.

Ash, Alec (n.d.). *Ian McEwan on the Books That Shaped His Novels*. Five Books. https://fivebooks.com/best-books/ian-mcewan-books-that-shape-his-novels/

Auster, Paul (1997). *Hand to Mouth: A chronicle of early failure*. Faber & Faber: London.

Auster, Paul (1993). *Leviathan*. Penguin: New York.

Babel, Nathalie (ed.) (2002). *The Complete Works of Isaac Babel*. Norton: New York.

Bakewell, Sarah (2016). *At the Existential Café: Freedom, being, and apricot cocktails*. Other Press: New York.

Barnes, Djuna (1974). *Vagaries Malicieux: Two stories*. Small Press Distribution: Berkeley.

Bashevis Singer, Isaac & Burgin, Richard (1986). *Conversations with Isaac Bashevis Singer*. Farrar, Straus & Giroux: New York.

Begley, Adam (2002). Ian McEwan, The Art of Fiction No. 173. *The Paris Review*, issue 162, Summer. https://www.theparisreview.org/interviews/393the-art-of-fiction-no-173-ian-mcewan

Beha, Christopher (ed.) (2012). *The Writer's Notebook II: Craft Essays*. Tin House: Portland.

Bell, Gail (2003). *The Poison Principle: A memoir of family secrets and literary poisonings*. Pan Macmillan: Australia.

Benedict, Elizabeth (ed.) (2009). *Mentors, Muses & Monsters: 30 writers on the people who changed their lives*. Free Press: New York.

Blain, Georgia (2008). *Births, Deaths, Marriages: True tales*. Random House: North Sydney.

Bolton, Gillie (1999). *The Therapeutic Potential of Creative Writing*. Jessica Kingsley Publishers: London.

Brodsky, Joseph (2013). *Watermark: An essay on Venice*. Penguin: London.

Brontë, Charlotte (2003). *Jane Eyre*. Penguin: London.
Bulgakov, Mikhail (2003). *The Master and Margarita*. Vintage: London.
Burnham, Sophy (1996). *For Writers Only*. Ballantine Books: New York.
Camus, Albert (1956). *The Fall*. Random House: New York.
Capote, Truman (2012). *Music for Chameleons*. Vintage: New York.
Carey, Peter (n.d.). *Author Q&A*. Gotham Writers. https://www.writingclasses.com/toolbox/author-q-a/peter-carey?page=2
Carver, Raymond (1985). On Writing. *Mississippi Review*, Vol.14(1–2), Winter. https://www.jstor.org/stable/20115383
Chandler, Raymond (2008). *The Big Sleep*. Penguin: Australia.
Chatwin, Bruce (1984). *On the Black Hill*. Penguin: New York.
Christensen, Kate (2013). *Blue Plate Special: An autobiography of my appetites*. Doubleday: New York.
Claxton, Guy (2005). *The Wayward Mind: An intimate history of the unconscious*. Abacus: London.
Connolly, Cyril (2009). *Enemies of Promise*. Chicago University Press: Chicago.
Corrigan, Maureen (2005). *Leave Me Alone, I'm Reading: Finding and losing myself in books*. Vintage: New York.
Damianakis, T. (2001). Postmodernism, Spirituality, and the Creative Writing Process: Implications for social work practice, *Families in Societies: The journal of contemporary human services*, Vol.82(1), January, pp.23–40
DeSalvo, Louise (2014). *The Art of Slow Writing: Reflections on time, craft and creativity*. St Martin's Griffin: New York.
Dessaix, Robert (2012). *As I Was Saying*. Random House: North Sydney.
Didion, Joan (2011). *Blue Nights*. Fourth Estate: London.
Didion, Joan (2006). *We Tell Ourselves Stories in Order to Live: Collected nonfiction*. Knopf: New York.
Dillard, Annie (1990), *The Writing Life*. Harper Perennial: New York.
Drewe, Robert (ed.) (2007). *The Best Australian Stories 2007*. Black Inc.: Melbourne.
Duras, Marguerite (1997). *The Lover*. Pantheon: New York.
Dyer, Geoff (2009). *Out of Sheer Rage*. Abacus: London.
Eiseley, Lauren (1 November 2010). The Mind as Nature. *The American Poetry Review*. https://www.thefreelibrary.com/The+Mind+as+Nature-a0242306448
Enright, Anne (2013). *Making Babies: Stumbling into motherhood*. Norton: New York.
Eugenides, Jeffrey (2011). *The Marriage Plot*. Fourth Estate: London.
Fallon, Michael (9 September 2008). *The Day the Music Died*. Mn Artists. https://mnartists.walkerart.org/essay-the-day-the-music-died
Farmer, Beverley (1990). *A Body of Water*. University of Queensland Press: Brisbane.
Ferrante, Elena (2016). *Frantumaglia: A writer's journey*. Europa Editions: New York.
Fitzgerald, F. Scott (2008). *The Great Gatsby*. Penguin: Australia.
Flaubert, Gustave (1979). *Madame Bovary*. Penguin: Middlesex.
Fox, Killian (9 September 2012). Meet the author: Michael Chabon. *The Guardian*. https://www.theguardian.com/books/2012/sep/09michael-chabon-telegraph-avenue-interview
Franzen, Jonathan (ed.) (2016). *The Best American Essays 2016*. Houghton Mifflin Harcourt: New York.
Franzen, Jonathan (2012). *Farther Away*. Fourth Estate: London.
Freud, Sigmund (1908). *Creative Writers and Day-dreaming*. https://static1.squarespace.com/static/5441df7ee4b02f59465d2869/t/588e9620e6f2e152d3ebcffc/1485739554918/Freud+-+Creative+Writers+and+Day+Dreaming%281%29.pdf
Funder, Anna (2002). *Stasiland*. Text: Melbourne.
Gaita, Raimond (2011). *After Romulus*. Text: Melbourne.
Gardner, John (1999). *On Becoming a Novelist*. Norton: New York.
Garner, Helen (n.d.). I. *Meanjin Quarterly*. https://meanjin.com.au/essays/i/
Garner, Helen (2019). *Yellow Notebook: Diaries Volume 1 1978–1987*. Text: Melbourne.

Garner, Helen (2008). *The Feel of Steel.* Picador: Sydney.
Garner, Helen (2005). *Joe Cinque's Consolation: A true story of death, grief and the law.* Picador: Sydney.
Gould, Emily (2010). *And the Heart Says Whatever.* Free Press: New York.
Gourevitch, Philip (ed.) (2006). *The Paris Review Interviews, Vol.1.* Picador: New York.
Gourevitch, Philip (ed.) (2009). *The Paris Review Interviews, Vol.4.* Canongate Books: Edinburgh.
Gourney, Douglas (30 December 2010). Michael Chabon: How to salvage a wrecked novel. *The Atlantic.* https://www.theatlantic.com/entertainment/archive/2010/12/michael-chabon-how-to-salvage-a-wrecked-novel/68665/
Greene, Graham (1999). *Ways of Escape.* Vintage: London.
Grenville, Kate (2021). *Lilian's Story.* Text Classics: Melbourne.
Grenville, Kate & Woolfe, Sue (2001). *Making Stories: How ten Australian novels were written.* Allen & Unwin: Crows Nest.
Hadley, Tessa (2019). *Late in the Day.* Jonathan Cape: London.
Hamsun, Knut (1967). *Hunger.* Picador: London.
Hemingway, Ernest (1996). *A Moveable Feast.* Arrow Books: London.
Hemley, Robin (2012), *A Field Guide for Immersion Writing: Memoir, journalism, and travel.* The University of Georgia Press: Athens.
Henley, Jon (13 May 2013). How Dan Brown and Other Authors Defeat Writer's Block. *The Guardian.* https://www.theguardian.com/books/shortcuts/2013/may/13/dan-brown-authors-writers-block
Hessler, Peter (2010). John McPhee, The Art of Nonfiction No. 3. *The Paris Review,* issue 192, Spring. https://www.theparisreview.org/interviews/5997/the-art-of-nonfiction-no-3-john-mcphee
Highsmith, Patricia (2016). *Plotting and Writing Suspense Fiction.* Sphere: London.
Holden, Kate (2005). *In My Skin: A memoir.* Text: Melbourne.
Jones, Gail (2015). *A Guide to Berlin.* Random House: Australia.
Juchau, Mireille (2016). *The World Without Us.* Bloomsbury: London.
Katsonis, Maria & Kofman, Lee (eds.) (2016). *Rebellious Daughters: True stories from Australia's finest female writers.* Ventura Press: Edgecliff.
Keret, Etgar (2016). *The Seven Good Years.* Granta Books: London.
Kerouac, Jack (1976). *On the Road.* Penguin: New York.
King, Stephen (2001). *On Writing: A memoir of the craft.* Hodder & Stoughton: London.
Klauser, Henriette Anne (2003). *With Pen in Hand.* Perseus Publishing: Seattle.
Knausgaard, Karl Ove (2018). *The End.* Harvill Secker: London.
Kofman, Lee (2020). At the Russian Restaurant. *Griffith Review,* issue 69, pp.199–209.
Kofman, Lee (ed.) (2019). *Split: True stories of leaving, loss and new beginnings.* Ventura Press: Edgecliff.
Kofman, Lee (2019). *Imperfect: How our bodies shape the people we become.* Affirm Press: South Melbourne.
Kofman, Lee (11 July 2017). *And More on Failure.* The Writing Life. https://leekofman.com.au/the-writing-life/failure/
Kofman, Lee (2016). Diamonds in the red alley. *The Lifted Brow,* no. 30, June, pp.76–80.
Kofman, Lee (29 August 2014). *That Damn First Draft.* The Writing Life. http://leekofman.com.au/the-writing-life/damn-first-draft/
Kofman, Lee (2014). *The Dangerous Bride: A memoir of love, gods and geography.* Melbourne University Press: Carlton.
Krauss, Nicole (25 May 2011). *On Writing 'Great House'.* HuffPost. https://www.huffpost.com/entry/nicole-krauss-on-writing-_b_764806
Kureishi, Hanif (2008). *Something To Tell You.* Faber & Faber: London.
Lamott, Anne (2008). *Bird By Bird: Some instructions on writing and life.* Scribe: Carlton.
Lawrence, D. H. (2008). *Lady Chatterley's Lover.* Penguin: Australia.
Livings, Jack (2005). Salman Rushdie, The Art of Fiction No.186. *The Paris Review,* issue 174, Summer. https://www.theparisreview.org/interviews/5531/the-art-of-fiction-no-186-salman-rushdie

Malouf, David (2014). *The Writing Life*. Knopf: North Sydney.

Mantel, Hilary (22 February 2010). Hilary Mantel's Rules for Writers. *The Guardian*. https://www.theguardian.com/books/2010/feb/22/hilary-mantel-rules-for-writers

Maran, Meredith (ed.) 2016. *Why We Write About Ourselves: Twenty memoirists on why they expose themselves (and others) in the name of literature*. Plume: New York.

Masson, Isidora (n.d.). Read Like a Butterfly, Write Like a Bee. *Journal*. https://vocal.media/journal/read-like-a-butterfly-write-like-a-bee

Marsden, John (1998). *Everything I Know About Writing*. Pan McMillan: Sydney.

McKeon, Belinda (2009). John Banville, The Art of Fiction No. 200. *The Paris Review*, issue 188, Spring. https://www.theparisreview.org/interviews/5907/the-art-of-fiction-no-200-john-banville

Miller, Henry (1969). *The Books in My Life*. Penguin: New York.

Miller, Henry (1965). *Nexus*. Grove Press: New York.

Miller Patti (2017). *Writing True Stories: The complete guide to writing autobiography, memoir, personal essay, biography, travel and creative nonfiction*. Routledge: Oxfordshire.

Moore, Lorrie (2009). *The Collected Stories*. Faber & Faber: London.

Moriarty, Liane (2020). *Three Wishes*. Harper Collins: Australia.

Munro, Alice (2013). *Dear Life*. Vintage: London.

Nabokov, Vladimir (2001). *The Gift*. Penguin: London.

Nabokov, Vladimir (2000). *The Annotated Lolita*. Penguin: London.

Nabokov, Vladimir (2000). *Speak, Memory: An autobiography revisited*. Penguin: New York.

Neiman, Susan (2003). *Evil in Modern Thought: An alternative history of philosophy*. Scribe: Melbourne.

Oates, Joyce Carol (2006). *Uncensored: Views & (re)views*. Harper Collins: New York.

Ofek, Lior (1998). *Bangkok Stories*. Gvanim: Tel Aviv. [In Hebrew].

Orwell, George (1946). *Why I Write*. https://www.orwellfoundation.com/the-orwell-foundation/orwell/essays-and-other-works/why-i-write/

Osborne, Glenys (12 January 2008). The Feeder. *The Age*. https://www.theage.com.au/entertainment/books/the-feeder-20080112-ge6lht.html

Oz, Amos (2005). *A Tale of Love and Darkness*. Vintage: London.

Oz, Amos (1991). *My Michael*. Vintage: London.

Parini, Jay (30 July 1989). The More They Write, the More They Write. *The New York Times*. https://www.nytimes.com/1989/07/30/books/the-more-they-write-the-more-they-write.html

Patchett, Ann (2011). The Writing Life: Examined in a Digital Minibook. *Nieman Reports*. https://niemanreports.org/articles/the-writing-life-examined-in-a-digital-minibook/

Paul, Pamela (ed.) (2014). *By the Book: Writers on literature and the literary life from* The New York Times Book Review. Picador: New York.

Pennebaker, J.W. & Seagal, J.D. (1999). Forming a Story: The health benefits of narrative. *Journal of Clinical Psychology*, Vol.55(10), pp.1243–1254.

Phillips, Robert (1978). Joyce Carol Oates, The Art of Fiction No. 72. *The Paris Review*, issue 74, Fall-Winter. https://www.theparisreview.org/interviews/3441/the-art-of-fiction-no-72-joyce-carol-oates

Popova, Maria (2019). *Figuring*. Pantheon Books: New York.

Popova, Maria (13 March 2012). 6 Writing Tips From John Steinbeck. *The Atlantic*. https://www.theatlantic.com/entertainment/archive/2012/03/6-writing-tips-from-john-steinbeck/254351/

Price, Leah (ed.) (2011). *Unpacking My Library: Writers and their books*. Yale University Press: Connecticut.

Prose, Francine (2007). *Reading Like a Writer: A guide for people who love books and for those who want to write them*. Harper Perennial: New York.

Proust, Marcel (2003). *Time Regained*. Modern Library: New York.

Pung, Alice (2006). *Unpolished Gem*. Black Inc.:Melbourne.

Redhouse, Nicola (2019). *Unlike the Heart: A memoir of brain and mind*. The University of Queensland Press: St Lucia.

Rilke, Rainer Maria (2008). *Letters to a Young Poet.* BN Publishing: Hawthorne.

Rimbaud, Arthur (1966). *Complete Works, Selected Letters.* Chicago University Press: Chicago.

Ripatrazone, Nick (12 November 2015). Why Writers Run. *The Atlantic.* https://www.theatlantic.com/entertainment/archive/2015/11/why-writers-run/415146/

Ronson, Jon (2015). *So You've Been Publicly Shamed.* Riverhead Books: New York.

Roth, Philip (1986). *Goodbye, Columbus.* Penguin: Middlesex.

Roth Pierpont, Claudia (2000). *Passionate Minds: Women rewriting the world.* Scribe: Carlton.

Rothman, Joshua (11 November 2018). Karl Ove Knausgaard Looks Back on 'My Struggle'. *The New Yorker.* https://www.newyorker.com/culture/the-new-yorker-interview/karl-ove-knausgaard-the-duty-of-literature-is-to-fight-fiction

Roy, Arundhati (2002). *The God of Small Things.* Penguin: New Delhi.

Rushdie, Salman (2012). *Joseph Anton.* Jonathan Cape: London.

Sampson, Fiona (ed.) (2004). *Creative Writing in Health and Social Care.* Jessica Kingsley Publishers: London.

Sayer, Mandy (1999). *Dreamtime Alice.* Vintage: Milsons Point.

Scambler, Graham (n.d.). Vienna's Cafe Central. *Graham Scambler.* http://www.grahamscambler.com/viennas-cafe-central/

Sebold, Alice (2002). *Lucky.* Picador: London.

Smith, Zadie (2005). *On Beauty.* Penguin: Australia.

Taylor, Irene & Alan (eds.) (2008). *The Assassin's Cloak: An anthology of the world's greatest diarists.* Cannongate Books: Edinburgh.

Tharp, Twyla (2006). *The Creative Habit: Learn it and use it for life.* Simon & Schuster: New York.

Todd, Olivier (1997). *Albert Camus: A life.* Carroll & Graf Publishers: New York.

Valentish, Jenny (2017). *Woman of Substances: A journey into addiction and treatment.* Black Inc.:Carlton.

Weaver Flaherty, Alice Weaver (2005). *Midnight Disease: The drive to write, writer's block, and the creative brain.* Mariner Books: Boston.

Weinreich, Regina (2016). Kerouac and Burroughs in Tangier. *CLCWeb: Comparative Literature and Culture*, Vol.18(5). https://docs.lib.purdue.edu/cgi/viewcontent.cgi?article=2974&context=clcweb

Weste, Linda (2020). *Inside the Verse Novel: Writers on writing.* Australian Scholarly: North Melbourne.

Wolff, Geoffrey (2013). *A Day at the Beach.* Vintage: New York.

Wood, James & Knausgaard Karl Ove (2014). Writing *My Struggle*: An exchange. *The Paris Review*, issue 211, Winter. https://www.theparisreview.org/miscellaneous/6345/writing-my-struggle-an-exchange-james-wood-karl-ove-knausgaard

Wood, James (2008). *How Fiction Works.* Picador: New York.

Yuknavitch, Lidia (2010). *The Chronology of Water: A memoir.* Hawthorn Books: Oregon.

Zunshine, Lisa (2008). *Strange Concepts and the Stories They Make Possible: Cognition, culture, narrative.* Johns Hopkins University Press: Baltimore.